The Druid's Primer

The Druid's Primer

Luke Eastwood

MOON
BOOKS

Winchester, UK
Washington, USA

JOHN HUNT PUBLISHING

First published by Moon Books, 2012
Moon Books is an imprint of John Hunt Publishing Ltd., No. 3 East Street, Alresford
Hampshire SO24 9EE, UK
office@jhpbooks.net
www.johnhuntpublishing.com
www.moon-books.net

For distributor details and how to order please visit the 'Ordering' section on our website.

ISBN: 978 1 84694 764 3
978 1 84694 765 0 (ebook)

A CIP catalogue record for this book is available from the British Library.

Design: Stuart Davies

UK: Printed and bound by CPI Group (UK) Ltd, Croydon, CR0 4YY
US: Printed and bound by Thomson-Shore, 7300 West Joy Road, Dexter, MI 48130

CONTENTS

A sword is useless without the hand that wields it,
So too is knowledge useless without wisdom.

Bendacht For Cech N-Oen Legfas
A blessing on all who read this

Acknowledgements

Many people have contributed to this book, many of them unknowingly. I'd like to thank all those who have personally helped me on my spiritual journey and helped me to arrive at this point in my life, in particular: Chris Woods, Barbara Lee, Herbie Brennan, Cait Branigan, Deirdre Wadding, Con Connor, Lady Olivia Robertson, Sarah Fuhro, Bev and Del Richardson, Mary Spain, Margaret Lawlor, Wil Kinghan, Liam McGrath, Elizabeth Bateman, Marlene Ffrench-Mullen, Mark Kavanagh, Ray Sweeney. I am also very grateful for the assistance of The National Library of Ireland and The National Museum of Ireland – Archaeology.

I'm eternally grateful to all the authors whose works I have read and used as source material for this book, without them this book would not have been written. Thanks to the staff at Moon Books for their patience and hard work. A big thank you to Cait Branigan for a final read through and continuity/accuracy check. I'd also like to thank all of my friends and family for their love and support, especially my daughter Amy.

A special thank you to my mentor and friend Hugh Brennan, whose knowledge and advice, over many years, has been invaluable to me.

Foreword

In the last twenty years or so, many have found themselves drawn to the practice of Druidry as a way of deepening their knowledge and connection to life. As we wrestle with the challenges that confront us in the 21st Century, it is a path that can offer us an alternative vision of how we might live and be in the world. The Druid quest is essentially a search for wisdom and knowledge; as a spiritual path or philosophy it seeks to honour the Earth, perceiving the material world as sacred. The practices of Druidry can enable us to enhance our relationship with the planet we live on - healing the psychological fissure that has emotionally separated us from our environment, each other and ourselves. It gives us a series of spiritual tools and approaches that aim to create a greater harmony with the Earth's cycles and seasons and, in doing so, rediscover a greater sense of belonging.

Druidry also understands the value in connecting to the gifts offered by a study of our ancient history. It seeks to draw from the spiritual taproot that reaches down into the rich soil of our cultural and spiritual past with the aim of feeding and nourishing our present. Druidry recognises the potential value of our ancestors' knowledge, especially when we can use its wisdom in ways that have relevance and meaning for contemporary life.

Luke's book represents a valuable resource for those drawn to explore this old, yet ever-developing spiritual path. His deep knowledge of original Celtic sources has been lovingly crafted in a way that those new to the subject will find accessible and informative. Those who have been travelling the path for a while now - but who may not be aware of the origins of some of their practices - will also find much to satisfy them here. *The Druid's Primer* is not only a good reference book; it takes a knowledge of the past and presents it in a manner that encourages the reader to explore further. Luke shares his insights in a sensitive and open manner that honours the spirit of the original texts and sources whilst leaving enough space for the reader to draw their own conclusions.

The Druid's Primer clearly illustrates the fact that Druidry is a living, growing spirituality, rooted in a fertile past. It shows us that humanity is an interconnected part of existence - dwelling upon a thread that connects the past to the present and on into the future. This thread leads us back to the wisdom already within us, inherited from all those who have gone before and from Nature herself. From this new sense of ourselves we can make that step into a deeper practice of Druidry, becoming sensitive and responsible caretakers of the life and resources we all share.

Philip Carr-Gomm

Introduction

What prompted me to write this book is the widely scattered and often hidden nature of Druidic and more generally Celtic knowledge. Many have written that there is little known about Druids or the ancient Celts, the truth is exactly the opposite – there is a mountain of knowledge and information extant, much of which can be traced back to antiquity. The problem is that these gems are scattered far and wide and much of this knowledge, where it is written, is in a style that is awkward and unpleasing to modern tastes. Much information and knowledge remains untranslated from the original texts and lies in the vaults of museums. However a massive amount of work in this respect did take place in Ireland, Britain, France and Germany during the 'Celtic revival' of the eighteenth and nineteenth centuries.

In more recent years, much work has also taken place in bringing to light ancient Celtic spirituality, most notably the work of John and Caitlin Matthews and Alexi Kondratiev. Even so, it takes a great quantity of time, effort and money to build up any kind of workable 'library' of knowledge that relates to ancient Druid practices or to using that knowledge in a modern context. There are many books on Druidry but few of them contain much source material that is of practical use. It has taken me some fifteen years to collect the sources necessary to prepare this 'distillation' of knowledge into what I hope is a practical and instructional compendium. I have written it as much for myself as anyone else. Being without the blessings of a photographic memory or sufficient time to frequently peruse my book collection at length, I felt I could make use of such a book as much as any other modern Druid.

The traditional structure of Druidic training has long since disappeared, leaving the modern Druid movement with the problem of creating a new model for transmission of knowledge and wisdom. Largely this means that modern Druids often have to train themselves. Correspondence courses exist and some are excellent ways of training. Some neophyte Druids are lucky enough to join a grove led by an experienced Druid who is able to pass on their own skills and learning. There are also workshops and courses, which can be highly worthwhile, but for most people it all has to fit within the framework of the working week, shopping, family and so on. Modern living does not lend itself well to the transmission of wisdom in the oral tradition, I suspect that by the Middle Ages there was an awareness that a process of loss was happening which may have led to the codifying (writing down) of much knowledge that had not already been forgotten.

The curriculum given in *Manners and Customs of the Ancient Irish* specifies a twelve-year programme for the training of a bard which includes oghams, grammar, philosophy, a huge number of tales and poems, study of the law, the language of poets, composition, improvisation, prophetic techniques, wisdom tales and orations. The final three years alone includes the learning by heart of 350 tales. Some of the areas of study, written in *Gaeilge* (Irish) are of unknown meaning and hence remain untranslated.

This book is not intended to be a substitute for such a programme of study but merely to disseminate core information which many consider essential to druidic training. I hope that it will make the job of training and acquiring druidic knowledge and wisdom a little less convoluted. I could spend the rest of my life improving and adding to this collection, however I hope it will encourage others in further mining of the rich seam of druidic knowledge.

Luke Eastwood, Co. Wexford, Ireland. 2011

I

Some History

There are a large number of histories of the Druids and the Celtic people. In these pages, I am not going to attempt to write a comprehensive history. Roman historian Pliny the Elder wrote a history of Rome and the known world comprising 31 books almost two thousand years ago, which is sadly lost. Two volumes of that epic work were dedicated to the civilization of the Celts, which was contemporary at the time of writing, albeit very biased against them. Given the size of that work, a history of the Celts and Druids up to present day (that is truly worthy of the title) deserves a substantial book in itself.

It is generally accepted that the Druids were Celtic or Proto-Celtic people who performed an important function in society with relation to religious practices, retention and transmission of knowledge, magical/healing arts and administering justice. There are various arguments that the Druids predate Celtic culture, and likewise there are disagreements over the time and number of migrations of the Celts across Europe. The validity of such theories, is extremely difficult to prove, however we can be reasonably safe in stating that the Celts dominated Europe for much of the first millennium BC — the Hallstatt and La Tène cultures are well known. It is known that the Celts settled northern Italy before 600 BC and sacked Rome in 390 BC. In 281 BC, Cerethrius invaded Greece, wreaking havoc across the Hellenic world and culminating in 279 BC when they sacked the Oracle at Delphi with limited success, according to some Greek sources, before returning north. Celtic influence extended into Asia Minor with the Galatian settlement in what is now northern Turkey, a culture that survived until the 6th century AD. They also colonised modern day Spain — Celt-Iberia flourished until crushing defeat by the Romans in 133 BC. Celtic dominance gradually declined under Roman and Germanic pressure, with them becoming confined to the western half of Europe by the 1st century BC. As Roman power increased only Ireland and Scotland remained untouched by Roman control.

It is said that Aedd Mawr[1] set up a Druid Order in Albion (Britain) around 1000 BC, supposedly prior to the influx of Celts. Likewise, in Ireland some claim that Druidry is pre-Celtic and was introduced to the invaders by the indigenous megalithic people. To give a definitive answer to this question is difficult, however the existence of megalithic sites such as Stonehenge, *Brú na Bóinne*, Avebury, Lewis and Knowth to name but a few, point to the possibility of this being the case. Whoever built these sites had a precise knowledge of astronomy, architecture and had religious reasons for creating them in the first place.

Various opinions exist regarding the meaning of the word Druid — the most popular being that it derives from the oak tree. Pliny believed that the name derived from the Greek *drus* (note the Irish for druid is *druí*, and oak is *duir*). In his *Historia naturia* he famously describes the picking of mistletoe from an oak tree by Gaulish Druids and he also claimed that the oak was their most sacred tree. There are various interpretations such as 'strong seeing', 'oak seers' but many of these seem to derive from the word druid which is an English word that itself might be derived from the latin *druides* or greek *druidae*.

Most of what is known of the ancient Druids is derived from outside sources, mainly Greek and Romans such as Posidonius, Livy, Strabo, Pliny, and Julius Caesar. Historians and especially modern pagans have rightly questioned the accuracy of the information we have received from classical sources. Much of what we read today is coloured by politics as is the 'official' history taught to children. Likewise I think it would be safe to say that most of the classical authors will have exaggerated or lied for political or sensationalist reasons, however I feel that it would be unwise to dismiss all of their accounts as completely invalid.

Archaeological evidence clearly shows that Celtic culture was widespread in Europe until around 225 BC when the Romans defeated Celtic tribes at the battle of Telamon. From this point on it appears that Celtic influence gradually diminished as first Galatia, Iberia (Spain) and subsequently Gallia Narbonensis (southern Gaul) came under Roman control. Julius Caesar[2] was instrumental in suppressing the Celts in the run up to the Christian age, firstly in the seven year Gallic war that culminated in the surrender of Vercingetorix, and secondly in Caesar's two British campaigns. In 43 AD, Claudius completed the job that Julius had begun; establishing a 400-year presence in what is now England. Romanization was a gradual process as large areas of North and West England were more or less ungovernable. Wales, particularly Mona (Anglesey) until a Roman annihilation campaign, became the Druids' stronghold and Scotland remained mostly unexplored.

Gaius Suetonius Paulinus famously exterminated the Druids at Mona and in 61 AD Boudicca's Iceni rebellion was finally crushed near Watling Street. Julius Agricola was charged with the job of conquering the entire Island, however he was recalled to Rome before any serious efforts could begin. The tribes north of the Pennines remained a constant threat, leading to Hadrianus ordering the construction of the fortified wall that still bears his name. Up until 410 AD when Emperor Honorius abandoned Britain to defend Rome itself, a gradual expansion and cultural integration took place. This is evidenced by the proliferation of Romano-Celtic deities, latinisation of the language and accounts of the time (e.g. Tacitus). Meanwhile it appears that Ireland was hardly touched by Rome, although the discovery of Roman coins and a few vague derogatory passages does indicate there may have been some contact between Rome and Ireland. In fact, Ireland posed a problem for Rome, especially in the latter half of the 4th century AD when the western coast of Britain was subject to frequent raids and settlement by the Irish.

> From here it is a two day voyage to the Sacred Isle,
> For by this name the ancients called the island.
> It lies rich in turf among the waves,
> Thickly populated by the Hierni [Irish].
> Avienus Ora Maritima, from the lost 'Massaliote Periplus, 6th century BC.

> Above Britain is Iuverna [Ireland], almost the same in area, but oblong with coasts of equal length on both sides. The climate is unfavourable for the ripening of grain, but yet it is so fertile with grass, not only abundant but sweet, that livestock eat their fill in a small part of the day... The inhabitants of this island are unrefined, ignorant of all the virtues more than any other people, and totally lack all sense of duty.
> Isidorus, C. AD 25

In the post Roman period, St. Patrick arrived in Ireland (perhaps 432 AD) from an already established Christian hierarchy in Wales. Waves of Saxons, Jutes and Angles arrived in England forcing the Celtic tribes further west and north until eventually they were completely cut off, forming the more-or-less modern Celtic enclaves of Scotland and Wales. Somewhere around this period Arturus, Ar Dhu or Arthur appears in history, most probably as a military leader who has since become entwined in various myths and romances that are codified from the *Mabinogion* onwards. It is also widely believed that many Celts fled to Amorica (Brittany) establishing a Celtic enclave over the 6th to the 9th centuries.

It is often stated that in both Ireland and Britain many Druids converted to Christianity, perhaps this was in name only in some cases. Archaeological evidence shows that pagan burials were still happening in the 7th century in Ireland, which clearly indicates a gradual rather than instantaneous transition to Christianity, taking place over at least two centuries.Whatever the case may be with the Christianisation of Ireland, it appears to have been a largely non-violent conversion[3], which would seem to make sense. The codification of what we now call Celtic literature would lend weight to the argument that much of the Druidic knowledge was retained via the ecclesiastical system. In Ireland the kings had to have a Druid to advise in matters of law and religion, a bard, physician and musician plus three 'supervisors' of his family were required. In the early Christian period the Druid was replaced by a Christian priest, other than that the structure of seven advisors was retained; the same arrangement was also applicable to the senior nobility. As late as the 10th century the head of the tribe received a Druid as a 'gift' during the tribal assembly held every seven years. It is also recorded as late as the 12th century that Druids still existed in Wales.

The Bardic schools were run by Druids or at least were under their supervision until the 6th century. These existed as fixed communities (e.g. Kildare) and as schools attached to a certain Druid or group of Druids. With the onset of Christianity, the main stream of education was ecclesiastical; however, the Bardic schools continued to exist alongside, the same is true of Scotland. Bardic schools continued to train poets, doctors, judges, musicians and historians.

It is clearly true that the Teutonic invaders arrived bringing with them their Norse paganism. Christianity and high culture was re-introduced to Britain via Irish saints such as Columcille (Columba), Brendan and Cieran (Piran). A degree of cross-cultural influences occurred between Celts, Romans and the Teutonic tribes and seemingly between the Celtic tribes themselves. Scholars generally divide the remaining Celtic peoples into two main categories — Q/K Celtic or Goidelic (encompassing Ireland, Scotland and Isle of Man/Monapia) the other being P Celtic or Brythonic (encompassing Wales, Cornwall and Brittany). Interaction between Ireland, Wales, Cornwall, Scotland and parts of England is clearly evidenced by the accounts of the early Irish evangelists as well as archaeological evidence of Irish settlements in Britain. Despite further inroads into Wales and Northern England by the Saxons, some level of integration and re-Celticisation appears to have continued following Roman abandonment, up until the arrival of the Normans in England in 1066AD.

The arrival of the Normans was the death knell for the remnants of Druidry and began a prolonged period of Celtic contraction as the Normans gradually increased their empire. Prior to William I, the island of Britain was divided into seventeen kingdoms[4] and Ireland into five. After the defeat of Harold II, the Saxon lands of the south quickly fell. Dumnonia (Cornwall) and the northern kingdoms of Mercia, Lindsey, Elmet and Deira were also absorbed into what became England. With military might and a restructuring of life into the feudal system, Celtic and Saxon laws were replaced with a more draconian form of government, further reducing what remained of the existing culture. Unlike the Saxons the Normans were not content with a loose arrangement of sub-kingdoms – they immediately made war on Wales (Cymru). Wales had become the stronghold of Britons following the Saxon invasions, and several attempts were made to retake parts of the North and East. After the battle of Chester c.613 AD, northern Britain and Wales were separated after their defeat by the Angle king, Ethelfrith. From then up until the Norman period Wales was mainly occupied in internal struggles between tribal princes and the king. Some conflicts occurred with the Danes and the Saxons; however up until 1066 Wales remained an independent nation with cultural and political independence. Rebellions against the newly arrived Normans in what is now Northern England were swiftly put down, the 'Harrying of the North' saw mass slaughter and burning of virtually all the farmlands, towns and villages in an unprecedented level of retribution, which ensured complete submission.

The next two hundred years, until 1282, was an era of constant war between Wales and England to retain Welsh independence from the Normans. In that year King Llewelyn, grandson son of Llewelyn ap Iorwerth was defeated and killed by Edward I of England so bringing to an end a separate existence for the Britons. It is from this period on that a new order of tyrannical baronies was imposed and the beginning of a gradual decline of *Cymraeg*, the Welsh language. The Bardic schools continued into the Norman period though, some notable names in that area being Gwalchmai, Cynddelw Brydydd Mawr, Hywel ab Owain and Fafydd ap Gwilym. An outward complicity and submissiveness allowed the Welsh to retain much of their culture and heritage, which is evidenced by the volume of Celtic literature that survives and the survival of the language and cultural activities (such as the *Gorsedd* and the National *Eisteddfod* of Wales) into the modern era.

The modern *Gorsedd* was founded by controversial Bard Iolo Morganwg (Edward Williams) in 1792, who claimed that it had been secretly maintained for hundreds of years, based on Druid ritual and principles. Likewise, the modern *Eisteddfod* began around the same time (1789) although the first recorded festival of this form was in 1176 at Cardigan Castle, home of Lord Rhys (which is still standing today).

Having succeeded in invading Wales (although the conflict was far from over) the Normans used overtures from Diarmaid mac Murchadha, the King of Leinster (south east province of Ireland/*Éire*) as an opportunity to further expand their territories. Henry II who was fighting to retain Norman lands in France agreed to send Richard de Clare, 2nd Earl of Pembroke (commonly known as Strongbow) to aid the deposed king. In return, de Clare married Mac Murchadha's daughter Aoife and was to inherit the Kingdom of Leinster. The campaign of 1167 was successful and by agreement with the *Ard-Rí* (High King) Rauirí Ó Conchubhair the Normans returned (temporarily) to Wales. This was not the first time that non-Celts had been in Ireland, in fact the Irish had long been fighting the Vikings and it was not until Brian Bóroimhe (Boru) united the country as *Ard-Rí* (High King) that they were finally held in check, although at the cost of his own life and that of his son Muechadh, in 1014.

Three years after the Normans left, they returned, landing at the Viking city of Waterford, which they soon captured. Dublin (*dubh linn*) which was also a Viking city was under siege from the Norman forces and fell before the Irish forces could come to their assistance. Henry himself arrived in 1171 with reinforcements enabling them to consolidate their foothold on Irish soil and in the treaty of 1175 Ó Conchubhair accepted Henry's rule in Leinster. By 1204 Dublin had become the Norman capital and the basis for the English 'Pale'. To begin with, Norman expansion led to a large degree of assimilation, with the Normans adopting Irish language, culture and customs. At this point the Normans posed little threat to Brehon Laws (*Dlithe na mBreithiúin/ Feineachus*) deriving from the pre-Christian period, to language, dress and the largely unchanged way of life. However, by 1366 the Normans felt it necessary to stop the 'creeping Gaelicisation' in its tracks with the Statutes of Kilkenny. This abolished Brehon laws, imposed English language and English names and even sought to eliminate the Celtic form of dress and horse riding and so forth. Further reintroduction and additions over time diminished Irish influence even so far as to ban those of Irish blood from trading around the capital (The Pale). From the Reformation onwards, English domination and suppression of the Celtic culture drastically increased, leading to several hundred years of rebellion and retribution which has only ended in relatively recent times (1921). Bardic schools survived into the 17th century and 'hedge schools' (illegal Gaelic speaking schools) attempted to stem the tide of Anglicization, but despite what has been described by some as cultural genocide, Celtic culture has survived into the modern era. Approximately two million died and two million emigrated of a population of eight million during the Irish famine of the mid 1840s. It is estimated that at that time two thirds of the Irish population spoke the native tongue; however within one generation it was largely abandoned for English. Continued emigration after the famine led to a steady decline in both the population and Celtic culture in Ireland, indeed, emigration was still very high up until the late 1980s.

Today Gaelic (*Gaeilge*) survives in pockets, mainly in the *Gaeltacht* areas of perhaps 200,000 people. Since the formation of the Irish Free State (1922) serious attempts have been made to re-establish the language and all Irish children now learn Gaelic at least up until secondary school. Cultural aspects such as art, music and literature have fared better and since the Gaelic revival of the 19th century great efforts have been made to preserve what remains of Celtic culture in Ireland.

Scotland had escaped largely untouched by the Romans; in fact, the Picti (meaning painted/tattooed people) and Calendonii were a constant threat to the Roman colony. Ancient Scotland (*Alba*) and Northern Ireland (*Banba*) were populated largely by Picts, although called that by the Romans they were a series of tribes often at war amongst themselves. They did however manage to unite against Roman aggression and although suffering crushing losses at times (e.g. Agricola's campaign against Calgath and his Caledonian tribe), it was these people who fought the Romans and remained unconquered. This may be hugely due to the abandonment of the Roman campaign to take the entire island, however we will never know if they could have succeeded, perhaps it was considered too much difficulty for questionable reward. By 105 AD, the Romans had withdrawn as far south as the Tyne River and in 122 AD the northern frontier was marked by Hadrian's Wall which ran from Solway Firth to Wallsend-on-Tyne. Some twenty years later a new Governor (Quintus Lollius Urbicus) attempted to regain territory lost fifty years earlier, his gains were consolidated by a second wall — the Antonine Wall, which was stormed in 161 AD, then retaken by the Romans and finally abandoned for good in 180 AD. By 214 AD the Romans had given up on Scotland completely and from this time were largely on the defensive. Hence, Romans had little impact both politically or culturally on Scotland, one can assume that life continued much as it had before. Little is known of the Picts themselves, however after Eumenius's poetry made the name Picti famous in 297 AD, all Scottish peoples seem to be have been lumped under the same heading, be they Celtic, Norse or indigenous tribes.

In 367 AD a simultaneous attack from the Irish *Scotia* arriving in the West, the Picts who overran Hadrian's Wall and a wave of Angles and Saxons in the South and East decimated the Roman forces. Although this was not the end of Roman Britain, it severely weakened the Roman presence and by 410 AD continued inroads by the Irish, Picts, Scots and Saxons made the territory untenable. It is often stated that the Scots (from Scotia or Dalriada) invaded the western half of Scotland at the beginning of the 6th century, however looking at archaeology and mythology, they would appear to have had a significant presence much earlier. After a significant period of living in close proximity and frequent warfare between the Scots and Picts (not to mention rebuffing repeated Viking attacks) in the mid 9th century Kenneth McAlpine (King of Dalraida) united the country by ascending to the Pictish throne. Discerning the cultural differences between the Scot and Pict is very difficult given their gradual merger. Pictish culture has often been regarded as the lesser and more simplistic of the two branches, however, gradual integration and domination by the Scots over hundreds of years makes it almost impossible to separate them. 'Pictish Oghams' as the stone are called in Scotland could be of either origin and the level of linguistic and cultural similarity prior to integration is hard to say. It is generally considered that the Scots were Christians and that the Picts retained the Celtic gods and gradually accepted the incoming ideas long before unification.

Trouble was brewing in the reign of Macbeth (MacBeathadh, 1040-57) perhaps the most maligned and famous of Scottish kings. Shakespeare's highly political play, portraying him as a murderer and villainous king, was highly inaccurate and was aimed at pleasing the English (Anglo-Norman) royalty. The truth it seems is that both Macbeth and Duncan had a legitimate claim to the throne. Subsequent to Duncan's disastrous invasion of northern England Macbeth met him in battle near Elgin in 1040, killing Duncan and emerging victorious to take the Scottish throne. Duncan's two sons fled to England, which was (largely) ruled by Edward the Confessor. In 1054 Malcolm, with the aid of Earl Siward (a Dane) and the support of Edward led an invasion of Scotland. Despite Macbeth's defeat, he maintained control of northern Scotland, leaving Malcolm to be installed by Edward as ruler of the Lothians and Strathclyde. By 1057, Macbeth's support was waning and Malcolm eventually succeeded in deposing him, supposedly at Lumphanan. Lulach (Macbeth's stepson) continued to fight Malcolm but was killed in 1058 enabling Malcolm III to become Scottish king.

The demise of Macbeth really marked the beginning of the end for the truly Celtic royalty and culture in Scotland. Up until this time, Saxon England had little or no effect on Scotland, Celtic traditions and thinly disguised Druidic practices continued to flourish. Stone circles continued to be in use, the lairds kept Bards and the Christian church failed to abide by much of the edicts of the Synod of Whitby (667). It was with the involvement of the Saxons and particularly the subsequent presence of the Normans that pre-Christian and Celtic influence was to decline.

Malcolm Ceann Mór (Malcolm III) had hopes of expanding his domain, and despite help from England in ascending the throne and an upbringing largely in the English court, he began a long campaign into northern England, which was ultimately unsuccessful. As a direct result of the Norman invasion of England many northern Celts and Saxons fled into the relative safety of Scotland. Margaret Atheling (later St. Margaret) with her brother and king-elect Edgar arrived in Scotland also, after a failed attempt to flee to Hungary. Malcolm, now a widower, fell for the reputedly striking beauty of Princess Margaret taking her as his second wife thus uniting the Scottish line with the now defunct Anglo-Saxon royalty.

William the Conqueror was not slow to see the obvious threat from Scotland to his newly established authority. He began with a failed attempt to subdue Northumbria. Malcolm seeing their weakened state invaded Northumbria himself, extending Scottish territory beyond Hadrian's Wall for the first time since the Roman period. This success was short lived, William II taking up the baton from his father, made inroads into Northumbria and Cumbria, finally provoking a reinvasion by Malcolm and his eldest son Edward. Both were killed at Alnwick, sending Scotland into a crisis. Donald III (Malcolm's younger brother) claimed the throne attempting to drive out English influence brought about by his brother and sister-in-law Margaret. His reign was short lived. Malcolm's other son Duncan, who had grown up in the English court, deposed him with the assistance of William II of England. Duncan, who had sworn loyalty to England, had an even shorter reign and his murder enabled Donald to resume the throne until William II again sent an army headed by Malcolm and Margaret's fourth son Edgar. Donald III was slain, and became the last of the Scottish kings to be buried on the western island of Iona, the traditional burial ground of the Dalraida line. Edgar I became king in 1097, marking the end of this period of turmoil and the beginning of 'Normanisation' of

Scotland. Feudalism was introduced and Papal authority re-established over the largely Celtic church.

Various attempts were made to re-establish Scottish independence, notably by William Wallace and Robert the Bruce, culminating in the Treaty of Northampton in 1328, which recognized Scottish independence. However, a weakened and divided Scotland allied itself with France in war against England with little success but remained independent until James VI (cousin of Elizabeth I) ascended to the English throne in 1603. With the Stuart dynasty uniting the Scottish and English crown, Scotland's fate was sealed as an independent and Celtic state. After becoming embroiled in religious and succession strife, culminating in Jacobite rebellion and the demise of Bonnie Prince Charlie, Scotland found itself financially and politically ruined. This led to further Anglicisation, extermination of the highland clans (who opposed the 1707 act of union) and the land clearances that saw as many as two million crofters and clansmen flee to America, Canada, Australia and New Zealand. Scots Gaelic (*Gáidhlig*) went into retreat rapidly as English language predominated with Georgian expansion, leading to the modern-day situation of scattered island communities in the north and west who are still able to speak their native tongue.

In both Britain and Ireland a huge shift occurred, not just in terms of who was in charge, but in the whole way of life and even the land itself. Celtic culture gradually receded with customs and language coming under threat. The end of the clans in Scotland and the flight of the earls in Ireland ended patronage for the Bards and the Bardic schools and this most probably led to the loss of the oral tradition that had managed to survive until this time. The land itself also changed dramatically with land enclosures and feudalism replacing the open landscape and commonage. It is said that an Irish squirrel (red that is, grey arrived much later) could travel from Antrim to Kerry without ever having to touch the ground, obviously almost the whole island was once covered in forest. A similar situation existed in Britain, but this changed earliest in the south with the arrival of the Romans. Further deforestation occurred with the arrival of the Normans, but it was in the late Middle Ages, when sheep and deer farming and ship building expanded, that whole forests began to disappear. In the past new trees had been able to grow without too much trouble as the population of sheep and deer was small and wolves were numerous. As time passed, wolves were hunted into extinction and the widespread use of land for livestock gave seedlings and saplings no chance of survival unless man protected them. Celtic buildings, mainly of the thatched roundhouse variety, were relatively simple and to use modern parlance — eco friendly. Later development favoured by the Saxons and Normans used more stone and more wood, which of course meant that more quarries were mined and more trees had to be cut down. Saxons built some of the earliest stone churches in Britain although these were rather modest in style and proportion; later Norman buildings were of elaborate and immense construction, obviously needing a lot more materials and labour. Druidic tradition forbade killing trees for trivial usage, although the Romans and Normans in particular had no qualms about such actions.

These changes in lifestyle have led directly to the landscape of Britain and Ireland that we know today —most of the highlands are grassland roamed by sheep and there are few or no trees, lowland areas are divided mainly into enclosed fields surrounding towns and villages. Henry VIII and Elizabeth I of England were particularly responsible for clearing forests and both were greatly interested in developing an impressive navy, which required large numbers of mature trees. However they did retain forests for their own use. Pockets of ancient forest survive today, particularly those that were used by aristocrats and royalty for hunting. However this is a tiny fraction of the immense woodland that once covered the British Isles.

Therefore, a clear pattern emerges – gradual military defeat at the hands of numerous invaders, which led to great cultural, social and topographical changes. It would be very easy to blame it all on the Normans – what a rotten bunch! However, the Normans were opportunists; if anything they seized every chance to gain new territories and exploited any weakness of their opponents. One must not forget that in both the case of Scotland and Ireland they were called upon for assistance, which gave them the 'foot in the door' so to speak. Another important factor in this transition was the division and infighting amongst the Celts, had they not been warring with each other they would have had a considerably stronger chance of resisting invaders or ejecting them subsequent to invasion. Only particularly brilliant leaders such as Vercingetorix of the Arveni in Gaul, Llewelyn ap Iorwerth in Wales or Brian Bóroimhe in Ireland had the charisma and skill to unite their people sufficiently to make a realistic defence against overwhelming force. Another factor that went against the Celts is that being on the fringes of Europe they soon became behind with the times as far as strategy and technology of warfare was concerned. The Romans copied the Celtic chariot but vastly improved it. They also borrowed and modified their armour designs, making use of these innovations against later generations of Celts. Later still, the Vikings proved a difficult adversary in part due to superior iron working that enabled them to make better quality swords. It was the Vikings that introduced better smithing, new weapons and horse spurs to Ireland, they also are thought to be the first people (apart from a few Romans) to use coinage in Ireland. When the Normans arrived in England they had the latest armour and weapons, which the Saxons and Celts did not, they also used cavalry to far greater effect and were already using modern chainmail that was common on the continent, this advantage was evident again in the conquest of Wales, Scotland and Ireland.

Having established hegemony in the British Isles, the

Normans were able to retain power largely due to their spectacular prowess in political manipulation – by keeping nobles fighting amongst each other instead of fighting the common enemy, control was retained. Revolts did occur regularly in all the territories, including Cornwall, however none had any lasting success, primarily because principalities and provinces failed to act in unison.

Moving on from conquest, various attempts at Celtic re-emergence took place, firstly in the late 13th and early 14th century Scotland re-emerged for a while as a powerful force, actually managing to re-capture parts of northern England. In Ireland in the 14th century, the Normans had been assimilated to such an extent that the English crown deemed it necessary to issue the Statute of Kilkenny. The Norman-Irish, now Gaelic speaking lords, were known as the 'Old English' so as to distinguish them from the later 'New English' who they opposed (in unity with the native Irish). Gaelic culture was still strong and a threat to English colonisation, hence the statute had to be reintroduced several times. However, despite attempts to recover, Celtic culture across the British Isles continued a gradual decline.

After centuries of military, political and cultural retreat, 'Young Ireland' formed in the 1840s, was instrumental in both a cultural and political revival. The likes of Synge, Yeats and Gregory were important in the preservation of Gaelic language and culture, as was the Gaelic League formed in 1893. This however did not include religious aspects of the ancient Irish culture as religious life had long ago become entirely dominated by the struggle between the Catholic and Protestant churches.

In Wales and England, interest in Celtic and megalithic culture began to grow in the mid 17th century with the work of John Aubrey (1629-97). He surveyed ancient monuments such as Stonehenge and Avebury and wrote extensively. Only his *Miscellanies* was published during his life, the remainder of his works being published in the 18th and 19th centuries. John

Toland and William Stukeley are two names greatly linked with the English Romantic Revival of Druidry, both of whom were familiar with Aubrey's work. The Ancient Druid Order (ADO) claims John Toland as its founder in 1717; however, his own writing seems to demonstrate his distaste for Druidry and priesthood in general, casting a shadow of doubt over that claim. The ADO list, a continuous line of 'Chosen Chiefs' from 1717 up to current time, including amongst their number William Stukely and the famed poet William Blake. Stukeley, a rather eccentric Doctor, Freemason and Anglican priest, not only lectured his congregation on Druidry but went as far as creating a Druidic folly in the grounds of the vicarage of Stamford. He also signed his letters as 'Chyndonax, Druid of Mount Haemus', which was a further indication that his whimsical notions had become seriously out of hand. Although he did draw attention to Stonehenge with his works, any serious connection with the Druids of old and any of their extant traditions and wisdom is very doubtful.

In 1781 another order — the Ancient Order of Druids (AOD) was founded in London by Henry Hurle, who like Stukeley was involved in Freemasonry; again with no more than romantic notions of a largely forgotten past as inspiration. Interest in the Celts and Druidry began to increase, with the offer of thirty pounds reward for genuine archaic knowledge being brought to light. The work of Edward Williams (better known as Iolo Morganwg) surfaced with an entire system of Druidic thought and practice which he had 'discovered' from Welsh documents attributed to 16th century Bard Llewelyn Sion. *Barddas* was translated by his son and accepted by the Welsh Manuscript Society as entirely genuine on publication (1862) forty years after Morganwg's death. Morganwg, it appears, fabricated most of the work, producing elaborate forgeries whilst in a debtors' prison. It was some 100 years after his death (he died in 1822) that his work was discredited, although more recent examination and cross referencing would indicate that much of the work was genuine although interspersed with his own compositions. Morganwg had used his ideas to resurrect the *Gorsedau* and *Eisteddfodau* in Wales, the modern form of which still uses rituals he devised or found. This led to revivals of the *Gorsedd* in both Cornwall and Brittany, the *Mod* in Scotland and the *Oireachtas* in Ireland.

Another famous fabricator appeared in Scotland of the 1760s. James Macpherson succeeded in palming off his own works inspired by Irish mythology as that of 'Ossian' an ancient Dalriadan Bard. His contemporaries were convinced as was famous classical historian Sir Edward Gibbon. Even now, his work is available as a 'genuine' Celtic text despite having been thoroughly discredited. William Butler Yeats and Lady Augusta Gregory (writing around the turn of the last century), although not guilty of fraud or invention, seem to have succumbed to the romantics' desire to sanitize the Celt to suit the mores of Victorian society. Their translations although doing much to publicise and retain Irish literature and culture leave much to be desired in terms of accuracy.

On the Isle of Man, The Manx Language Society (*Yn Cheshaght Ghailckagh*) was formed to resurrect the dying language. It was recorded in 1875 that 12,000 people spoke the language but by 1955 this had fallen to just six people! Although it is not widely spoken, and probably never will be again, Manx has at least been saved from extinction. In 1904 the *Handbook of the Cornish Language* was published by Henry Jenner in an attempt to revive the language that had been more or less dead since 1800. The Cornish Society continues his work and both Cornish language and cultural identity has re-emerged after a long period of decline since the 11th century. Important translations by Guest, O'Curry, Skene, Stokes, Rolleston and many others in the Victorian period have provided the basis for recovering Celtic texts for a largely non-Celtic speaking people. In fact, those who are fluent in modern Irish, Cornish, Scots, Breton or Welsh would probably have extreme difficulty in trying to read the original texts in their corresponding language as the modern forms are now vastly different from those of the medieval and earlier periods. Sadly, many Gaelic texts still lie untranslated in university and museum vaults, hopefully this will not always remain the case.

The repeal of the Witchcraft act in Britain in 1951 prompted the public emergence of two figures who have been hugely influential in modern paganism – Gerald Gardner and Ross Nichols. Gerald Gardner founded the Wiccan religion that has now become global, and his friend Ross Nichols (who left the ADO in 1964) began the Order of Bards, Ovates and Druids (OBOD). Nichols devised the eightfold year that has become central to modern paganism based on his knowledge of ancient festivals, however, we can never be sure if the ancient Celts or Druids had an understanding of their year in such a manner. Nichols also incorporated elements of Robert Graves's ideas from *The White Goddess*. Graves's Tree Calendar is seemingly pure invention, derided by Celtic experts of the time and even by his own father and grandfather who were both serious Irish academics. Graves's work did bring to light the rather obscure Ogham alphabet, however his work was deeply flawed and modern attempts to re-evaluate Ogham (eg. by Damien McManus and Niall MacCoitir) are still far less widely accepted than Graves's work, despite Graves's own admission that he had made some serious errors.

More recently, the late Alexi Kondratiev, John Matthews, Caitlin Matthews and Ronald Hutton have done much to clear away the mist created by romanticism and wild speculation of Victorian writers, by returning to extant Classical and Celtic sources. Various Druid orders now exist around the world, all of which, except a handful (such as ADO, AOD, Insular Order of Druids) began in the latter half of the 20th century. Some orders and Druids might like to claim a continuous link with the ancient

Druids or at least as far back as the last of the Bardic schools; unfortunately I have found no evidence to suggest that this is the case and no serious scholar I have come across has given weight to any such claims.

The sad truth is that Druidry began fading away with the onset of Christianity, going into its death throes with the passing of the Bardic Schools and the end of patronage by nobility. There are still tiny Druidic remnants, so I am told, the last remains of that ancient spirituality that may well be gone in less than a generation if it has not already disappeared[5]. Modern Druidry is, at best, a reconstruction or re-interpretation of a lost religion or spiritual system. Dubious claims within Druidry as well as dubious scholarship still exists and is in fact quite widespread. However cheap reproductions of translations of the source material and careful use of the internet make building a more accurate picture of what Druidry (and more broadly Celtic culture) once was more achievable.

It is my belief that only by having as complete an understanding as possible of the Druidry of the past, can it be practiced now or in the future. If there is little or no continuity between the 'old Druidry' and the 'neo-Druidry' then it would be as well to give 'neo-Druidry' a different name altogether. Having briefly looked at over two thousand years of history, we can now proceed to examine what remains of the body of Druidic knowledge that we are fortunate enough to have access to.

II

What is a Druid?

There is not always agreement amongst modern Druids regarding what defines a Druid. The general concensus among historians and definitions to be found in a dictionary or encyclopaedia are something along these lines:

A Druid is a member of the priestly or learned class in ancient Celtic society. In most cases, this is confined to the inhabitants of Ireland, Britain and France/Belgium in the pre-Christian era. The derivation of this word is often linked with the Greek and Roman words used to describe them (see previous chapter) and is generally regarded to mean 'very knowledgeable' or 'oak seer'. From the testimony of the Greeks and Romans it would appear that Druids were the uppermost echelon of Celtic society, superior in some respects to rulers. Comparisons have been drawn with Brahmins (the uppermost caste in Hindu society), who also performed priestly functions. Early Irish manuscripts that describe society and in particular the colours worn by different sections of society would indicate that Celtic culture was very hierarchical, at the pinnacle of which was the Druid caste. However, one must be careful in making comparisons between one culture and another, especially where language is concerned. Some have tried to make linguistic links (despite different alphabets) between Hindu and Egyptian words and those of the Celtic languages; the same is also true of some practices. Most of this is speculative and not based on any recorded or found evidence of links between cultures. Quite possibly apparent linguistic similarities are a mere coincidence rather than due to some common values or past associations. At least commentary by classical writers was contemporaneous with the ancient Druids (even if biased) and was largely gleaned from first hand observations. These original accounts are arguably as good as or better than third-hand information received through the filter of many hundreds of years of recapitulation and distortion.

Diodorus:
The Gauls have certain wise men and experts on the gods called Druids, as well as a highly respected class of seers. Through auguries and animal sacrifice these seers predict the future and no one dares to scoff at them. ...It is the custom among the Gauls to never perform a sacrifice without someone skilled in divine ways present. They say that those who know about the nature of the gods should offer thanks to them and make requests of them, as though these people spoke the same language as the gods. The Gauls, friends and foes alike, obey the rule of the priests and bards not only in times of peace but also during wars. It has often happened that just as two armies approached each other with swords drawn and spears ready, the Druids will step between the two sides and stop the fighting, as if they had cast a spell on wild beasts. Thus even among the wildest barbarians, anger yields to wisdom and the god of war respects the Muses.

Julius Caesar:
Throughout all of Gaul there are two classes of people who are treated with dignity and honour. This does not include the common people, who are little better than slaves and never have a voice in councils. ...The two most powerful classes mentioned above are the Druids and the warriors. Druids are concerned with religious matters, public and private sacrifices and divination. ...the Druids are the judges on all controversies, public and private. If any crime has been committed, if any murder done, if there are any questions concerning

inheritance, or any controversy concerning boundaries, the Druids decide the case and determine punishments.

Posidonius, Pliny and Caesar wrote at length on the Celts and the Druids of Gaul in particular, and to a lesser extent on those of Britain, which gives us a wealth of information, much of which has been corroborated by archaeological evidence and later Celtic sources. Of course it is difficult to discern what is true, and what is fabricated for the excitement of the classical reader. However it would appear that the classical accounts are in the most part worth examining – usually fairly unemotional, often incredulous and generally less inclined to turgid hyperbole than much that has been written in later eras.

The earliest Irish and Welsh writings of history, mythology and residual wisdom are from 6th century, but from mainly the 9th century onwards are attributed to monastic scribes. It is often said that writing did not arrive in Ireland until the arrival of Christianity, conversely it is well known that the Druids were able to speak and write using the ancient Greek alphabet, which was used in mundane or 'housekeeping' affairs, as stated by Caesar. It is also widely accepted that the Druids were familiar with and revered the teachings of Pythagoras (c.540-510 BC), sharing his belief in metempsychosis or 'transmigration of souls'. One would therefore be inclined to conclude that transfer of Druidic knowledge by oral tradition was a matter of choice rather than due to ignorance of other methods. This proves to be highly inconvenient for the modern would be Druid, given the absence of any surviving Druids to teach or explain their beliefs and practices. Likewise, with the exception of Pythagorus' theorum (received via Euclid) and brief mentions by later writers there are sadly no known writings of his philosophy, his religious society or his mathematics. It is known that the Celts' territories extended into the Balkans, Greece and Turkey so it is not unreasonable to expect that some degree of cultural interchange took place between the Celts and Greeks.

> Posidonius:
> The teachings of Pythagoras prevails among the Gauls, that the souls of humans are immortal and that after a certain number of years they will live again, with the soul passing into another body. Because of this belief, some people at funerals will throw letters into the funeral pyre, so that those having passed on might read them.

By careful analysis of Classical writings, those of monastic scribes and archaeological evidence we can begin to build an imperfect but plausible picture of what a Druid was and what functions they performed. We must be careful to note that there may have been considerable differences within Druidry within Ireland, Britain and Gaul. Caesar rather casually states, 'the system is thought to have been devised in Britain and brought thence into Gaul.' No evidence or justification is given for this remark and nowhere else does such an earlier statement exist. However, based on this one line great claims have been made about the origin of Druidry. Revival writers such as Julius Pokorny tried to justify this stance but archaeological evidence would seem to indicate the reverse as it is quite clear that the Celts migrated westwards across Europe and it is most likely that Druidry was introduced to Ireland and Britain via Europe. As far as Ireland is concerned, extant Classical texts are of little help, with only a few derogatory mentions of Ireland and sadly, Pytheas's *On the Ocean*, which probably included Ireland, no longer exists. We do though find that information to be found in the Irish sources does often corroborate what is stated in Classical sources, which in those cases, in the absence of further information, we must assume to be of some validity.

Classical sources (Strabo, Diodorus, Timagenes) refer to three classes of Druids – these being the Druids (philosophers &

judges), Vates (diviners and healers) and Bards (singers, poets and storytellers). There would appear to be some measure of overlap between classes, especially between Vates and Druids, both it appears could perform prophesy, and both might be concerned with sacrifices[6]. In Ireland the structure appears to concur with that given by classical sources — *Druí (Draoi), Fáith (Fáidh) and File (Bard).* It is thought that the Gauls used similar terms — *Druid/Drus, Vátis* and *Bardos.* This threefold structure has been used in modern Druid orders and often is hierarchical — Bard, Ovate and Druid ascending in that order. In reality, we cannot be entirely sure if the hierarchy was structured as is often found today, we do know however, that in Ireland there were several stages within each class, requiring considerable time and study to reach the highest level.

We now have a rough picture of what a Druid was in terms of function; however, contrary to popular thought, it appears there was considerable disparity between the Druidry of Ireland, Britain and Gaul. Much of the opinions of the romantic era that have also been carried down into the modern era, are derived from Iolo Morganwg's *Barddas* but are unfortunately quite erroneous. The preface to the book makes a lengthy comparison with the contents of Morganwg's work on British Bardism and the accounts of Julius Caesar and other classical sources. It makes the assumption that the contents of *Barddas* is a genuine inheritance of the pre-Christian Druids and attempts to unify British and Gaulish Druidry. However, where differences occur it is attributed to corruption of the 'pure' British form which occurred in Gaul at some indeterminable time. Not only are the arguments often illogical but they demonstrate arrogance in assuming British Druidry to be both superior and also progenitor of Druidry elsewhere, without realistic supporting evidence.

Arguments are given by some that Druidry is native to the British Isles and was practised by the aboriginal peoples, later being adopted by the conquering Celts[6]. Attractive as this theory may be, I think it unlikely that the Celts would adopt 'wholesale' a foreign religious system. Mythology suggests some retention or absorption of the indigenous culture as is often the case but I find it hard to believe that Druidry supplanted an existing religious system and spread into Gaul, Iberia and Cisalpine Gaul from Britain and/or Ireland. One need only look at subsequent history to observe the transfer of religious ideas from conquering peoples to the defeated, albeit with some retention of earlier beliefs. The Roman influence in Gaul is undeniable through evidence of the fusion of Roman and Gaulish deities and the arrival of Christianity, via the Roman Empire some three centuries later. This largely replaced or overlayed the existing pagan system in all of Europe, again with some retention of earlier beliefs and assimilation of pagan practices. Why then would the Celts, preceding the Romans, not have followed this same model of dominance? Surely, their own religion and theological ideas were not so weak as to be annihilated or absorbed by the religion of the people they conquered. This suggestion seems to go against the grain of known history and the observed and recorded effects of a militarily advanced culture interacting with an older one. It cannot be proven definitively one way or the other, but the introduction of Druidry into western Europe by the migrating Celts, with some degree of absorption of native beliefs, seems to be the most logical and likely source of the origin of Druidry in Europe.

It appears to me that the differences between what is known of British and Gaulish Druidry and that of Ireland are often conveniently skipped over, when in truth there is a huge body of medieval literature that paints quite a different picture of the practice and beliefs of the Irish. It is quite obvious that there is a significant overlap between the different streams of Druidry, but the differences in their development are also of great importance in gaining a fuller understanding of ancient Druidry.

It is generally accepted that the Celts arrived in Western Europe, Britain and Ireland at different times, and according to the earliest accounts from different locations. For example the Milesians came from Iberia (Spain), the British who apparently were descended from Brú (Brutus) were claimed (however unlikely) to be from Troy. Archaeological evidence would seem to support the idea of a staggered spread across Europe, concurring with the ancient accounts and accepted academic view. This being the case it is most likely that the culture and religious practice of the Celts diverged to some extent due to their physical isolation. Naturally, this isolation would also explain why the languages, which have a common root, diverged considerably between Ireland, Britain and Gaul.

Like the Druids of Gaul and Britain, the Irish Druids held a high position in society and performed similar functions, having to take a considerable number of years in their training. The three tiers of the system were open to both men and women and Irish mythology testifies to the significant role of women as Druids and - as warriors.

Gaulish Druids were supposedly under the leadership of a single Druid who was elected via a council or assembly of Druids, *Barddas* claims a similar arrangement in Britain. In Ireland no such arrangement seems to have existed, Druids were localised and generally attached to some form of noble or monarch. For instance, King Laegaire had a number of eminent Druids in his service, of whom it is said Lucetmail and Lochru foretold the coming of St. Patrick. The Druid's sphere of influence appears to be linked to the master they served as well as their own eminence, with no supreme authority over the entire country.

In Ireland, there is ample record of auguries from the use of the hide of a slaughtered bull, observation of clouds and heavenly bodies, sleeping on a burial mound, listening to bird song to the use of Ogham rods made of yew. However, there are few recorded accounts of the use of human sacrifice in Ireland (Strabo and Diodorus only) and unlike in continental Europe there is no significant archaeological evidence found suggesting the practice. There are tales in Ireland, Scotland and Wales of giants eating their human captives and Strabo stated that the Irish ate the corpses of their male ancestors, although Strabo actually visiting Ireland is unlikely. To eat in the presence of the dead was certainly customary a century ago in Ireland and it has been stated that in earlier times it was the custom for the food to be actually laid upon the corpse[8]. Perhaps this custom is some symbolic form of transfer of faculties of wisdom from the dead to the living. We cannot be sure, but it would appear likely that human sacrifice or ritual cannibalism was not practised (if at all) by Druids in Ireland to the same extent as those in Gaul. However, one should not be overly shocked by the concept of human sacrifice in the context of the ancient world. After all Roman historian Livy (Livius Titus) recorded of the 2nd Punic War (218-201 BC between Rome and Carthage) that the Romans themselves offered human victims to the gods, it still being a common (but declining) practice in the ancient world until the common era.

The Gauls are said to have followed the teachings of Pythagorus, namely the doctrine of transmigration of souls, which they believed immortal. It was generally regarded that men would be reborn as men, although in *Barddas* it claims that the British Druids believed that wrongdoers could descend to animal form also. The story of Taliesin's birth[9] would seem to confirm a belief in shapeshifting, possibly interpreted as rebirth in different animal states. In Ireland, there is no explicit reference to metempsychosis although mythology recounts the transformation of men into animals or living on in the otherworld beyond death. The concept of *Find* or the personification of wisdom echoes a belief in rebirth with the seer Find depicted as baby, man and old man most famously in the story of his avatar Fionn mac

Cumhaill. Although it is not explicitly connected to metempsychosis, it is clearly along similar lines of thought, whereby divine knowledge is transferred from the old to the young, the three forms being linked to the goddess of the land and the waters of the Boyne, which symbolised divine wisdom.

Gaulish Druids, according to classical sources, were forbidden from committing any of their wisdom, history or practices to writing, using Greek for mundane affairs and according to Julius Caesar, Ogham script on wooden staves. This was not the case in Ireland as the *Annals of the Four Masters* reveals:

> It was this Cormac, son of Art, also, that collected the Chroniclers of Ireland to Teamhair, and ordered them to write the chronicles of Ireland in one book, which was named the Psalter of Teamhair. In that book were entered the coeval exploits and synchronisms of the kings of Ireland with the kings and emperors of the world, and of the kings of the provinces with the monarchs of Ireland.

The death of Cormac mac Art, at the hands of the Druids for what they regarded as heresy is dated as 266 AD. Various annals copied from earlier texts exist today and if we are to believe the above quotation, Irish history was codified from long before the monastic scribes. There is no mention in any known Irish text of a prohibition of recording Druidic lore or practice; however, the majority of extant volumes that have been examined or translated are mythology or histories.

Trees, it is well known, were of great importance to the Druids. Pliny cites the oak as supreme among trees to the Gauls in the now famous account of the collection of mistletoe. Mistletoe is not native to Ireland and was only introduced in the 19th century; hence, it is far less likely to have had such importance in Ireland. In Ireland, trees were categorised from 'noble of the wood' downwards in the medieval texts and one can only assume this is a residual categorisation from much earlier. Oak was a prominent tree but perhaps no more so than yew and hazel and possibly others such as rowan, elder and hawthorn.

So, one can see that in defining what a Druid is or what a Druid does is dependent on what region you are considering, as clearly practises, although bearing similarities, were not uniform in the Celtic world. Bearing that in mind, defining Druidry now is further complicated for the modern Druid. Many authors have discussed the philosophy, path or meaning of Druidry at great length, however ultimately each individual has to discover the secrets for themselves. I believe that is through action that we gain as much insight as study and introspection, which bring to mind the Chinese proverb: 'to see is to know, to do is to understand'.

I will be looking in greater detail at the specifics of Druidic practice further into the book, drawing together what is known of ancient knowledge, pagan survivals and modern practice (derived from both), gleaned from as many verifiable sources as I am able to access. Through studying and actively using this knowledge, I believe this gives a stronger and more complete understanding of what Druidry is than any amount of musing and speculation can provide.

What then does practical Druidry entail in a modern context? Obviously the core areas of the Bard, Ovate and Druid must continue to exist in some form, otherwise the modern practise would not be worthy of the title Druidry. In a modern western environment, it is difficult for a person to spend the twelve or as many as nineteen years necessary to complete the training undertaken by the ancients. In the modern world of written and computer storage the memorisation of hundreds of poems, wisdom tales and the history of a family, tribe or people may seem obsolete. The practice of medicine, astronomy/astrology, divination, law and moral guidance has been undertaken by specialised professionals, mostly in a secular rather than spiritual way, which does not preclude the would be Druid from also becoming versed in these skills.

Because so much has changed about society, secular and religious practices and the shape and feel of both the human and natural world it is not possible to exactly recreate Druidry of the ancient Celts. Even if it were possible to recreate Druidry in its original form, one must wonder if it would still be relevant or viable. A much used term is 'the spirit of Druidry', which I interpret as recreating the key elements of ancient Druidry in a form that is adapted to modern man, whilst remaining as true in spirit and practice to its roots as is humanly possible. If we can do that then Druidry is real and not simply a lifestyle choice or a laughable parody of a long dead spirituality.

Ultimately, Druidry is not about slavish adherence to antique practices and dogma, nor about re-inventing it in a form that is convenient and user-friendly. Although maintaining a high degree of continuity between ancient and modern Druidry is essential, above all I believe that it is about finding our own truth, a connection to our inner selves, a connection to spirit and the Earth. To us, in the early twenty first century, this presents a great spiritual challenge in a time that offers perhaps the greatest challenges to humanity and to the future existence of life on this planet.

III

Gods and Goddesses

Modern Druids may be pantheists, monotheists, Christians, Buddhists or even agnostics, such has the world changed since the time of the ancient Celts. To have a greater understanding of the Celtic deities and their relevance in modern Drudry I feel that it is useful to look at deity in a wider context.

It cannot be known for sure, but many believe that humankind's earliest gods were the sun and moon, which have come to represent the divine male and female. Others believe that the earliest gods were feminine, there being some archaeological evidence (e.g. Willendorf Venus) to support this view. Whatever the earliest form of god was, there has clearly been a transition over the millennia in what and how we worship. The prominence of matriarchal religion in the ancient past is clear and its gradual decline and replacement by patriarchal religion can be fairly easily traced. The most ancient form of Judaism discovered, revered both a male and female god, however, by the time their religion was codified the feminine deity had been displaced and forgotten. Vestiges of a greater feminine importance still exist in modern Hindu religion – the male gods are coupled with their lesser known female consorts (with the exception of Kali), however the male gods derive their power from the female which would indicate a previously equal, if not higher status of the feminine. Even the Hindu process of blessing the home can involve sacred earth taken from a brothel, a clear throwback to a feminine fertility rite.

As time has passed, male domination in both secular and religious life has increased as the patriarchal religions – Judaism, Christianity and Islam have spread around the world, replacing belief systems that honour either both sexes or particularly the feminine. This has been a gradual process. In some cases the feminine has been retained to some extent – such as the Marion cult in Christianity replacing the worship of Ishtar, Demeter or Isis, which was still common around the time of the fall of the western Roman empire.

The ancient Celts appear to have a religious system in many ways not unlike that of the Egyptians, Greeks or Romans. It is clear that a multitude of gods and goddesses existed in Ireland, in Britain and Gaul. It is not entirely clear if the Celts' view of their gods is comparable to that of the Egyptians or Greeks. The destruction of the Greek statues of their gods by the Celts at the sacking of the Oracle of Delphi would indicate a lack of respect for their pantheon and it said that the Celts laughed at the Greeks' statuary. The situation as regards Celtic deity is far more complicated with several 'layers' existing, presumably developments over different stages in history. The gods of Gaul, Ireland and Britain are not all the same, in fact they rarely concur exactly. The Gaulish pantheon seems to have a rough correspondence with the Roman gods, as the archaeological evidence would indicate, but this may largely be due to assimilation of Roman values for example the god Jupiter-Taranis. The same is also true of the Roman period in Britain, which saw Roman gods also coupled with Celtic deities. In both Gaul and Britain, deity was also highly local in nature with gods local to tribes, places and features of the natural world such as rivers.

In Ireland it appears that gods of different periods coexisted. The Book of Invasions (*Leabhar Gabhala Erin*) gives an indication of how this came about with the chronicling of the arrival of different mythical peoples from the arrival of Banba onwards, giving us a combination of ancient and maybe native deities and mythical peoples/gods such as the *Tuatha dé Danann (people of Danu/Dana/Anu)*. The Fomorians (*Fomoire*) appear throughout the Book of Invasions as the nemesis of each invading tribe, although they appear to be sea-faring folk based on Tory Island in the north or perhaps even from Scandinavia, as suggested by authors such as Charles de Kay. Little is known of them apart from a few names such as Cichol or Conand. *Cath Maige Tuired* (The 2nd battle of Moytira) gives further detail, especially of Balor, in the Fomorian conflict with the Tuatha Dé Danann. Some regard them as ancient gods of fertility, wild and uncontrolled, brought under the yoke of the gods of the tribe (Tuatha Dé Danann) who have knowledge of agriculture. Unlike the Tuatha dé Danann, who also appear in Gaulish, Welsh and Scottish culture, the Fomorians are particular to Ireland.

Throughout the Celtic and ex-Celtic countries, there is much evidence of many localised deities but later folklore and codified information ties places to particular deities for instance the huge number of wells dedicated to or associated with Brighid. In the case of Wales and Scotland there is great similarity with Irish deities and mythology for instance Bran, Brighid and Lugh are commonly found in one or both countries, but it is as likely that many of these were exported through colonisation/settlement as it is that they share a common root. Lugh is the only deity I could find that appears in all of the British Isles, as well as Gaul and Iberia.

In all cases, with the Celtic deities, it is difficult to ascertain with certainty their place and period of origin as little was recorded until quite a late stage. What information does exist is often of little help in trying to gain a more detailed picture. What the mythology does though is give us ample information about the character of the gods and in some cases shows us something of their function.

To further muddy the waters, the Universalist strand in Druidry seems to have its roots in the writings of Edward Williams, in particular *Barddas*. Throughout this work, much of which is probably fraudulent, deity is referred to as God in the masculine singular, very much in line with Judao-Christian thought. My personal feeling is that either earlier compendiums (from which the author claims to have drawn) or the author himself altered the druidic teachings so as not to conflict with monotheism.

At the end of this hypothesising one must ask does it matter if there are many gods, gods as aspects of the one, or just one god. To the modern mind, I do not think it is so difficult to reconcile the gap between polytheism and monotheism and it is perhaps best left to the individual to work with whichever model of deity feels most comfortable. Some would argue that to be a Druid is also to be a pagan and that other faiths are mutually exclusive. Pagan derives from the latin *paganus* meaning someone outside the jurisdiction of Rome, although the modern definition is a member of any religion other than Christianity, Judaism, Islam, Hinduism or Buddhism. Within these pages it is my intention to simply present the knowledge and understanding as best I can and not to express my opinion on who qualifies as a Pagan or a Druid. What I will say is, that to call oneself a Druid it is essential to have an understanding and appreciation of Celtic deities – the practice of Druidry, by definition, being primarily Celtic in nature.

Having taken a brief overview of Celtic deity, we will now proceed to specific descriptions of the most common deities among the pagan Celts:

Áine

The Irish goddess of love and fertility, appearing in Irish literature as a lady of the otherworld. She was described as daughter of Manannán and elsewhere daughter of Eoghabhal (foster son of Manannán). The name Áine means brightness and is a term that in antiquity was applied to deities of both sexes. In one story, Étar falls for Áine but dies of a broken heart following her rejection of his advances. King Ailill Ólom of Munster attempted to force himself on her but she used magic to kill him, although in another version of the same story Fearcheas (a Druid allied to Ailil) kills her father Eoghabhal and rapes Áine. Her worship was linked to agriculture, being a fertility goddess, with celebrations in her honour at the summer solstice as late as the end of the 19th century. This is borne out by her appropriation by the Eoghanacht (the dominant people of Munster) who linked her with the prosperity of the region, Cnoc Áine in Limerick being named after her. Mediaeval scholars describe Áine as her father's champion, ridding the area of his foes through magic and the four regions around the hill were allotted to Uainidhe, Fear Fí, Eoghabhal and Áine herself. By way of legitimising their rule, Norman lords (the Geraldines) linked themselves to Áine and thereby to the land, of which they had control. Áine was common in Irish folklore, often appearing in disguise to help beleaguered farming families or seen among the fields or at the midsummer fires. Several Cnoc Áine hills exist around Ireland reflecting her importance as a goddess of the land.

Aonghus

Also known as Angus, Oengus or Aonghus Mac Óg, Oengus mac ind Ócc (son of the two youths), Oengus an Brogha (of the palace), Oengus mac in Daghdha (son of the good god), he is best known as the Irish god of love. He is son of Daghdha and Bóinn and resided at Brugh na Bóinne (Newgrange) in Co. Meath. Aonghus is a divine love child conceived by a trick performed on Ealchamar (the husband) to get him to leave and then a spell to make nine months seem as but a day to him. Aonghus was born without Ealchamar realising what had happened and his mother said of him, 'young is the son who was begotten at the dawn and born between that and evening,' hence the epithet *Mac Óg* or more correctly '*maccan óc*' or '*in mac óc*' meaning 'the young boy'. Aonghus as the Maccan corresponds with the Welsh Mabon or Romano-Celt Maponos – the divine child of light. Daghdha brought him to Midhir who raised Aonghus for nine years until revealing his true parentage. Daghdha then met Aonghus at Uisneach telling him to go to Brugh na Bóinne at Samhain to demand residence for one day and one night. After taking possession of it for a day and night he refused to give it up to Ealchamar who sought judgment from Daghdha, who ruled in Aonghus's favour thus tricking Ealchamar out of his home. Another version gives Aonghus tricking Daghdha himself instead in order to take possession of Newgrange. This site, most clearly linked with the winter solstice and the rebirth of the sun, can obviously be connected with the analogy of the young God (or Maccan/Mabon/Maponos) replacing the old who is spent, for instance the sun. Aonghus is portrayed fighting along with his father in the second battle of Moytirra, he is also shown to be accompanied by four birds hovering over him, said to represent kisses. He magically spots Caer, who is disguised among 150 swans, in order to win her hand in marriage after her initial rebuffs. He also features in the story of Dairmuid and Grainne, managing to save Dairmuid from Fionn mac Cumhaill (Finn Maccool). However Aonghus cannot save Dairmuid from his predicted fate – death at the hands of the great boar Beann Ghulban, although Dairmuid manages to kill the boar before he himself dies.

Arianrhod

Daughter of the Welsh Goddess Don (equivalent to the Irish Danu), she was also niece of the king of Gwynedd Math. Math could only sleep if his feet were held in a virgin's lap; this role was performed by Goewin until she was raped by Gilvaethwy. When it was suggested that Arianrhod take her place, her purity was tested by having to step over Math's wand. As soon as she did this she gave birth to three sons – Dylan, Lleu and Gwydion. Arianrhod of the silver wheel appears as a virgin yet is also mistress of Gwydion. In the triads she appears as one of the three blessed ladies of Britain, perhaps having two aspects of an Earth-goddess – as both fertile mother and virgin. She was described by the poet Taliesin as 'beauty famed beyond summer's dawn'.

Arthur

Although strictly speaking not a god, in the earliest accounts of him he possesses supernatural ability and is linked with Annwn the Welsh Otherworld. His name is linked with Arturus, Artorius or Arcturus and he may have originally been a Celtic deity that has become humanised. He was a warrior without equal who functioned as the monster-hunting protector of Britain from both internal and external threat, some of these, such as the Saxons he defeats as described in the Historia Brittonum, but the majority of his opponents are supernatural, including giant cat-monsters, Twrch Trwyth the demi-god Boar, dragons, dogheads, giants and witches. Arthur was a figure of folklore and localised magical wonder-tales particularly in Wales, he was the leader of a band of superhuman heroes who roamed the land much like Fionn mac Cumhaill and the Fianna in Ireland. The early Welsh Arthur had a close connection with the Welsh otherworld, Annwn. He is seen to make attacks on otherworldly fortresses in search of treasure also freeing prisoners, however his company in the earliest sources includes former pagan gods, and his wife Gwenhwyfar and his possessions are clearly otherworldly in origin, which may indicate his own origin as a forgotten deity or demigod. References to Arthur such as the group of death-songs known as Y Gododdin refer to his prowess; elsewhere he supposedly slew 960 men by his own hand at the battle of Mons Badonicus (Mount Badon). One saga gives Arthur in a daring raid on Ireland where he steals Fionn mac Cumhaill's hounds; indeed he is mentioned several times in Irish myth. However, Geoffrey of Monmouth's Latin work *Historia Regum Britanniae* (completed in 1138) is the basis of the romantic character that we have become familiar with since the Middle Ages and up into modern times, which gives

Arthur as ruler of a British Empire encompassing Iceland, Norway and France as well as the whole British Isles. At this point, we must really discount any genuine value in the legends as flights of fancy, as extracts from other myths and stories were heaped upon an already inflated and doubtful version of events given by Geoffrey (Galfridus). It is also interesting to note that the 'discovery' of the grave of Arthur and Guinevere in 1191 raised the remaining funds needed to complete rebuilding of Glastonbury Abbey (which burnt down in 1186) following the death of its main benefactor, Henry II, in 1189. The Holy Grail (perhaps also representing Daghdha's/Cerridwen's cauldron), the round table, Lancelot, Excalibur, Glastonbury, his return in time of need and so forth, were all later additions in the romances of writers such as Chrétien de Troyes or Thomas Malory. Popular and intriguing as these works may be, they have little in common with the ancient historical or mythical Arthur of the Romano-Celtic people and it has become extremely difficult in these later works to distinguish the Celtic remnants from the medieval whimsy and assimilated myths and folklore.

Belenus

Also known as Bel or Baal, Belenos he was a solar deity in Gaul and Britain, compared by Julius Caesar to the Greek Apollo. In Wales, he was known as Beli and in Ireland as Bile, god of light and fire the 'Bright One' an accolade often given to ancient deities. It is widely believed that Bealtaine or Beltane, heralding the return of summer, is derived from his name and in whose honour the Bel tine or good fire is lit. He is also connected with the summer solstice and herbs harvested at that time such as henbane (Belenos herb) or St. John's Wort, which were thought to possess solar properties. Although Bel was clearly known and worshipped throughout the Celtic world there is little recorded or known about him.

Bóinn

Also known as Boann, she was the water goddess and mother of Aonghus. She is associated with the River Boyne and the Newgrange tumulus in Meath (Brú na Bóinne). It is thought the older name bóu-vinda is associated with the cow, her name meaning 'illuminated or wise cow'. 'Vind' had several meanings in reference to wisdom, brightness and the colour white. This parallels the Vedic literature that symbolises sacred rivers as milk that flows from a mystical cow, to this day the cow being sacred in Hindu communities. It was said that the source of the Boyne was the Sidh of Nechtan, a well surrounded by nine hazels, in which lived the salmon. Nechtan is another name for Nuadha, given as Bóinn's husband. The well supposedly could only be used by Nechtan and his cup bearers, all others would be blinded by its waters. However, Bóinn approached the well to find that three great gushes of water came from it hitting her in her foot, hand and one eye, which was blinded. As she ran away from the well, the water followed her all the way to the sea, by which manner the Boyne River was formed. It was said that drinking of the Boyne in June could make one a seer-poet, and the power of the water from the well of wisdom, incorporates the idea of the light of inspiration blinding the receiver. The association with Find (the personification of wisdom) originating with Bóinn is carried forward to Fionn mac Cumhaill, much associated with the Boyne, who accidentally eats of the Salmon of Knowledge when he burns his thumb. The bright brow or illumination that he receives, like his Welsh equivalent Gwion (Taliesin) who drinks the water splashes from Cerridwen's cauldron transforms him into a seer — an obvious metaphor for the connection between the sacred waters and divine wisdom.

Bran

It is important to distinguish between the Irish Bran (Bran mac Feabhail) and the Welsh Bran the Blessed, the former being a hero of some importance the latter being the son of Llyr the sea god. The Voyage of Bran (mac Feabhail) is one of the most important Irish *immrama* or *iomramh,* detailing otherworldly journeys. Bran (meaning raven) is visited at his palace by a lady bearing a silver, musical branch covered in white flowers from an apple tree in the realm of Eamhain (otherworld). After describing its wonders in song she invites him to visit, disappearing with the branch despite Bran clutching it with both hands. Sailing westwards with three times nine crew, Bran encounters Manannán who confirms her story of great wonders awaiting them and instructs them on how to reach the island. On the way, they encounter a strange island where all the inhabitants laugh and stare, one of the crew who disembarks immediately begins to do the same. They encounter a second island, the island of women where they remained for a year in great splendour and happiness only to discover that in fact many years had passed. Neachtan, one of the crew, longing to return to Ireland leaves and Bran decides to accompany him, not before the women advise them not to set foot on land. Sadly Neachtan jumps from the boat and ages to a pile of withered bones on touching the soil of Ireland, whilst Bran who does not leave the boat realises he recognises no one and he is now a figure of legend, such is the time that has elapsed. Having no other option, Bran returns but not before writing the story of his adventures in Ogham. This like the story of Oisin (who dies of age on his return) indicates the strange temporal quality of the otherworld where either much larger or smaller time elapses than in the everyday physical world.

Bran the blessed, also known as Bendigeidfran was a Welsh king and otherworld god. Bran's sister Branwen was betrothed to *Ard-Rí* (High King) of Ireland Matholwch when he visited Bran's court at Harlech. Her half-brother Efnisien, not being consulted, decided to cut off the ears, lips and tails of all Matholwch's horses as a great insult. Bran narrowly avoided a war with the Irish by offering replacement horses and a magic cauldron which Matholwch took back to Ireland along with his bride and before long they had a son – Gwern. However, after some time, Branwen to her shame, was mistreated and reduced to the status of a cook. Having managed to dispatch a bird to Bran to tell him of her disgrace and upon hearing this Bran sailed with a great army to Ireland to avenge her. In the battle, the Irish used the cauldron to revive their warriors until it was broken by Efnisien at the cost of his own life. In the slaughter that followed, every adult Irishman was slain and only seven of the Welsh warriors survived, who brought back the head of Bran (as instructed by him) who was killed in the battle by a poisoned arrow. Bran's head was still able to eat and to talk and it is said that for eighty years his head entertained the court with his stories. A later myth claims that his head was buried in London facing east to ward off invaders from Europe, King Arthur was also reputed to have made use of the magical power of Bran's head.

Brighid

Also known as Brid, Bridie, Bride, Brigandu, Brigantia and Brigit, the Romans associated her with their goddess Minerva. Her name means 'the exalted one', probably one of the primary Celtic goddesses of ancient times she is also a mythical lady of the Tuathe Dé Danann and St. Brigit in Christian tradition. Traces of her worship exist in Gaul and Britain as well as Ireland, the country with which she is most associated. Described as the daughter of Daghdha in *Lebor Gabála Érenn*, she fulfils many functions – goddess of poetry, protector of children, the hearth and home, goddess of smithing and crafts, of healing and midwifery. She was a triple goddess, sometimes appearing as three sisters, other times as three ladies of young, middle and old age. One story has her born with the sunrise (indicating she may have originally been a solar goddess), with a burst of flame emanating from her forehead that reached from earth to the heavens. She also possesses a warrior aspect, favouring the spear or arrow as weapons, as well as being sacred to smiths, most of whom would have manufactured weapons as well as more mundane items. She is strongly associated with the elements of water and fire, with many sacred wells and springs named after her. She possessed two oxen named Fea and Feimhean as well as Torc Triath, a mystical boar or king of the swine. She is also associated with milk and the birthing of animals as is Imbolc or Oílmeg, which is generally regarded as the festival of Brighid marking the beginning of spring. Brighid like Danu is attributed motherhood of Brian, Iuchar and Iucharba, indicating mother-goddess aspects or perhaps even a common origin. Brighid is also associated with bees, via the otherworldly apple orchard that she kept. The bees collected the pollen bringing it back into the ordinary world – mention of it is in the song '*Brid Thomais Mhurchu*' of unknown date. Interestingly the late Joe Heaney recorded a song of the same name in *Gaeilge* but the lyrics are completely different.

St. Brigit

This is a clear example of a pagan survival into Christianity. In both Ireland and Scotland she was, and perhaps still is the most important female saint and was often referred to as 'the Mary of the Irish'. The most official version of her origin is that she was daughter of a druid and that she had predicted the arrival of Christianity in Ireland. She is said to have received baptism from St. Patrick himself although she is claimed to have died in 524 AD and Patrick himself died some 65 or more years earlier in 457 AD (according to the *Annals of the Four Masters*). In folklore she is claimed as the midwife to Mary and hence her invocation by women in labour. It is said that Brigit became a nun and abbess at Cill Dara (Kildare) meaning 'Church of the oak tree', which many believe was formerly a druidic site of some significance. It is here at the abbey that a shrine was kept with nineteen virgin nuns who tended the perpetual fire. Such a practice was common throughout the pagan world and it is most likely that it was originally a shrine to the goddess Brighid, one can imagine that her following was so strong that it was necessary to absorb Brighid and her rites into the Christian fold in order to gain otherwise reluctant converts. No men were allowed to enter the abbey and supplies and so forth were brought in by women only. In the 13th century, the Catholic Church decreed that priests must be admitted to the abbey and that the sacred flame be extinguished as it was a heretical pagan custom. Various accounts exist of miracles performed by St. Brigit but there is scant historical biographical information, even within the authorised Latin biography — *Vita Brigitae* which was compiled by Cogitosus around 650 AD. In the 1960s, St. Brigit was decanonized by the Vatican II council who declared that there was insufficient proof of her historical existence and outside of Ireland and Scotland she is not widely known. Much of the attributes of Brighid are common to St. Brigit, which together with the known historical information leads me to believe that they are in fact one and the same.

Cailleach

The land goddess manifesting as an old crone, the Cailleach was found throughout Britain, Ireland and Western Europe. She is equated with the Greek goddess Demeter as crone, sharing the same qualities of extreme age and associations with the land in winter, the otherworld and the dead. In Ireland she is called Cailleach Beare, associated with the Beare peninsula in Co. Cork, however in earlier times she had three aspects — Cailleach Bólas and Cailleach Corca Duibhne being her two 'sister' hags. She is described in the *Yellow Book of Lecan* as mother of the tribes, having seven periods of youth, seven husbands and fifty foster children. Cailleach is often associated with standing stones, it being said that she transformed animals or people into the stones as well as being responsible for the formation of lakes and mountains – a clear demonstration of her power as land goddess. She was portrayed as guardian of sacred wells and hilltops and keeper of woodlands. In Scotland, she came to be the female spirit of the wilderness and protector of wild animals, a clear throwback to her primal role as land goddess. She is also linked with the harvest, the last sheaf of wheat or barley was known as the Cailleach indicating her importance in the agricultural cycle. In Legend Niall of the Nine Hostages becomes High King of Ireland when he alone of the candidates recognises the crone as the land goddess. He not only gives her the kiss she requests but offers to lay with her, where upon she transforms into a comely maid and they mate thus confirming him as rightful king and uniting the tribe with the land.

Cerridwen

Cerridwen was a Welsh fertility goddess, most famously appearing in the transformation story of Taliesin, the most famous of Welsh bards. In lake Tegid, Cerridwen lived with her three children, Morvran (who became a fierce warrior alongside Arthur at Camlan, his final battle), Creirwy a girl of unsurpassed beauty and brightness and finally Afagddu a dark boy of unspeakable ugliness. Cerridwen uses her cauldon (associated with fertility) to produce three drops of inspiration for Afagddu, like Brighid, Cerridwen was worshipped by the Bards. Cerridwen may well also have been a corn goddess – referred to as goddess of grain and her association with the pig, a common symbol of the corn spirit. A similar association with the pig is the case with Demeter, the pig being an embodiment of the corn spirit. In fact, in the story referred to earlier Cerridwen (as a hen) eats Gwion Bach who has transformed into a single grain of wheat, whereafter he is reborn of her as the magical child Taliesin.

Cernunnos

The name of this god is thought to mean ' the horned one'. Most famously depicted on the Gundestrup cauldron, which was found dismantled in a bog in Jutland, Denmark (now kept in Dublin). Cernunnos is usually shown with horns or antlers, often bearded and sometimes with animal ears, wearing a torc and clutching a ram-headed serpent. He is often equated with Bran, Castor and the Greek Pan. In modern paganism he is also known as Lord of the Animals or Herne the Hunter. There are many archaeological finds linked with this god in continental Europe, including an altar in Paris. Cernunnos is sometimes three-headed and hence is possibly part of a triad, which might explain the association with various other gods. He is often interpreted as the Gaulish Dis Pater (especially in the seated/squatting position on the ground as was a typical of Gauls) and also due to the serpent he is often seen as some form of underworld god. As there are no contemporary accounts or mythology referring explicitly to this god it is difficult to be certain of his characteristics, however he remains of great significance to many modern pagans.

Crom

Often referred to as Crom Cruach, Cenn Cruaich or Crom Dubh, Crom represents the archetypal pagan opponent of St. Patrick and Christianity. He is mentioned in accounts of Patrick in early literature, as Cenn Cruiaich he was said to have twelve sub-gods and it is said his statue at Magh Sléacht was demolished by St. Patrick, whereafter it sunk into the ground. It is often supposed that Crom was invented as a prototype of the Christian Satan, the sub-gods perhaps given to encompass the whole of the Celtic pantheon. Regardless of Christian invention or an earlier origin, as Crom Dubh meaning 'black stoop' or 'dark croucher' he was after Patrick interpreted as an emanation of the Devil. Some folklore shows Crom as a human sinner who was redeemed at the last moment by Patrick's intervention as demons arrive to take his soul away. He is also shown giving a cauldron or a bullock to Patrick. Patrick weighs the gift against his letter of thanks, which is miraculously heavier thus convincing Crom to convert. The Sunday closest to Lughnasa (1st August) was known as 'Crom Dubh's Sunday'. This festival associated with Lugh who defeated Balor having gained the association of Patrick and Crom, thus replacing the earlier personalities.

Daghdha

Also Dagdae, Dagda, Dagán or Eochaid Ollathair he is the principal male deity of the Tuatha Dé Danann, also sometimes associated with the Gaul's Dis Pater (Sucellos) as claimed by Julius Caesar as their ancestral god. Also given the name Eochaidh meaning 'father of many' there is an overt link to sexual productivity. He was sometimes depicted in a short tunic revealing his bare buttocks perhaps in reference to his sexual fertility, which is bore out in the accounts of his mating with Mór-Ríoghain (Morrigan) as she stood astride the River Unshin, and also his union with Bóinn (Boann) which begat Aonghus Mac Og. He is a warrior of great strength as described in the two battles of Magh Tuiredh (Moytirra) bearing a huge club that required eight men to lift it, which was dragged around on wheels. The club was terribly destructive, the rough end being capable of slaying nine men in one blow, but its opposite end was smooth and could be used to heal and even revive the dead. This bears great similarity to Sucellos, whose name has almost the same meaning – good striker) and who possessed a mallet and jar with properties similar to Daghdha's club and cauldron. He was also possessor of a magical harp that played three kinds of music and a great cauldron, which provided an endless supply of food. The cauldron could also be used to heal the sick and injured or revive the dead. Sometimes paired with Danu in the manner of Isis and Osiris, he is more accurately husband of Mór-Ríoghan, although he is also said to have accounted for the birth of Aodh, Brighid, Caomh and Dian Céacht by various women of the Tuatha Dé Danann. The Brugh na Bóinne (Newgrange in Co. Meath) and Grianán of Aileach in Co. Donegal are both attributed to Daghdha.

Danu

Ancient goddess mentioned in much of Irish mythology and also in place names. Progenitor of the Tuatha Dé Danann (people of Danu). she is also known as Anu, Ana and Dana. The name is highly similar to Danüv, from continental Europe, most probably a river goddess linked with the Danube. Similarity also extends to Dånu the Sankrit (Hindu) river goddess and Dôn in Welsh Mythology. The old Irish word '*anai*' meaning wealth is probably linked with the prosperity and fruitfulness of the land and it is said that the province of Munster (South West Ireland) derived its rich landscape from Anu. To this day two mountaintops near Killarney, Co. Kerry are named after her (Dá Chích nAnann or Two Paps of Anu). An early text refers to Ireland as 'iath nAnann' or 'land of Anu', confirming her position as goddess of the land. Some early writers identify Danu with Mór-Ríoghain (Morrigan) and Brighid, perhaps both instances being a subsequent emanation or avatar of the earth goddess. Little exists in literature with regard to Danu, however she is said to have been mother to three sons — Brian, Iuchar and Iucharbar, hence the Tuatha Dé Danann are also known as 'fir tri ndea' or 'men of the three gods'.

Tuireall (Tureen and also alternatively named Dealbhaoth) is claimed as their father, but in other accounts he is also claimed as Danu's own father or entirely different paternity is given. The story often referred to as 'the first sorrow of Irish storytelling' is the Sons of Tureen, a truly woeful tale of vengeance and mercilessness also involving Lugh, however there is no reference to Danu in any of the versions I have encountered, which strikes me as strange given their more obvious link to her.

Dian Céacht

God of healing and mythical physician of the Tuatha Dé Danann, he most famously made a silver arm for Nuadhu after the first battle of Moytirra. He is described as 'the healing sage of Ireland' and 'god of health', he and his three sons feature in the first battle. Dian Céacht and his daughter and two sons feature as physicians in the second battle, he with his daughter Airmeith (Airmid) having charge of a magical spring that restored dying gods to life. After Dian Céacht makes the silver arm for Nuadhu, his son Miach sets about further healing the king by transforming it into a flesh arm and after nine days, it grows skin and has full mobility. Dian Céacht being upset by his son's interference strikes him on the head with a sword three times and each time Miach cures himself of the wound. A fourth blow was then struck cutting his head open and destroying his brain. After his 365 herbs sprouted from Miach's grave, Airmeith collected these but Dian Céacht mixed them up so that no one would fully know their healing properties. He also put every type of herb that grows in Ireland into a well, situated between Moytirra and the shore of Lough Arrow (in Sligo). This well, named Tiopra Sláine was reputed to belong to Dian Céacht as his well of healing. He was mentioned elsewhere in healing of Midhir, one of Mór-Ríoghan's sons and Tuirill (Tuireann) the father of Brian, Iuchair and Iucharba. Clearly Dian Céacht, although vengeful and withholding his knowledge, was the primary god of healing and health; the legends point to him as the source of herbalism and physicians' skills.

Donn

Irish God of the underworld, not to be confused with Don the Welsh name for Danu. His name means 'brown' or perhaps originally 'dark', he is believed to be an aspect of Daghdha relating to death. Donn was thought to convey the dead to Tir na nÓg from his island home on Teach nDuind (house of Donn) where the souls of the recently deceased gathered. He was also referred to as an ancestor of those who have died, for instance the death of Conaire refers to Donn in this way. In Limerick he was thought to inhabit a hill (Cnoc Fírinne) and the dead were brought to a cave at the summit of this hill. It was said that Donn could ride out at night on a horse across the land or even in the sky and whisk away people into the otherworld. He is also possibly linked with the Gaul Dis Pater and Greek Hades.

Ériu

She is the goddess who gave her name to Ireland, one of the three triple goddesses who met the invading son of Mil (Milesians). The myth states that the land would be theirs if they gave their names to the land, in effect giving reverence to them as goddesses of the land. The three goddesses Ériu (Érin, Éire), Banba (Banb) and Fódla (Fotla) are each names for Ireland, the latter two now less known were often used in poetry to refer to Ireland. Éire has been, and is still used in writing and ordinary speech to mean Ireland and from it is derived Érainn meaning the people of Ireland. Ériu is said to be of the Fomhóire people (fomors) – the mother of Breas who taught Lugh the skills of agriculture in exchange for his life. This may indicate her as an earlier goddess of sovereignty of the land prior to the arrival of the Tuatha Dé Danann. She was shown giving a drink to successive kings of Ireland – the spouse representing the forces of nature joined to the ruler of the land. It is also considered that she is represented in myth also by the powerful triple goddess Macha and Fir Bolg Goddess Tailtiu, foster mother of Lugh who died clearing the plains of forest for the Tuatha Dé Danann.

Lir

Although given as the father of Manannán, he appears to be later in origin, the earliest sources being from the 12th century, he was a king of the Tuatha Dé Danann but little is known of him. It is thought that Leicester in England is named after him or the welsh equivalent Llyr. Some have speculated that Lir was the basis of Shakespeare's tragic play *King Lear* and it is indeed possible he was inspired by the story of the *Children of Lir*, another tragedy, albeit with a very different course of events. The *Children of Lir* is the main source of Lir's mention in Celtic literature but Lir plays a fairly minor part in the story. It is commonly accepted amongst academics that this story is based on a British or French legend 'The Knight of the Swan', it had little impact on folklore on its arrival but has become one of the most loved and well-known Irish legends in modern times.

Lugh

Lugh, Lugus or Lleu is the most well known Celtic solar god. Julius Caesar wrote of the Gaulish 'Mercurius' who he described as inventor of the arts and presider over commerce, although not mentioned by name it is generally agreed he was referring to Lugus. The name is still present in modern place names derived from the Gallo-Roman capital Lugudunon (Fortress of Lugus) for example Laon, Lauzun, Laudun, Loudon and most famously, Lyon. Like the Irish who celebrate Lughnasa, the Gauls celebrated a great festival (at Lyon) associated with Lugus at the beginning of August — the time of first harvest. In northern Spain, a Celtiberian stone inscription (in Latin) mentions Lugus twice. It is also possible that Lugh is the source of the name London — derived from Lugdunum perhaps. Lugh was certainly worshipped in Britain and is particularly well known to the Welsh as Lleu, bearing a strong mythical connection to the Irish Lugh of the Tuatha Dé Danann. Although in earlier times he was clearly a solar deity, in Ireland he became Lugh Lámhfhada (Lugh the long-armed), mythical hero and father of Cú Chulainn. It is also thought that the word leprechaun, which is still current in Irish folklore, is a corruption of the word Luchorpain meaning 'little stooping Lugh'. Lugh was recognised as a highly skilled warrior, who replaces Nuada (deposed after losing an arm) at the second battle of Magh Tuireadh as war leader in order to defeat his grandfather Balor, champion of the Fomorians. In fact, Lugh's conception was engineered by Cian of the Tuatha Dé Danann who impregnated Ethlinn (who was hidden away on Tory island) in order that the prophecy that Balor, who can only be killed by his grandson, could be fulfilled. Interestingly Lugh is half Fomorian and Dé Danann, one analysis of the story concludes that Lugh's role is to suppress the violent force in nature, symbolised by the Fomorians, so that the battle may end and peace be restored to the land, so that the fruitful and nurturing aspect of the earth goddess can be called upon. This theory would tie in well with Lugh's festival Lughnasa (also the word for August in Irish) which is in celebration of the time of harvest. The fact that Lugh instituted this festival in honour of his foster mother Tailtu (who died clearing the plains of Ireland) clearly embodies an earlier goddess linked harvest lore. In fact, the Irish myth relates closely to Greek, Persian and ancient Babylonian harvest cults and it is possible these stories have a common origin or one culture borrowed the concept from another. Lleu Llawgyffes (accurate arm) features in Welsh literature but with a less clearly defined role than in Irish sources. However, it is thought that his cult probably migrated to Ireland via Wales or Gaul perhaps around the time of Jesus of Nazareth. Like the sun, which can scorch as well as nurture, Lugh has a negative side. He is somewhat of a trickster and hence likened at times to the Norse Loki. He also proves to be highly unforgiving and vindictive as evidenced by the story 'The Sons of Tureen' (Tuireall). In one version of the story Lugh who now, thanks to the three sons, possesses the pigskin of Tuas, which heals all wounds, refuses to give it to Tureen to save his dying sons. In disgust, King Nuada banishes Lugh forever from Ireland for his vengefulness and lack of mercy (although this would seem to contradict the events of the 'Second Battle of Magh Tuireadh' mentioned earlier).

Macha

Linked with Mór Ríoghain, Macha is described as the goddess of war, however her name refers to a pasture or field hence it is likely she may originally have been a goddess of the land. To the Ultonians (Ulster) she represented sovereignty hence the royal settlement Eamhain Mhacha, which was named after her, as is the modern city of Armagh (Ard Mhacha). One account of Macha tells that she was daughter of Aodh, one of three kings who took turns of seven years each to rule Ireland. After her father's death, she was refused his right and so fought in battle and won her term. She refused to relinquish the throne to the five sons of King Díthorba and defeated them in battle and subsequently married the other King Ciombaoth. Later she encountered the sons of Díthorba again in Connacht whilst disguised as a leper. After sharing their food each one tried to lie with her one by one, except she beat each one and tied them up, dragging them back to Ulster with her where she made them build a majestic rath for her – Eo-muin (or Eamhain) Macha. The more well known story relates how Macha was married to an Ulster farmer named Crunnchu who boasted to king Conchobhar mac Neasa that his wife could outrun the king's horses. His chariot horses were said to be the swiftest in Ireland, so such a boast could not be left unchallenged and so the heavily pregnant Macha was brought forth to run against them in order to save her husband's life. She won the race but collapsed at the finish and died giving birth to twins. However, before she died she cursed the Ultonians (Ulstermen) for ten generations that in their hour of greatest need every man would be struck down with the agonies she suffered and be as helpless as newborns. This curse is evidenced during the cattle raid of Cooley, which leaves Cú Chulainn to single-handedly defend Ulster against the forces of Queen Maeve/Meadhbh. Interestingly Cú Chulainn's horse was known as the Grey of Macha – another link with horses. In Gaul Macha is linked with Epona the horse goddess and an engraving found in France shows her riding upon Epona's back. Sometimes she is depicted on horseback with a foal also running alongside – a clear suggestion of fertility.

Manannán Mac Lír

Manannán, formerly Manandan and in some sources formerly Oirbsiu, is the Celtic lord of the otherworld and of the sea. In Connacht (Ireland) Oirbsiu is said to have died and a great lake burst forth from his grave, elsewhere other lakes are associated with Manannán or his offspring. The epithet Mac Lír means 'son of the sea' associating him with the lesser known sea god Lír. In Wales he is known as Manawydan fab Llyr, similarly replacing the earlier Manawyd. He is associated with Mona, which was the Roman name for the Isle of Man, Anglesey and Aran. It is thought his name is derived from the Isle of Man but all three islands are east of Ireland, where it was often supposed that otherworldly realms lay in the sea to the east for example Tir Tairngire (land of promise), Maggh Meall (pleasant plain) or Eamhain Abhlach (place of apples). Eamhain Ablach or Mana is given as his dwelling place, although in some accounts this is given to the west in the Atlantic Ocean. Manannán in modern thought is more associated with the sea, somewhat like the Greek Poseidon, although he in fact has many qualities other than otherworld and sea ruler – a skilled warrior whose boat 'Wave Sweeper' could direct itself over the waves and whose chariot could travel over water as easily as land. He was also a master craftsman, a magician and a trickster. He possessed many magic items such as the magic cloak that he shook between Fand (his wife) and Cú Chulainn that they might not meet again. He seems to appear and disappear at will and appears to the wife of King Fiachna offering to save him from defeat in battle in exchange for her lying with him. In another version, he appears disguised as her husband, to lie with her – whichever being the case Mongán is conceived from their union. This story relates to the conception of Arthur in Welsh myth and also connects with Fionn mac Cumhaill (reincarnation). Manannán also shows his skills and generosity to the Tuatha Dé Danann after their defeat by the Milesians advising them to retreat into the hills and mounds of Ireland, from which originates the *sídh* (cairn-dwelling). In addition Manannán bestows three gifts – the *féth Fiadha*, a cloak that concealed them, the second a magical feast that through its celebration kept them forever young (feast of Goibhniu) and the third was a herd of magical pigs who after being slaughtered and eaten would revive again the next day. Here it is clear that he is not one of the Tuatha Dé Danann, indicating he is an earlier deity. However, in some accounts he is listed among the Tuatha Dé Danann as is Lír his father, although I would consider him to predate them, the association with Lír being a later addition. In another example of his skill, it was Manannán who enables Aonghas Mac Og to displace Ealchamar from Brú na Bóinne by use of a spell forcing him to leave the tumulus. Manannán is also said to possess mighty weapons such as a great shield, a shirt and knife, which later find their way to Fionn mac Cumhaill.

Mór-Ríoghain

Mór-Ríoghain is also known as Morrigan or Morrigú in triplet form. She is also a triple goddess linked to Neamhain, Macha and Badhbh (Badb) as a triad of aspects contained within Morrigú the war goddess, whose name means 'great queen' or possibly 'phantom/nightmare queen'. She is also linked with Anu as an emanation of the goddess of the land, in this aspect presiding over conflicts surrounding the land. Dá chích na Mórrígna, the two paps of Morrigan are to be found near Brú na Bóinne/Síd in Broga (Newgrange) in Co. Meath, and she is mentioned elsewhere in the Irish landscape. As Badb she is linked to the Gaulish Bodua. Badb meaning 'scald crow' is a well-known form (as recounted in the Cú Chulainn saga) perhaps as crows were often seen feeding off the dead at battlefields. Badb is also consort to Nét, a war god of the Tuatha Dé Danann, and hence also linked with the Spanish equivalent Neton. Neman (Neamhain) is also given as Nét's consort, and she may well be Nemetonia of the inscriptions founds at Bath who was linked to Mars (the Roman equivalent of Nét/Neton). As Macha she was married to Nemed who defeated the Fomorians, also taking part in the battle of Magh Tuireadh (with Mór-Ríoghain and Badhbh) to bring a magical rain of hailstones on the Fomorrians (Fomhóire) as well as flinging spears at them. The heads of slain enemies were often devoted to Macha. Morrigan features heavily in the accounts of the Tuatha Dé Danann, she is given as wife of Daghdha, as well as playing a significant role in Cú Chulainn's fate after he scorns her sexual advances. In modern terms, she is associated with death (often compared with the Vedic Kali) and the dark fertile aspects of the land, which perhaps with Anu and Brighid is her more ancient role as earth goddess.

Nuadhu

Also Nuada, was a mythical king and battle leader of the Tuatha Dé Danann. He is equated with Nudd in Wales and Nodons in northern Britain, there having been a temple dedicated to him a Lydney in northern England. His image is sometimes shown fishing or with dogs, associating him with hunting, in fact his name can be interpreted to mean 'catcher'. In Irish tradition he is associated with the Boyne and Brú na Bóinne, as husband of Bóinn, however he is displaced from his home by a trick of Aonghus and/or Daghdha, elsewhere Nuadhu is also given as husband to Nemain. Nuada features extensively in the two battles of Moytirra, between the Tuatha Dé Danann and the Fomhóire (an earlier and more malign race of gods). Nuadhu is forced to step down as king after gaining a blemish (he loses his arm). Bres is made king until a magical silver replacement is made enabling Nuadhu to regain his kingship, however this angers Bres (who is half Fomhóire) leading to the second battle of Moytirra. Nuada and his wife Nemain are killed by Balor, the Fomhóire leader, but the war is won and Ireland is free from their malignant influence. Nuadhu is also linked, like his wife Bóinn, with the Boyne River, the Salmon of Knowledge and Fionn mac Cumhaill. The elderly seer Finneigás who was supposed to receive the wisdom of the salmon but is unwittingly denied it by Fionn, is also known as Nuadhu Finnegéas, echoing Aonghus gaining the Brú from Nuadhu.

Oghma

Oghma, the Celtic god of eloquence and knowledge, was known as Ogmios to the Gauls who was equated with the Greek Heracles. The Roman writer Lucian described Ogmios's 'smiling face' whilst the Irish Oghma possessed the epithet *grianainech* which translates to the same meaning or alternatively 'sun faced'. Oghma's parentage is somewhat confused, given as son of Brighid, son or brother of Daghdha and son of Ealadha (who name means art or poetry). A champion of the Tuatha Dé Danann, despite being made to carry firewood, he features particularly in the second battle of Moytirra, slaying Indech one of the leaders of the Fomhóire (Fomorians). In some versions, he is also slain but in others, he goes on to capture a magical sword that recounts its deeds and also to recover Daghdha's magical harp. Oghma was attributed the invention of the Ogham alphabet, which the sagas describe as being widely used and state that a large collection of writing existed. Of course, today all that remains are stone inscriptions and the medieval writings on Ogham, which leads some to presume that it was used only for boundary markers etc. In addition to his skill as an orator and poet Oghma performed the function of escorting the dead to Tir na nOg, much like the Greek Hermes (although Tartarus was a less pleasant place).

Rhiannon

In Welsh mythology, Rhiannon was daughter of Hereydd or Heveidd Hen (the Ancient one) and in the Mabinogion is linked with Pwyll and later Manawyddan. Pyll, prince of Dyfed, agrees to rule Arawn's kingdom Annwn (land of the dead) for a year and kills Arawn's enemy Havgan at the end of that time. Pwyll saves Rhiannon (who appears from a fairy mound riding a white horse) from an unwanted suitor Gwawl and then marries her. Llwyd, given as either the friend or father of Gwawl, curses Rhiannon and Pwyll so that she is barren for many years. Eventually Rhiannon gives birth to her son Pryderi but he is stolen and Rhiannon is accused of eating her child and is disgraced until Teyrnon, who finds the boy in a stable, restores him to his parents. During her long period of disgrace, she is forced to act as a beast of burden, like a horse or donkey for any visitors to the palace, in order to atone for her supposed crime. It is most likely that both Pwyll and Rhiannon were gods whose significance was lost, however her name a corruption of Rigantona, meaning 'great queen' signifies that Rhiannon was of some importance as an otherworld or land goddess. Rhiannon appears to have a clear connection with horses, she being swifter on horseback than any other and there is also a clear link with the otherworld through her magical birds. Rhiannon also appears in the story of Bran, where Pryderi (her son) and Manawyddan bring Bran's (talking) head to Wales. Her magical birds charmed the bearers of Bran for seven years and it is said that her singing could wake the dead or send the living into a death like sleep. Rhiannon married Manawyddan who was then able to finally lift the curse of Llwyd.

Taranis

This Gaulish god was equated with Jupiter or Zeus by the Romans, his name meaning 'Thunderer', although to the Celts he was not king of the gods. He has been depicted with a wheel, thought to symbolise the sun and holding a trident/mallet to represent lightning. Monuments to him have been found across Europe and as far west as Britian. Taranis is said to have fought and defeated a great sea serpent with his mallet and thereby saving the land from flooding and devastation.

Tlachtga

Tlachtga is an Irish goddess/druidess associated with Samhain (Halloween). In myth, she was the daughter of blind Munster Druid Mogh Ruith, who died giving birth to triplets at the hill bearing her name. The Samhain fire ceremony at Tlachtga (Hill of Ward) was resurrected in recent years and takes place every October 31st. Her name in English mean 'Earth spear'.

Some additional known Celtic gods & goddesses

Sulevia, Belisima	Gaulish, thought to be equivalent to Brighid or the Roman Minerva
Sulis	Romano-British goddess, associated with Bath in England
Agrona	a Gaulish goddess of war
Albiorix, Smertrius	Romano-Gaulish equivalent to the Roman Mars
Teutates	Gaulish meaning 'god of the tribe' possibly in reference to many gods
Goibhniu	Irish blacksmith god of the Tuatha Dé Danann
Modron	Welsh goddess equated with Morrigan
Erecura	Gaulish earth goddess
Camalus	a Gaulish god of war and sky
Grannus	a Gaulish god of healing and mineral springs
Aoife	Irish warrior goddess who trained with Scathach on the Isle of Skye
Damara	Gaulish, a fertility goddess

Esus	Axe wielding forest god of the Gauls
Nantosuelta	Gaulish river goddess
Abnoba	a Gaulish goddess of rivers and forests
Nodens/Nudens/ Nodons	a god of healing, the sea, hunting and dogs
Coventina	Gaulish goddess of wells and springs
Sucellos	a Gaulish god of love and time
Damona	Gaulish cow goddess, perhaps equivalent to Bóinn
Rosmerta	Gaulish goddess of fertility and abundance
Amaethon	Welsh god of agriculture
Debranua	a Gaulish goddess of speed and fat
Artio	Gaulish goddess of the bear
Souconna	goddess of the Saone River in Gaul
Arawn	King of the Welsh otherworld realm of Annwn
Nemetona	Gaulish/British goddess of sacred groves
Alisanus	Gaulish god of rocks and stone

There were literally hundreds of Celtic gods and goddesses, many of them particular to a local area or an individual tribe, most of which, if we know the name, there is little or nothing known of their function or how they were worshiped.

IV

Myth and Legend

There are a wide selection of books that are collections of Celtic myth and legend and have been translated into English and other languages; there are also a fair number of volumes that summarise the entire body of Celtic myth and legend that has made it into the public arena. Hence I am not going to explore these myths in any detail, this has already been done more extensively and better than I could ever hope to do.

I leave it to you, the reader, to explore the literature; however, care must be taken in this task. Much of the Celtic texts were translated from old and middle Irish, Welsh, Scots Gaelic and so forth in the 1800s and 1900s both by scholars and gifted amateurs. In the last century, much of this work has been revisited and re-interpreted in view of the mis-translation and blatant re-writing that took place so not to offend the public and fit in with the social mores of the time. In modern society, which is more secular and multi-religious, the impetus to put a Christian gloss on the past is not so strong; also moral values being more relaxed nowadays there is no longer the need to 'tone down' sexual and violent episodes within the texts. In order to gain a true understanding of the texts (if like me you are not fluent in the ancient Celtic languages), it is necessary to use some discretion in selecting source information. In some cases, it is an interesting exercise to read more than one version in order to be truly aware of the enormous differences in style and meaning that can be derived from the same original. Another reason for reading multiple versions is that the original texts of the same stories differ to varying degrees and it is interesting to make comparisons between them, as no doubt there were differences in the oral stories and histories depending on who told them.

From my own experience of the modern Druid, I can say that many of those I have met do not take the mythic poetry and wisdom tales particularly seriously. In general, although there are always exceptions, I find many Druids to have scant or weak knowledge of the linguistic tradition of Druidry — that which should be the primary concern of the Bard. I can understand why this is the case, the modern world does not lend itself to the prolonged, in-depth study and memorisation of poems and stories, study of Ogham or *Coelbren* does not usually extend beyond an understanding of the alphabets and their use in modern divination. As documented by O'Curry and various other sources[10] an understanding of grammar, rhyme and metre and composition was an integral part of study into the medieval period and on until the demise of Bardic schools:

1st Year:	Oghams, elementary grammar, 20 tales.
2nd Year	50 Oghams, 6 easy lessons in philosophy, some specific poems, 30 tales.
3rd Year:	50 Oghams, 6 minor lessons in philosophy, some specific poems, 40 poems, grammar.
4th Year:	Law of privileges (*Bretha Nemed*), 20 *Eman* (births) poems, 50 tales.
5th Year:	Grammar, 60 tales.
6th Year:	The secret language of poets, 40 *Nuath* (twins) poems, 70–80 tales.
7th Year:	*Brosnacha* (miscellanies), the laws of Bardism.
8th Year:	Prosody (structure of poetry — metre and versification), glosses (obscure words), *Teinm Laeghda* (illumination of song), *Imbas Forosnai* (illumination of foresight), *Dicheltel do Chennibh* (ad lib incantations), *Dindsenchas* (land lore).
9th Year:	A specified number of compositions of the type: *Sennet**, *Luasca* (3 springs over the head), *Nena**,

	Eochraid (keys), *Sruith* (streams) and *Duila Feda* (wisdom tales).
	* The meaning in English is unknown
10th Year:	More of the above as part of a total of 175 such tales.
11th Year:	100 of the compositions known as *Anamuin*.
12th Year:	120 *Cetals* (orations), the 4 arts of poetry. During this year and also years 10 and 11 — mystery of 175 tales and 175 tales learned by *Annruth*

I am not about to suggest that the modern Druid should attempt to undertake a similar programme, which would require twelve years of uninterrupted devotion; however, once can clearly see the great importance of language and mastery of all its aspects. Obviously replicating this knowledge is impossible as much of what was taught was lost and there is no record of the techniques of teaching or specifics of much of the material studied. Anyone who has read the treatise on language and grammar within *Auraicept na n-Éces* (Scholar's Primer) is more than likely perplexed by its contents, it being the case that many of the terms of reference are incomprehensible to almost all of us of the modern age. What we can do though is to seriously study what literature remains, learn to appreciate (and perhaps compose) prose and poetry and read the wisdom tales and myths that we are lucky enough to still possess.

It is important to gain familiarity with the literature of the Celts for several reasons, most obviously because it provides a window on the lives of the Celts. These stories tell us much about the way of life, beliefs and structure of society as it stood in pagan and early Christian times. They also provide illuminating information regarding the deities of the Celts, their history and the history of the people and the land. Not least of all is the underlying wisdom that is embodied within the myths and legends — on a surface level, they are just interesting stories, but they have a deeper purpose. Within them lies powerful symbolism and mysteries that resonate to those who are able to interpret them. For example, the story of Taliesin is not simply an interesting oddity – the symbolism of the cauldron, Afagddu, the horses, the shapeshifting all have significance in terms of Druidic wisdom. In the tragic story of The Sons of Tureen, the adventures of his three sons are described at length following their slaying of Lugh's foster father Cian. Like Heracles of Greek myth, they were set a series of seemingly impossible tasks, which against the odds they completed. This exciting and tragic story throws considerable light on the tricky and vengeful side of Lugh's character. Like the sun, which he sometimes represents, that warms and gives life, it is also highly destructive and merciless in its negative aspect. The story illustrates how Lugh uses the sons to collect objects that are later of use against the Fomhóire, but when they have fulfilled their *geas* (a form of oath or taboo) and are needful of his mercy, he is immovable in his desire to punish them, which in turn leads to his own expulsion. Above all, I believe this is a cautionary tale about the pointlessness of revenge, as no one is the victor here and all pay a heavy price.

Another prime example is the tale Diarmuid and Gráinne, a Fianna romance that clearly alludes to the battle between *Samradh* and *Geimredh*. The light and dark halves of the year are represented by Diarmuid and Fionn, Gráinne herself being the goddess of the land. The boar who kills Diarmuid (who is symbolic of the Maponos/Mabon) also dies in this enactment of the cosmic boar hunt, illustrative of the cycle between the sun and the fertility of the earth.

These are just three examples. Dedicated trawling through the body of translated myths takes considerable time and effort but yields great dividends. I have heard it said that nothing worthwhile comes without effort and indeed, I've often found that to be the case. It may seem a daunting task just to read the whole of the *Táin* or the *Mabinogion*, however there are some more readable (but faithful) modern translations available. For those who don't read frequently or at length these modern versions make it less arduous to pursue what is an essential aspect of Druidic learning. It has taken me a very long time to read the bulk of the Celtic myths but I consider it well worth making the effort to do so.

V

Elemental Forces

Most people with an interest in the occult or the esoteric arts will be familiar with the four elements, which are well known in the modern western mystery tradition via Hermeticism. This model is generally as shown in the diagram below, but in this case with various relevant correspondences attached to each direction.

Direction : North
Element : Earth
Quality : Physical
Season : Winter
Ritual : W. Solstice
Age : Elderly
Animal : Bear
Magical Tool : Lia Faíl
City : Falias
Guardian : Morfessa

Centre
Spirit (nwyvre/neart)

Direction : West
Element : Water
Quality : Emotional
Season : Autumn
Ritual : A. Equinox
Age : Maturity
Animal : Salmon
Magical Tool : Cauldron
City : Murias
Guardian : Semias

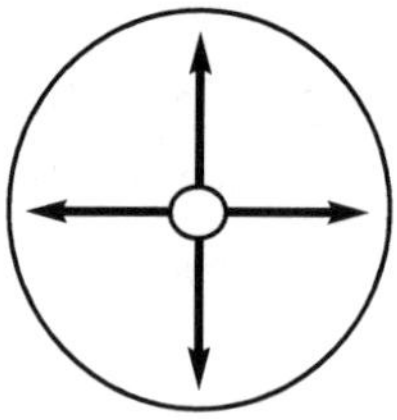

Direction : East
Element : Air
Quality : Mental
Season : Spring
Ritual : S. Equinox
Age : Youth
Animal : Hawk
Magical Tool : Sword
City : Finias
Guardian : Uscias

Direction : South
Element : Fire
Quality : Vitality
Season : Summer
Ritual : S. Solstice
Age : Adulthood
Animal : Stag
Magical Tool : Spear
City : Gorias
Guardian : Esras

Most of these correspondences are fairly obvious and well-known to pagans who are at all familiar with the neo-pagan wheel of the year or eightfold year. The magical tools or hallows (holy objects) are the four treasures of the Tuatha Dé Danann – Lugh's spear that never misses when thrown, Nuada's sword that no opponent can escape from, the cauldron of Daghdha that can satisfy any hunger and finally the Lia Faíl or Stone of Destiny which screamed out (at its site in Tara) when touched by the rightful High King (*Ard Rí*). All four objects are also associated with Tuatha Dé Danann cities, although the Lia Faíl was brought to Ireland with the arrival of the Tuatha Dé Danann. Interestingly the stone still exists, it was lent (or some say stolen) for the crowning of one of the Scots (*Dalraidian*) kings but was never returned. It became known as the Stone of Scone (where Scots kings were crowned) until it was taken by Edward I of England to Westminster Abbey in 1296. It was since then been used for coronation of all English kings and queens (although briefly stolen and repatriated by Scottish nationalists) until its official return to Scotland a few years ago. The current 'Lia Faíl' to be seen at Tara is an entirely different shape, located at 'Cormac's House' mound; the original stone is thought to have been located near the 'Mound of the Hostages'. Some historians claim that the Scottish stone is in fact not the Lia Faíl and the stone at Tara is the original stone, if that is the case, I find it odd that such a sacred item was moved from its original location for no apparent reason.

These treasures or hallows are also reflected in Welsh tradition which lists the thirteen treasures of Britain, the four cities paralleled by Dinas Affaraon – city of the *Pheryllt* or Druid alchemists. An alternative set up of the four elements (given by Alexi Kondratiev) gives the elements and cities associated with different directions as shown below.

Direction : North
Element : Air
Function : battle
(*cath*)
Animal : Eagle
Magical Tool : Sword
City : Finias
Guardian : Uscias

Centre
Sovereignty (flaith)

Direction : West
Element : Fire
Function : knowledge
(*fios*)
Animal : Stag
Magical Tool : Spear
City : Gorias
Guardian : Esras

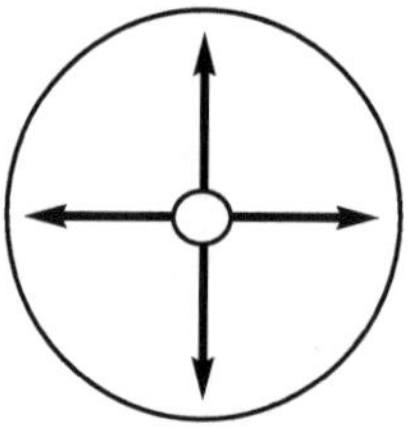

Direction : East
Element : Water
Function : plenty
(*bláth*)
Animal : Salmon
Magical Tool : Cauldron
City : Murias
Guardian : Semias

Direction : South
Element : Earth
Function : song
(*séis*)
Animal : Boar
Magical Tool : *Lia Faíl*
City : Falias
Guardian : Morfessa

There are three main ancient references to the four cities and they were described as being located on islands in the four corners of the world — no specific directions were formally allocated to them in *Lebor Gabála Érenn*, the battles of Moytirra or the *Yellow Book of Lecan* although they can be interpreted to fit more than one system. French author Michel-Gérald Boutet gives the treasures located in the same directions as Kondratiev but gives a different model again with respect to the elements, associating the spear with earth and the stone with fire. Hence, it is a matter of opinion, taste or instinct when deciding which model to use as it is clearly not possible to find a definitive answer to this dilemma.

As one can see, these two models illustrated are quite different and there are arguments for both. It is indeed true that the boar is associated with the corn spirit and thereby the goddess of the land, however its placement in the south I find questionable. Water is reflected from east to west, there being some argument that in ancient times the otherworld and the sea were associated with the east. This being true perhaps, in later (but still ancient) times the west was and still is associated with water in Celtic tradition. The treasures seem to be in agreement in both models and these of course also correspond to the more familiar symbols found in the tarot – cup/grail (cauldron), sword, wand (spear) and pentacle (stone). The more well-known system has in its favour its association with the physical movements of the sun, for example the obvious connection between south and fire via the solstice and the sun's midday position.

There is also a third way of looking at the elements, this being a threefold system and vastly different again, not connected with animals or the *séta* (treasures) or directions of the compass. This is of course the triad of land, sea and sky. This system is linked to the *dúile* and thereby the world tree linking the three realms and also the three cauldrons (which I will discuss more later).

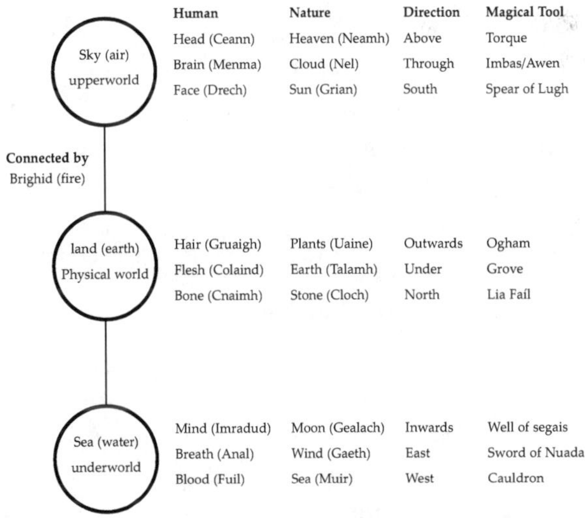

The idea of fire connecting the realms and connecting the *dúile* within the self is personified by Brighid the goddess of fire, fire of the hearth and home, of poetry and inspiration, fire in the heart and head. Fire is also central to druidic ritual and it is fire that warms the three cauldrons of warming, vocation and knowledge – hence there is good argument for the fourth element seen as a cosmic bridge between worlds.

> *Caite didiu bunad ind archetail & cach sois olchenae? Ní ansae; gainitir tri coiri i cach duiniu .i. coire goriath & coire érmai & coire sois.*
>
> What then is the root of poetry and every other wisdom? Not hard; three cauldrons are born in every person – the cauldron of warming, the cauldron of motion and the cauldron of wisdom.
>
> (From the Cauldron of Poesy, trans. Erynn Rowan Laurie 1995/1998)

The *dúile* themselves are divided between the three cauldrons in the same manner as above, they correspond roughly with the Chakras of Vedic tradition and are mentioned by both Amergin (*Ollamh* to the Milesians) and Taliesin (the primary bard of Wales) as central to the mysteries of the self and the cosmos. Roughly equivalent to the Irish concept of land, sea and sky, is the Welsh triad of *calas, gwyar* and *nwyfre. Calas* means 'solidity', representing the earth and its associated image being the stone. *Gwyar* means 'blood' or 'fluid', representing water and a waterfall or river its associated image. *Nwyfre* means both 'sky' and 'heaven' and also represents the life force or spirit within living things, its associated image being a clear blue sky. *Nwyfre* is a Welsh term used much in modern Druidry, the equivalent concept in Irish is *Neart*. It was believed that these three elements are forms of a primal substance called *mandred* and all existence is comprised of various combinations of the three elements.

Accordingly, we have three somewhat different views but they are not necessarily mutually exclusive, at least not between a fourfold and threefold system. I do feel that, ritually speaking, it is important to decide on the four directions and their correspondences so far as any work with the compass points is concerned otherwise confusion is likely to reign. I can see strong arguments for use of the Eagle for air and the Boar for earth as totems as they were both highly significant to the ancient Celts (although both are now almost extinct in Celtic or ex-Celtic lands). The bear does not seem to have any particular significance in Celtic culture beyond that of other European cultures and has not been as widespread in the most western parts of Europe as elsewhere; in fact they are now sadly extinct in the British Isles and most of western Europe.

I think it is quite conceivable to overlay or move between models one or two and model three, depending on your purpose or nature of the ritual. The Celtic worldview is well defined but has a flexibility perhaps not evident in the more rigid Greek or Roman paganism. Themes of the cycle of the moon and cycles of the sun, the land and the tribe run concurrently and independently but seemingly without being in conflict and in fact, forming a cohesive whole. Hence, I think it is possible to work with the elements in the form of the four directions and the three realms without any conflict of ideology.

In ancient Ireland and Scotland, we can see the great importance of the elements in the way that people swore upon them as we (mostly) now swear upon the Bible. For example, King Laoghaire swore upon the elements to not exact taxes of tribute from the people of Ulster; having reneged on his oath he died, supposedly killed by the elements. Oaths that included sun and moon, water and air, day and night, sea and land were common (*grian agus ésca, usci agus aer. lá agus adaig, muir agus tír*) or by swearing by the three realms for example 'if I break my *geis* may the earth swallow me up, the sea drown me or the sky fall upon me'. Such retribution was a very powerful image in the Celtic psyche and such oaths were not taken lightly. Ptolemy I (4th century BC) recorded that Celts 'feared nothing except that the sky might fall down on them'.[11]

Residuals of this attitude carried into the Christian era, indeed the final section of the Irish prayer St. Patrick's Breastplate (trans. by Kuno Meyer) refers explicitly to the power of the elements:

Atomriug indiu	I arise today
niurt nime	Through strength of firmament,
soilse gréne	light of sun,
etrochtae ésci	brightness of moon,
áne thened	splendour of fire,
déne lóchet	speed of lightning,
Lúathe gáithe	swiftness of wind,
fudomnae maro	depth of sea,
tairisminge talman	solidity of earth,
cobsaide ailech	firmness of rock.

What is most important here, of course, is a true and deep understanding of the elements within the wider universe and ourselves. It is so easy for us to divorce ourselves from nature in modern society, even the language we use regarding nature is indicative of our attitude that it is something separate and not of us, or us of it. Learning to unlearn this division is essential to communing with the land and ourselves. It is through the elements that flow through all earthly existence, that we can find our connection to the cosmos and the divine force that passes through and inhabits all living things.

In order to do this when we are not familiar with the process it is vitally important to escape from the urban, artificial environment. Becoming exposed to the raw elements, living (even for a short time) in a more naturalistic way opens us up to the influence and connection of the elements, which is always there but which we generally ignore. Sometimes a sort of 'shock therapy' of direct exposure is necessary with some people to re-awaken their senses to the reality of the physical and spiritual world. Even for those familiar and 'connected' it is necessary to maintain this relationship by direct contact with the wild elements as modern life has a tendency over time to sedate or switch off this connection.

Meditating or journeying through the three realms or the four elements is also a powerful way of internalising the outer manifestation of elemental forces and in doing so reminds us that we can find them within ourselves at any time, even if we are in a concrete building that is air conditioned, heated and lit by artificial means.

If nothing else is gained from Druidic study or if you chose a different path, to know the elements is a powerful and enriching gift for any person; however I would also consider it to be a basic foundation and an essential platform for further growth and Druidic understanding.

VI

Cosmology

Cosmology means the study of the nature and origins of the universe, a subject that plays a part in all the religions known to man. To understand the Celtic view of the cosmos, perhaps the best place to start is with the Self. The Self can be viewed as a microcosm of the cosmos, both being comprised of the same elements in terms of the *dúile*. To the Celts, the centre of their world was where they are, the centre of the Self and their home. As the member of a tribe, they understood the connection between themselves and the rest of the tribe and the cosmos, symbolised by the *bile* or sacred tree of the tribe. The fire that was sacred in the home and also in ritual connects the three realms, gives inspiration to the seer and poet (fire in the head) and warms the three cauldrons of warming, vocation and knowledge.

Amergin is credited with the poetic tract that describes the three cauldrons and the nine elements of *dúile*, furthermore the song of Amergin (from *Lebor Gabála Érenn*) beautifully describes the mystery of the cosmos, a section of which is given below:

I am wind on sea
I am ocean wave
I am roar of sea
I am bull of seven fights

I am vulture of cliff
I am dewdrop
I am fairest of flowers
I am boar of boldness

I am salmon in pool
I am lake on plain
I am word of skill
I am point of weapon (that poureth forth combats)

Who smootheth the ruggedness of a mountain?
Wo is He who announceth the ages of the Moon?
And who, the place where falleth the sunset?
Who calleth the cattle from the House of Tethra?
On whom do the cattle of Tethra smile?

This strange riddle written by the *Ollamh* of the Milesian people of Ireland (arriving after the Tuatha Dé Danann) illustrates his connectedness with all of creation, note the House of Tethra is another name for the Celtic otherworld.

The parts of us are analogous to parts of the cosmos when viewed in the light of the connection between all things in the universe. The sense of oneness that is to be found in this ancient way of perception that is to be found in 'uncivilised' cultures and also is embodied in Taoism, the ancient religion of China. Returning to the cauldrons, these embody the nine elements of the *dúile* as follows:

Land, sea and sky are also synonymous with the three realms of the physical world, the under/otherworld and the upperworld, which is discretely symbolised by the sacred tree or world tree.

The world tree is alluded to in Celtic literature but is more explicit in Siberian and more famously Norse folklore. To the Norse the world tree (*Yggdrasil*) connected the nine worlds and was supported by three giant roots, description of which survived into later times perhaps due to the late Christianisation of Scandinavia; in the Celtic kingdoms and Europe generally, the cosmic tree is lost or only partially described.

However, the importance of the *bile* or sacred tree in the Druidic or Celtic view cannot be underestimated. Sacred trees are clearly linked with royal sites of inauguration and the power of sovereignty. In Ireland, the *Bile Buadha* or tree of power acted as the symbolic centre of the tribe and was venerated and sacred to all people of that tribe. Strangely, the ancient Irish were not above destroying the *Bile Buadha* of another tribe. In fact, this destruction occurred several times in an effort to destroy the power and morale of enemies — for instance the 'Annals of the Four Masters' describes how the sacred trees of the O'Neills in Tyrone were uprooted by a rival Antrim tribe.

A *bile* was often to be found near to a royal fort or residence and was also considered a doorway or link to the otherworld, tales of the magical branch or magical fruit of trees abound in Celtic literature. Even now 'fairy trees' are commonly found in or near by remains of a *rath* (fort), mound or other ancient site, especially in Ireland. Five great trees were especially sacred in ancient Ireland — five being the number of the ancient provinces, the trees were *Bile Tortan* — Tara; *Craebh Uisnigh* — Uisneach (centre); *Craebh Daithi* — Westmeath; *Eo Mugna* — Kildare and *Eo Rossa* — Carlow.

The Nordic legends describe the creation of the universe and also how the first man and woman sprung from an ash and a rowan tree (or alternatively from a giant's armpit); unfortunately no truly ancient Celtic cosmogony survives either in literature or folklore. Julius Caesar stated the Gauls believed themselves all descended from the god Dis Pater but no myth relating to this claim exists. What have survived are various accounts of the arrivals of the Celts in Britain and Ireland, which are clearly written by Christian clerics. For instance, the account of the 72 races, languages, Nimrod's tower and Fenius Farsaidh from *Auraicept na n-Éces* (Scholar's Primer) is clearly borrowed from the biblical story of the Tower of Babel. Also surviving into literature via Scottish poet James Thomson is the concept of the three circles of manifestation, more famously described by Iolo Morganwg in *Barddas,* which closely relates to the Irish concept of the three realms and the Pythagorean concept of metempsychosis.

The three circles of existence are *Abred, Gwynfyd* and *Ceugant,* illustrated generally as three concentric circles. *Abred* represents the physical realm of living creatures of the land, sky and sea, it is essence the middle world or the trunk of the world tree. All life emerged from *Annwn,* the underworld, or roots of the world tree, depicted here as a cauldron containing the jumbled elements that make up all living things. The circle of *Abred* expands outwards from the lowest forms such as algae, stretching out to humans at its outer limit. It was thought that all existence progressed outwards towards the realm of *Gwynfyd,* much as plants reach towards light. Through various incarnations, the soul would progress into higher forms or failing that, slip backwards — say from an animal to a plant. At the human level, it was thought our consciousness can enable a progression into *Gwynfyd,* 'the White Life', or realm of the soul, this being like the upper world or high branches of the world tree. In this realm, the soul journeys towards perfection, those at the outer edge again being higher or more developed than those preceding. The upper limit of *Gwynfyd* cannot be breached by the soul, beyond it lays *Ceugant,* which initiated the whole manifestation starting from its centre. *Ceugant* is the beyond, infinity wherein dwells the divine power of the cosmos. This model can be represented in several ways, with one realm contained within the other or interlinked in a hierarchical or non-hierarchical manner. The left hand model is from *Barddas,* Ross Nichols gives an inverted version of the same with Ceugant at the centre[12], which he attributed to the early Celtic Church.

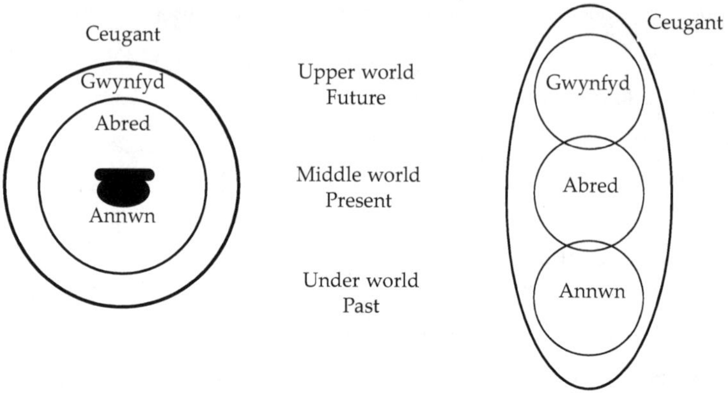

The three realms can be seen to tie in with the three states of time and *Ceugant* can be viewed as destiny or the hand of the fates that is interacting within these realms. In the above diagram, the progression is clearly hierarchical with a progression outwards, or with the 'triple knot' on the right – upwards. A third way of depicting this is shown below, the three realms are interlinked but one is no higher of more prominent than the other. This is the shape of the triskele, sacred symbol of the druids and Neolithic peoples.

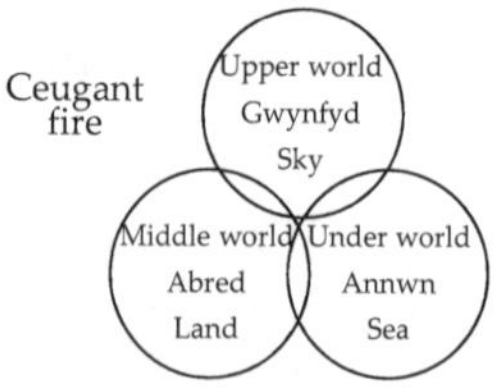

From personal experience I find the triskele model to be closest to my practical knowledge of the three realms, in the process of journeying to the upper or lower world, although it appears that you are going somewhere, I feel that the same time and space exists although seemingly different from ordinary reality. There is no chasm like between heaven and earth or hell of the Christian tradition; to the Druid it is a matter of a shift in perception enabling the experience of another dimension of reality. I see the three realms as co-existent in the same place — linked yet separated from each other in the same way that past, present and future are separate yet linked; each realm is discrete yet joined to the other to form a whole. The triad and the number three is extremely important in Druidry and can be interpreted in many ways, for instance: maiden, mother, crone; sun, moon, earth; mother, father, child; dark, light and the life force created by this polarity. There are many more possibilities besides, and perhaps it was partly the concept of the holy trinity — father, son and holy ghost that enabled St. Patrick to win over the Irish people who were already familiar with a threefold rather than dualistic way of looking at the world.

Although it is generally accepted by academics that there is no extant Celtic creation myth, I have received the following via an OBOD member, which was received orally from their grand-parent. It is impossible to guess how old this story is, whoever wrote it had some knowledge of the deities across the Celtic world as opposed to say just Ireland or just Wales. Apart from its modern style, this to me would indicate that it was written in the last two hundred years, prior to this, the term 'Celt' was not commonly in use from the time of Julius Caesar who used '*Celtae*' to refer to the people of Gaul. Regardless of its origin it is still an interesting document and hence presented here in full:

> Once upon a time, there was no time and that was when there also were no gods and no man walked the surface of the land. But there was the sea, and where the sea met the land, a mare was born, white and made of sea-foam. And her name was

Eiocha. On the land, near where the land met the sea, a tree grew, a strong and sturdy oak. On the oak, grew a plant whose seeds were formed of the foam tears of the sea. To sustain her, Eiocha ate the seeds, these white berries, and they were transformed within her. Eiocha grew heavy with child and gave birth to the god, Cernunnos. So great was her pain in childbirth that she ripped bark from the one tree and hurled it into the sea. The bark was transformed by the sea and became the giants of the deep.

Cernunnos was lonely and he saw the giants of the deep who were numerous, so he coupled with Eiocha and of their union came the gods, Maponos, Tauranis, and Teutates, and the goddess, Epona. Eiocha soon tired of the land, being a creature of sea-foam, and she returned to the sea, where she was transformed into Tethra, goddess of the deep water, sometimes called Tethys.

The gods and goddess were lonely for they had none to command nor none to worship them. The gods and goddess took wood from the one oak tree and fashioned the first man and the first woman.

Cernunnos also made other animals from the one oak tree, the deer and the hound, the boar and the raven, the hare and the snake. He was god of the animals, and he commanded the oak tree to spread and grow, to become a forest home for his children.

Epona also made animals, but she made only the horse, mare and stallion alike, in remembrance of Eiocha who was no more.

Teutates took limbs from the one tree, and fashioned a bow, arrows, and a club.

Tauranis took limbs from the one tree, and fashioned thunderbolts made of fire and noise. He would leap to the top of the tallest trees and hurl his weapon at the ground. The ground would shake, the grass would burn, and the animals would run in fear.

Maponos also took limbs from the one tree, but he fashioned not a weapon but a harp. He stretched strings of the winds from its limbs and spent his days in Cernunnos' forest. The winds would join in the melodies and the birds as well. And all Cernunnos' animals would come from near and far to hear Maponos play.

The giants of the deep saw the gods and goddess happy on the land, and the giants were jealous, for they had none to command nor none to worship them. So the giants plotted against the gods; they would overwhelm them with the sea and take the land under the water. But Tethra in the deep sea heard the murmuring of the giants in the waves and she remembered her days as Eiocha and so she warned her sons and daughter. The gods were prepared the day the giants came against them.

The gods took refuge in the one oak tree. Tauranis hurled his thunderbolt and split the land, and the sea overflowed its boundaries. Maponos broke the sky and hurled it at the giants. Teutates' deadly aim with the bow and arrows from the one oak tree cut down many of the giants. The giants of the deep were not without weapons; they had the strength of the waves.

The gods overwhelmed the giants, but could not destroy them. The giants of the deep were driven back into the sea, and Tethra bound them in the deep waters. But a few escaped Tethra and fled far from her reach. They called themselves the Fomor, and built a life on the outer edges of the world. But the Fomor dreamed of conquest, and vowed to once again take the land from the gods. Of their later battles, our histories tell us much.

The sea returned to its bed and Maponos repaired the sky. And the gods looked for Epona as she had been absent from the victory. Epona had rescued one man and one woman from the watery and fiery destruction, and the three of them waited deep in Cernunnos' forest. From this man and this woman Epona saved would come our mighty people. The gods and the goddess left the deep of Cernunnos's forest and returned to their home near the one tree of oak which still stood strong and sturdy, and the sacred berries where still white as sea-foam.

Where the fiery pieces of the heavens Maponos had torn from the sky had mingled with the waters of the sea, there were born new gods. The god Belenus and his sister Danu sprang from where the heavenly fire had been but little quenched. The god Lir sprang from where the waters of the sea had almost quenched the fire of heaven. From Lir, as the histories tell, there would come the mighty Manannan, the beautiful Branwen, the wise Bran. But from Danu many children would come, the Dagda, Nuadha of the Silver Hand, the wise Dienceght, the smith Goihbhio, the fearsome Morrigan, the gentle Brighid. The Children of Danu and the Children of Lir are the two mighty races our songs tell of, ever opposite.

Having looked at the basic concepts of the structure of the cosmos, let us now look at the Celtic conception of the physical world around us. It is a widely held belief that the Celts lived their lives in terms of winter (*Geimredh*) and summer (*Samradh*), night proceeding day and a year based on the cycles of the moon. Even today, the day begins at night time (12.00am), whereas the Celtic day began at nightfall, older man being rural and living much of life outside was probably far more comfortable with night than modern men. Many western people today never use their night vision, they never see the stars due to light pollution or the fact that they spend their nights almost always inside. The Celts, the Druids in particular, clearly had an understanding of astronomy and astrology — this is evidenced by the classical writings that state this, together with the two Gaulish calendars found in France, the most complete and most famous being the Coligny calendar of the Sequani tribe in Gaul. This calendar, discovered in 1897, was made in the form of a bronze tablet. Unfortunately it was in pieces, which although painstakingly reconstructed comprise less than half of the original tablet; consequently reconstructing the calendar has been somewhat difficult, although extensive work to understand it has taken place in the last two decades.

The reconstructed Coligny Calendar discovered in 1897.

The Coligny calendar is basically a five year, lunar calendar of twelve months per year, plus an intercalary month every two and a half years, which reconciles the cycles of the sun and the moon over that five year period. There is some dispute over where exactly the calendar begins – the first month *Samonios* can be interpreted as marking the winter solstice (late December), alternatively May 1st is given due to the theory that *Samonios* is derived from samon, 'summer'. As May 1st marks the beginning of the summer half of the year in traditional Celtic lore, *Samonios* could possibly be May 1st. However it is also often interpreted as marking *Samhain* (being November by modern reckoning) particularly as three days are marked corresponding with the more ancient three-day celebration of *Samhain* – the festival on the 17th of *Samonios* called the TRINVX SAMO SINDIV – 'the three nights of *Samonios*' today. If one looks further back again it is likely that the whole month of November was a sacred time of celebration and the thinning of the veil between the worlds. Then again, the winter solstice has a period of three days in which the sun appears to stand still and this could equally be relevant. On the basis of seeing the year starting at 31st October modern pagans generally regard this as a pagan New Year's Day. It is also often claimed that the solstices and equinoxes were not celebrated by the Celts, however there is a large body of evidence that goes against this theory. Extensive work by Benigni et al points to a winter solstice start to the Coligny calendar plus marking of the equinoxes and the summer solstice. Comparison is made to the sacred calendar of Eleusis (used by the ancient Greeks) and the astronomical and agricultural cycles of the Neolithic peoples of Europe.

Neo-pagan	**Olmsted Hypothesis**[13]	**Gaulish**	**No. days**
November/May	Late June/Late December	Samonios	30
December/June	Late July/Late January	Dumannios	29
January/July	Late August/Late February	Riuros	30
February/August	Late September/Late March	Anagantios	29
March/September	Late October/Late April	Ogronios	30
April/October	Late November/Late May	Cutios	30
May/November	Late December/Late June	Giamonios	29
June/December	Late January/Late July	Simivisonnos	30
July/January	Late February/Late August	Equos	29
August/February	Late March/Late September	Elembivios	29
September/March	Late April/Late October	Edrinios	30
October/April	Late May/Late November	Cantlos	29
	Ciallos (intercalculatory month)		30

It is quite clear that the Neolithic peoples who built (amongst others) the great circles of Carnac in France, Stonehenge in

England and the three temples of Newgrange, Knowth and Dowth in Ireland had a definite understanding and reverence for the sun and celebrated significant moments in its passage.

Some have described these people as proto-druids, whether this is the case or not is impossible to say. What is known is that the Neolithic peoples were conquered and assimilated by the westerly spreading Celts and the importance of these sacred sites is retained as evidenced by the literature and folklore that remains. Myth and legend clearly allude to the solar cycle and its connection to the land and tribe – something that is unmistakeable and in my view indicates that the solar festivals were celebrated, although it is impossible to say if they were of less, greater or equal importance to the four 'fire' festivals. Maybe the Celts inherited the understanding of the solar festivals from the Neolithic peoples, or perhaps it was already part of their belief system. A parallel to the former theory is the assimilation of Taoism into Buddhism in China. Rather than destroying Taoism, the Buddhists finding it to be complementary to their own beliefs simply absorbed it in its entirety, such that it still exists today in its own right and as a facet of Buddhism. I see no reason why the colonising Celts would not have absorbed some of the beliefs of the conquered peoples if they proved to be complementary to their own worldview. The fact that so many pre-Celtic sacred sites still remain in the Celtic and ex-Celtic countries is indicative of their respect for these sites, otherwise they may well have dismantled them as has occurred in lands further south or east where other cultures became dominant. Some claim that the Druids predate Celtic culture and that it was absorbed by the Celts, as opposed to the view that the Druids were by definition Celts – either way all that we know of the Druids has come to us via Celtic culture itself or classical reports about the Celts.

Our modern calendar is very much taken for granted, however the Gregorian calendar used in the western world was adopted in 1582 in Roman Catholic countries and later by the rest of Europe and its colonies. Before this, the Julian calendar was in common use since the time of Julius Caesar (45BC) when he reformed the Roman calendar which was at the time over two months out of synch. In relatively modern times New Year's Day has been a moveable feast, for example in France prior to 800,AD it was celebrated on 1st March; it has also been as early as 20th December and later still — 25th March and 1st April. It is said that April Fool's Day originates from the continuing practice of some to celebrate New Year on April 1st in Britain and Ireland despite a law being passed to further update the calendar in 1751, thus jumping forward twelve days from the then current date of 20th December and fixing New Year at 1st January. In China, the Muslim world and various other cultures the calendar is somewhat different from the one modern westerners are familiar with; hence in respect to the Celtic/Druidic calendar I see no reason why it should be adapted or 'massaged' to fit our preconceptions or convenience. The roots of the western calendar lie in the cycles of the moon (355 days) which gives rise to months; the later 365 day calendar was solar based. In its present form it is displaced from the solar events of the solstices and equinoxes such that it no longer has any meaning with relation to the cycles of moon and sun. This has disconnected us from living by the rhythms of nature, that our ancestors lived by for many millennia. By becoming familiar with the phases of the moon and the sun, observing it first hand and living by it we immediately begin reconnecting with the natural world. Of course, it is still necessary for most of us to live by clocks and cheat the seasons, but by noting the positions and phases of the sun and moon and also the stars it reminds us that there is a realm outside of human existence, which is far larger and far older than we can imagine.

This naturally leads me to the fact that the Druids had a knowledge of astronomy and astrology. Apart from references to this in the Celtic literature Julius Caesar clearly stated: 'They have a great many other teachings as well which they hand down to the young concerning such things as the motion of stars, the size of the cosmos and the earth...' And also from Pompomius Mela, AD18-75: 'These profess to know the size and shape of the world, the movements of the heavens and of the stars, and the will of the gods.'

Unfortunately, whatever star lore and astronomical or astrological systems existed seems to have been lost. It is well known that the ancient Egyptians, Babylonians, Greeks, Israelites, Romans, Indians and Assyrians were also well versed in astrology. In the last century, it has become clear that it was also a cultural development in Tibet, China and South America. However, the only system in current common usage, in Western culture, is that of the Ptolemaic dynasty of Macedonian royalty who ruled Egypt up until the death of Cleopatra in 30 BC. Up until the 17th century astrology and astronomy were considered as more or less the same discipline, the Ptolemaic system owed its ideas largely to Aristotle and Claudius Ptolemaeus, author of the *Almagest*. Although the Ptolemaic astronomical model of the cosmos has long been superseded, the astrological system is still with us today.

Some writers have attempted to reconstruct a Celtic astrological system; however, these are merely an attempt to adapt the Ptolemaic model by superimposing Celtic names on a clearly Greco-Egyptian system. As such, I feel that any Celtic astrological system is invalid, having absolutely no historical basis and often consisting of wild hypothesising. It is indeed sad that Druidic astrology is lost to the world but that is the unfortunate truth. It is well known that the Druids knew Greek language and it is widely believed that they knew and followed the teachings of the Greek philosopher and mathematician Pythagoras; it is therefore not unreasonable to suppose that they may have been conversant in the Greco-Egyptian astrology of the time. It would indeed be preferable to have access to a Druidic astrological system, however in the absence of any verifiable system, I do not see why we cannot make do with the current system, inherited from the Greeks, which is well tried and perfectly acceptable as a divination and evaluative tool. This is something that we will look at further later on.

So now, we have a fairly good idea of the Celtic understanding of the universe. Obviously, times have changed considerably and what was once highly relevant might not be deemed to be appropriate today. The Celts believed that the place of the soul was the head (not the heart) and the head cult was prominent in early Celtic kingdoms, so much so that it was thought that to possess someone's head gave you their power/life force and in some cases even control over their soul.

Overall, one could say that the Celtic/Druidic view of life and the cosmos is more in synergy with the natural world and more holistic than modern western-style culture. Certainly the Celts did not have the modern obsession with longevity, with materialism (although they loved beautiful possessions and extravagance) or with rational control of nearly every aspect of life. Much as we might regard some of the ancient Druids' practices as savage, for example human and animal sacrifice, I am sure that the lack of fairness, honour and the domination of financial considerations in almost all that we do would seem barbarous to them. When looking at the 'savage' practices of the ancients we must also consider the general 'savagery' of the times – times in which the comfort zones we take for granted just did not exist and human life was far more at the mercy of fate and the unpredictability and often violent capriciousness of nature. The Druids were clearly capable of rationality however, I believe that they had not become dominated by that aspect of the self and so had a more complete sense of themselves and their place in the world.

The Irish concept of *Dán* embodies much of what the Celtic world-view is about. *Dán* means art, poetry, destiny, fate and ability. Druid Jason Kirkley considers it synonymous with the Chinese *Tao,* which is in turn linked to the concept of *Ch'i* and the discipline of *Feng Shui*. I would consider *Dán* to be intimately connected to the *dúile, find* (the personification of wisdom) and *imbas/awen* - the light of inspiration that is so important to druids.

Everything that we do stems from our perception of ourselves and the universe around us. If we are able to find the 'centredness' to form a harmonious relationship as a part of the world, rather than embody forces of domination and abuse, then we have some chance of understanding the sacredness at the core of Druidry, neolithic/indigenous cultures and what is still present buried within many of the world's religions.

I believe that the problems that the world is experiencing now is the culmination of a fractured model of existence that denigrates an often unconscious but vital and potent part of ourselves. I see modern Druidry as one the methods by which humanity can reconnect to essential but neglected aspects of ourselves and thereby reconnect and re-establish equilibrium with the planet that we have thrown into turmoil.

VII

Inspiration

To the modern Druid inspiration or bright knowledge is as essential now as it undoubtedly was to the ancient Druids. To the Druids of old this was referred to as *imbas* or *awen*. The term *imbas* is probably best known in relation to *Imbas Forosna* (meaning illumination between the hands) which is a technique of divination, something that we will look at later.

Illumination is central to the Bardic arts, as highlighted by the Welsh story of Taliesin and his rebirth from uncultured youth (Gwion Bach, meaning little innocent) to inspired poet and seer of the radiant brow. The story, of which there are many versions, is essentially a tale of initiation, indicative of the personal search for wisdom as well as being a metaphor for shamanic journey. After his several transformations, gestation within the goddess and the leather bag he emerges fully aware. He received three gifts – poetry, prophesy and shape-shifting, these being equated by some to the three facets of Druidry – Bard, Ovate and Druid.

I have been a sow, I have been a buck,
I have been a sage, I have been a snout,
I have been a horn, I have been a wild sow,
I have been a shout in battle.
I have been a gushing torrent,
I have been a wave on the long shore.
I have been a gentle rain.
I have been a speckled cat in a forked tree.
I have been a circle, I have been a head,
I have been a goat in an elder tree.

I have been a cran-bag well filled,
— A sight to behold.

This story of illumination is paralleled by the Irish story of Fionn MacCumhaill who at the age of seven meets Finnéigeas 'Fionn the Seer' who has just caught the salmon of knowledge. Fionn was charged with the job of cooking it, but was warned not to eat it. However, Fionn burned his thumb, on the skin of the cooked fish, and sucked it thus gaining the gift of wisdom that Finnéigeas had intended for himself, just as Gwion accidentally received *Awen* from the three drops out of Cerridwen's cauldron.

Another aspect in Fionn's story is that the old Fionn is an emanation of the archaic Celtic seer *Find,* which in turn the young Finn himself becomes. This ancient personification of wisdom is particular to the Boyne valley, as well as Fionn MacCumhaill, *Find File* the mythical Leinster king and Morann the judge are associated with the wisdom and skill of Bóinn and Manannán. Many of Manannán's possessions find their way into the hands of Fionn in the folklore, the crane bag being of particular significance. The bag made from the skin of the goddess Aoife (in the form of a crane) held symbols of Manannán's great powers, and is used today by Druids to contain magical tools and objects of inspiration. The concept of *Find* ties in with what we know of Celtic ideas of reincarnation and demonstrates the eternal wellspring of wisdom that can be drawn on through the ages.

The Druid revival inspired by the Welsh sources brings us the story of the three rays of light — a creation myth of sorts. The giant Einigen, who was said to be the first being, saw three rays of light descend from the heavens, these also being the three syllables of the true name of God — O I U. It is said only those inspired by *Awen* can correctly pronounce these syllables. In the three rays was contained all the wisdom that ever existed or ever will be. Einigen took three staves of rowan and carved all of this knowledge upon them, but others worshipped the staves instead of reading what was inscribed upon them. Einigen's anger at the stupidity of men caused him to die on the spot and the three staves set root inside his huge skull and were growing out of the jaw. Men happened upon the three trees and read the words carved upon them, thus gaining great wisdom and passing on this bright knowledge on down generations through the Druids.

These three rays form the symbol that is familiar to most modern Druids, and which is discussed at some length in *Barddas*. The three rays are also said to represent the rays of the rising sun of the solstices and equinoxes as if shining against a menhir or standing stone so that a shadow is cast upon the ground forming the shape.

Shown with three dots over the downward pointing lines is the symbol of *Awen,* which itself can be broken down into three syllables when said or chanted Ah-oh-en. *Awen* or *Imbas* is the inner illumination that inspires the power of prophesy, poetic vision and any activity that draws upon the creative energy in the universe — it could equally well be called divine inspiration. This very closely mirrors the Vedic *Om,* which is now widely known in western alternative and New Age circles and today is often used in chant and meditation in much the same way.

Some rather bizarre methods of reaching a state of transcendent awareness were used by the ancient Druids, particularly in relation to divination. Rites and practices involving sacrificial slaughter have long since disappeared but some methods and have survived via the Bardic schools long enough to be documented.

> I must not omit to relate their way of study, which is very singular. They shut their doors and windows for a day's time, and lie on their backs with a stone upon their belly, and plaids about their heads, and their eyes being covered they pump their brains for rhetorical encomium or panegyric; and indeed they furnish such a stile from this dark cell as is understood by very few...
>
> (From Martin's Description of the Western Islands of Scotland)

The same technique is recorded as being used in the Bardic schools of Ireland, which were secular institutions, however deprivation of a similar nature was also used by Christian religious orders to induce a state of religious ecstasy. Indeed, the same technique is taught to Bards in modern Druid orders as a method of gaining *Awen/Imbas*.

The use of darkness is a valuable tool in the process of 'tuning-in' to the divine energy, the source of creativity and wisdom, after all, it was in darkness that Taliesin spent his final gestation period floating on the sea before finally emerging into the world again. The darkened room helps to pull one away from the every-day concerns of the world and create a space to precipitate that shift in mental state that is essential to receive inspiration. Likewise, the stone on the belly draws our attention to the breath and away from distractions.

Meditation, sitting up or lying down, may have the same effect; some prefer to stare into a candle flame or to listen to either soothing music or a guided relaxation. I do not believe that it is particularly important what method is used so long as it works. Above all, it is important to achieve the right state of mind and relaxation. Before attempting to access the power of *Awen/Imbas* it is essential to shake off stress and anxiety, otherwise this process is very difficult if not impossible. Becoming relaxed is often easier said than done. From personal experience I can say that using yoga, *Tai Chi* or breath work are excellent methods of achieving the necessary calm and relaxation. It is also important to create the right circumstances for this to happen. Avoid arguments or stressful situations prior to meditating, avoid coffee, tea, chocolate, cigarettes and in fact, anything that will have a stimulating affect on the mind or body.

Tiredness is another factor that can be either beneficial or detrimental. Extreme tiredness, as is the case for fasting, can sometimes induce a high level of clarity, however it can also have the opposite effect for instance total loss of focus and concentration and even falling asleep. From my own experience, I have found that working in conditions of extreme tiredness is far more effective in the open air, exposed to elements such as the breeze by the sea.

Once the right conditions have been achieved, one can begin to meditate, perhaps chanting *Awen* or *Imbas* three, six or nine times as a prelude to this. Careful control of the breath is key to the inner calm that is required to receive illumination, also focusing on the breath helps to keep the mind free of distraction. It is natural that thoughts about the day and everyday concerns will pop into the mind; trying to fight this can be counterproductive and cause agitation. Perhaps a better solution is just to observe the thoughts without fully entering them and allow them to pass, then returning to the focus of the breath. In essence, the art of receiving *Imbas/Awen* is to simply be, to not really think of anything, but to be open — straining to find it paradoxically can ensure that you never find it!

It is impossible to demonstrate or fully explain illumination; it is an individual experience that cannot really be taught. The best that can be offered is a few pointers to facilitate the process and increase the chances of success. In my experience, illumination is like a sea that rises and falls. At times wisdom and creatively will flow freely and often with unexpected speed, at other times it is not forthcoming or is very limited. The level of connectedness seems to be proportional to one's own emotional and spiritual state – in a state of anger or personal anxiety it is likely that the experience is much diminished, sometimes this lack arriving just when illumination feels most needed. Finding your centre and groundedness against a backdrop of chaos and difficulty is essential in order to maintain that connection through the different and often difficult periods we experience in life. Over time, each individual finds creative visualisations or physical techniques that help bring the self into balance and create the harmonious frame of mind that makes the opening for illumination to enter – each of us has to discover that through trial and error as this is different for everyone.

The physical state is an often forgotten factor in this equation – poor health, abuse of drink and drugs, bad diet and sluggish metabolism can often have a detrimental effect on spiritual abilities. When one considers the integration of mind, body and spirit it is quite obvious that depletion or damage to one area will affect the other areas, but with modern linear or rational thinking it is easy for us to overlook this.

Although it is impossible to adequately describe what illumination is, there are methods of meditating and exercises known that are generally found to be effective in achieving that state of being, mostly utilising the energy within the self or the energy of the elemental forces that surround us. To that purpose, I present overleaf two methods that may prove useful. Again I would highlight that these are performed most successfully in a relaxed state; slow, deep and regular breathing is a vital component in their execution. I strongly recommend that these be used where you will not be interrupted with no sudden sensory intrusions; this can be very powerful on a beach or in a woodland, so long as you have total privacy.

Essential Force Visualisation:

- Sit or lie down in a comfortable position and breathe deeply.
- Close your eyes and focus on the breath, becoming more relaxed with each breath.
- Visualise your life energy – nwyfre, chi, essence, soul force (whatever terms suits you) and see it manifest as an object, plant or creature than embodies its essential qualities.
- Cup your hands and see it sitting within your joined hands.
- Visualise this image growing in strength and size until it envelopes your entire physical body.
- Remain in this state and allow the energy of the visualisation to penetrate.
- To end, visualise this image shrinking again into your hands and then being absorbed back into yourself.
- Take your time to open your eyes and get up, strive to retrain the sense of calm and relaxation.

Even if done for just a few minutes the above exercise can have quite enlivening effects. Most people I have seen try this have received some benefit, with practice it can become a great gift that increases centredness and spiritual/psychic abilities.

Light Body Exercise:

- Sit or lie down in a comfortable position and breathe deeply.
- Listen to the sounds, feel the earth, smell and taste the air.
- Close your eyes and breathe in and out deeply at least three times.
- Sense tension in your body and allow it to disperse on the out-breaths.
- As you relax, sense the energy of the earth beneath you and

feel it pass upwards through the body slowly. Sense it as a golden light that fills and surrounds the physical body, bringing relaxation, rejuvenation and strength as it rises up. Feel it pass through the three cauldrons (or chakras if you prefer) and sense its effect as it does so.

- As it reaches the crown of the head become aware of the energy of the cosmos above and feel a white ray penetrate your crown and descend through your body until the two energies are fully intertwined within and around you.
- Remain in this state and allow the energy of the visualisation to penetrate.
- To end, visualise this body of light begin to fade, focus on the breath and become more aware of the physical sensations of the body. As you do this, it helps to ground you and return you to everyday consciousness.
- Take your time to open your eyes and get up, strive to retrain the sense of calm and relaxation.
- Eat or drink something if you do not feel fully grounded on completion.

There are several variants of the above exercise (e.g. the Celtic Cross of Light) taught by different Druidic orders and also by Celtic Shamanic Practitioners, although they are in principle the same, the method may differ. If you are not familiar with this already, it is important to try this as a preparation for spiritual journeys and as a means of accessing illumination. Do not be discouraged by early failure, it might take several attempts to receive noticeable results and indeed it may take weeks or months to become fully comfortable with this technique. Other techniques such as using a candle, cards, scrying bowl or a stone on the belly might work equally as well, I suggest that experimenting is best to find what is most effective. Herbie Brennan's excellent book *Astral Doorways,* although not a Druidic text, elaborates on techniques and the principles involved and is a valuable resource for anyone who is not already experienced in meditation or spiritual journeying.

As with all skills, it takes time and effort to acquire them, for those who are not naturally gifted. It has often been said that we all possess spiritual ability from birth but often lose it as we become socialised in the ways of modern living. Speaking for myself, I can state that this seems to be the case, the natural sensitivity I had as a child was gone by the time I was a teenager and has only returned after many years of effort to rekindle the flame that was snuffed out in my youth — such is life.

Above all, remember that practice and perseverance are essential in the development of any ability. Do not be deterred by initial failure, this is normal and nothing to feel bad about, be patient and persevere and you will eventually succeed.

VIII

Immrama

With the recent surge of interest in Shamanism, there has become a general greater awareness of the shamanic role in Celtic culture and in Druidry. Shaman is a term originally applied to the religious practitioners of Northern Asia, Lapland and Northern Canada (Inuit people). Whether accurate or not, this term has been broadened to embrace the Native American Medicine-Man, South American Shaman and Celtic Seer. I first met a Shaman around 1990, it was the first time I'd really heard of what it involves, although I had a vague idea of the definition. In this case, she was trained in the Native American methods and did not equate her practice to Celtic spirituality or Druidry.

The integration or overlapping of Shamanism with modern Druidry is a phenomenon that has occurred mostly in the last decade, so much so that Celtic Shamanism has become synonymous with the otherworld journey or *Immrama*, astral travel and psychic healing. It is quite clear that the *Fáidh* (Ovate) performed roles that included interaction with the upper and lower worlds, for instance existence beyond that of everyday reality; however the term Shaman was not employed in relation to Druidry or Celtic spirituality until very recently. This does not mean that Druids did not perform shamanic activities, but their role was not viewed in such terms in literature or folklore prior to the New Age fashionability of Shamanism.

In ancient Irish and Scottish Celtic culture, there were stories of *aeachtra* (adventure) and *iomramh* (sea voyage) as vehicles by which the hero was to arrive at wisdom via experience and ordeal. This concept survived into the Christian era for instance in the voyages of St. Brendan, who encountered mythical islands and strange monsters. It is also embodied in a physical form in some of the severe pilgrimages undertaken for spiritual renewal and purification, for example climbing Croagh Patrick in bare feet, the horrific and dangerous ordeal of the Sceilig Mhichíl (Skellig Michael island, Co. Kerry) pilgrimage. In later times, this was for the forgiveness of sins rather than to gain insights or wisdom, although the tradition is deeply rooted in pagan Celtic mysticism. In Christian tradition, St. Michael is associated with guiding souls of the dead to heaven. It is thought that this island was formerly associated with the otherworld god Donn, in fact a smaller island south called Teach nDuind (house of Donn) was believed to be where the dead were assembled before being escorted to Tir na nÓg, although folklore gives accounts of the same gathering of the dead occurring on Sceilig Mhichíl.

Before moving on to the 'meat and potatoes' of the *Immrama* (*iomramh*), it is wise to take a look at protection, an area that is essential to any would-be Shaman or Druid who is intent on journeying into other realms. A well known saying 'curiosity killed the cat' is worth mentioning here as there are obvious risks in undertaking astral activities. One should have a reason or purpose for undertaking such work, curiosity is not sufficient justification! I know first-hand of two people who have experimented in working with the otherworld without any prior knowledge or experience (and more importantly no one to assist) and ended up in significant difficulties.

I myself have had two very unpleasant experiences whilst engaged in astral travel. On the first occasion I encountered by pure chance a dark figure that exuded malevolence. At this stage in my life, I was somewhat inexperienced but I had some grasp of the basics of self-protection and a certain respect for that which is beyond my capacity – I ran. I instinctively willed myself to move away as quickly as possible and I appeared to do so almost at light speed, although it took a while to re-orient myself I managed to lose whatever entity I had run into. On the second occasion, whilst in my psychic grove a purple eye appeared spontaneously, I felt I should not look at it but found myself doing so, upon which I gave it the energy to manifest a ghostly creature above me. I used light to banish this creature with some effort and return to my normal consciousness; however, some of this energy returned with me and for three days strange manifestations appeared in the house, growing stronger. Fortunately, I was able to draw on the support and knowledge of a more experienced Druid who advised me on how to protect myself and remove the presence successfully.

This was not a pleasant experience, but luckily it left me more able, more prepared for all eventualities and also more respectful of potential dangers. I have no wish to scare the reader, after all, in more than ten years of astral work these are the only two truly worrying experiences that I have had. Working in the upper and lower realms is generally unproblematic, but like our every-day reality where car crashes happen and bad people do exist, it is better to be prepared for all eventualities. This aspect of magical work is not an area I wish to explore further here and hence for more information I would direct the reader to Dion Fortune's excellent guide *Psychic Self-Defence*. Although this is a witchcraft/occult book, its principles are universal and the techniques discussed are relevant to any magical practitioner, including Druids and Shamans.

As I stated earlier, one should have some reason for journeying in the upper or lower world, this is not a game and I do not recommend attempts to wander aimlessly in the astral realms purely for pleasure or out of sheer curiosity. It is clear from the accounts of Druidic practice that journeying was undertaken for the purpose of divination, to obtain some certain knowledge, healing or to communicate with either divinity or the dead.

The famous Irish story of the recovery of the *Táin Bo Cuailgne* (Cattle raid of Cooley) is a prime example of a *Filé* undergoing an otherworld *Immrama* in order to obtain lost knowledge. Murgan

(Muirgen) son of the *Ollamh* Senchan is charged with the job of recovering the *Táin* for Guaire the *Ard Rí* of Ireland, after searching the land he and the bard Eimena arrive at a lake in Connaught where they discover a standing stone on which is written in Ogham 'Fergus son of Roy is here'. Murgan sings an incantation over Fergus' grave after which a cloud appears around him for three days. During that time, Fergus' spirit appears to Murgan and recites the entire saga to him, until he has it committed to memory.

Sleeping upon a burial mound was a common Druidic practice as a means of communicating with the spirits of the dead, the dead appearing in dreams, which the Druid would recall on waking. This method is still valid today, however use some caution — for instance it is said that to sleep upon the Mound of the Hostages at Tara in Ireland would induce madness or even death. Perhaps before making use of a burial mound or other sacred site, it is wise to find out something of its history or any lore related to it. In general the energy or *nwyfre* of ancient sites is often extremely strong and conducive to entry into other realms, this may also be stronger at certain times of year when the veil between the worlds is thin, for instance at *Bealtaine* or *Samhain*.

Various techniques are useful in making that step of crossing the threshold. Use of the techniques described in the last chapter is an excellent preliminary to this process, from a trance/meditative state the lifting of the veil becomes easier. This process can also be aided by creative visualisation of the journey for example travelling through a cave, tunnel or woods perhaps. Drumming or chanting is also a powerful method of making the transition into another realm. At first it is often better to find a neutral or personal space such as a grove or perhaps the world tree. From here, one can take whatever time is needed to compose oneself and then journey onward into the upper or lower spheres.

Within this alternative reality, we are often able to call upon the help of guides — what witches refer to as familiars. These are often in animal form (which is discussed later) but also appear as human. Some people have only one guide they are aware of while others have a great multitude. From my discussions with others, it appears to be a very individual experience and one should not be overly concerned about how many guides or power animals exist — building a working relationship is far more important.

The journey or *Immrama* is a vital part of initiatory experience, whether self-initiated or initiated by a grove/order the secrets of the self are accessed within these realms consciously, just as they are accessed subconsciously in dreams. Within these realms, the seeds of action can be sown that are manifested in the physical world later, within the upper world we can directly access divinity and angelic or demonic forces and interact with them. Some fifteen years ago, whilst travelling in India, I had a quite amazing transcendental experience in the upperworld. Having left my body I travelled upwards out of the house, up beyond the earth, beyond the solar system and onwards seemingly forever towards a tiny star. This star became a pulsing golden globe, which as I approached created an amazing sense of well-being and completeness. As I eventually entered the centre of this globe, I felt at one with the universe, supreme Godhead or whatever you might choose to call it. This was such an enlightening and superlative sensation that I did not wish to return, however as is inevitable, it had to end. At this point in my development I remained paralysed while in a trance and I had to wait a long time before I made it back into my physical body and was able to relate my experience to others.

Physical paralysis or disconnection from the body is quite common in beginners, it can take considerable time and practice to be able to retain control over the body whilst mainly or partly elsewhere. Likewise, I was totally unable to speak whilst in a trance state. Eventually I managed to do this but even now I find my speech is more slurred than usual and it often requires considerable effort to control it and/or my body. From a safety perspective it is important not to disturb someone is such a state unless there is an emergency such as a fire. To physically bring someone out of a trance state can be traumatic and possibly dangerous, it is important that the traveller return to their every-day consciousness in their own time and be fully grounded before resuming 'normal' activities.

In the example just given, I had taken a small amount of marijuana as an aid, this being a common practice amongst the Sadhus in India where I was staying. I have made many upper-world journeys since but rarely as clear as this, although I attribute the power of the experience to the setting, frequent yoga and my relaxed, open state and not the use of a drug, the drug merely helped facilitate the experience. Psychedelics, used wisely, frugally, responsibly and in the right circumstances can precipitate strong experiences. However, I do not recommend regular use, if at all, not least because of the continued affects of ingestion sometimes long after the return to every-day consciousness. As a general rule, I do not use drugs as a spiritual aid, having found other techniques that are at least equally effective, without any side-effects or drawbacks. Shaman's such as Terence McKenna and Carlos Castaneda have written extensively on the subject of psychotropic drugs, a highly interesting area but one that requires both caution and great responsibility if it is to be of benefit rather than dangerous.

With regard to underworld/otherworld journeying, this is often related to accessing subconscious parts of the self and healing. Certainly it is through a personal *Immrama* that we can access the three cauldrons mentioned earlier and gain an understanding of aspects of ourselves that are difficult to verbalise. Through working on the three cauldrons and journeying through the three realms, a common shamanic practice, we can hone spiritual/psychic sensitivity and develop a greater internal balance — a process roughly equivalent to working on the *chakras* of Vedic tradition. Within the otherworld realm, we might meet particular deities such as the Cailleach or Cernunnos or equally we might be able to meet our ancestors, spirits of the dead or the *sidhé*.

As far as the *sidhé/síd* or fairies are concerned, they can be tricky as they are often quite ambivalent towards us. Folklore describes them as tricky, sometimes treacherous or dangerous, which might explain why they were often feared. The whimsical Victorian image of tiny fairies is far from the truth, the rural Celt such as in Ireland or Wales regarded them as taller than humans and had a healthy respect for the *sidhé* and usually avoided them, hence the common habit of wearing an iron pin which was supposed to deter them. In a modern context, it may often prove difficult to contact the *sidhé* both in the otherworld and the everyday world due to the urbanisation and general detachment of modern life. It may be necessary to make several attempts, offering food and libations and spending time on the land where you wish to contact them. One thing is for sure, if the *sidhé* do not wish to be seen then they will not be. Establishing the right conditions for contact is important and it might also be necessary to sing or chant to them in the manner of the ancient Druids who use this method to receive otherworldly knowledge.

In the same way that the popular view of fairies is distorted, so too is the common view of angels. One must not forget that it was an angel that was sent by the god of the Jews to smite the firstborn sons of the people of Egypt. As any Cabalist would know, the angelic beings are not all nice and fluffy as certain New Age gurus would have us believe. From my limited experience of angels, they are striking and somewhat intimidating looking creatures. In one particular instance I was able to see a huge figure with outspread wings that radiated a bright light that made it difficult to see, although its energy was clearly benevolent it was harsh and uncompromising, there was nothing remotely 'cute' about it. As I understand it, certain apparitions may in fact be only thought-forms as opposed to a real entity. Santa or the Easter Bunny are so well known that they can conceivably exist as a thought-form. I surmise that what certain writers have described with regard to fairies and angels is in fact a thought-form constructed from the consciousness of myriad imaginations; I believe that when you experience the energy of the real thing there is no question about its validity!

One other important point to note is that just as in the every-day world our senses vary from one individual to another, so too is that the case in the astral realms. Taking myself for an example – I have excellent eyesight. I would consider that I have good powers of observation and I have also used my vision creatively as a graphic designer and artist. However, in the astral realm, my vision is one of my weaker senses, at times I am not able to see entities or spirits even if I am able to feel or hear them. In general, my intuition seems to be strongest, I receive understanding as thoughts, feelings or aurally and sometimes when I cannot see anything, I have to trust in the senses that are more receptive. I've found that working with others, for instance a fellow member of our Druid grove who has excellent psychic vision but weaker instinct and aural receptivity, we are able to build a more complete understanding of the situation. Seemingly, it is quite normal that one sense is far more sensitive than the others are and one should not be overly upset about say a lack of vision or aural ability. Of course, all the senses become more receptive with practice and familiarity, but we all have different natural skills and inclinations in each realm of existence – a fact that I personally was greatly surprised to discover but now fully accept.

The use of journeying is an essential aspect of modern Shamanic and Ovate healing skills. This can be as simple as working on the cauldrons or *chakras* or a more complex operation such as soul retrieval, (where a part of the self has been lost or shattered), or a healing ritual for the land or for ancestors affected by some traumatic event. Largely, this becomes an important part of the Druid's or Shaman's work — an area where they can be of service to others as well as themselves. From my own personal experience, I can say that it is an important aspect of self-development as a Druid and also as a tool for working collectively in a grove for ritual, healing or learning purposes.

IX

Animism & Animal Worship

Animism is the belief that all natural objects (such as plants and animals) possess a soul. It can also be defined as the belief in a non-material force (spirit, *nwyfre, prana* or *ch'i* if you will) that permeates all material existence in the universe and thereby animates it. Pythagoras and Plato espoused this hypothesis but this is also an aspect of druidic thought.

At one time, the Celts may well have directly worshipped animals and plants as deities but within historic times, plants and animals especially have become symbols of the divine or of divine attributes. The importance of animals in Celtic paganism and ancient religion in general is well documented for example the Greek Zeus appearing as a bull, Lugh transforming into an eagle or Mór-Ríoghain appearing as a crow. In the Celtic world, cow/bull and swine cults are well known as too is the divine serpent. Animals have several aspects to their sacredness — as symbols of the fertility and vitality, as representations of gods and goddesses and as totemic symbols. Particular attributes are associated with certain animals, and various animal cults existed, specific examples of which I will discuss later. Animal worship is connected with Celtic culture through sacramental eating of animals, animal taboos and also totemism — the connection of families or tribes to a particular animal. These aspects of Celtic culture are no longer with us but we can see many modern parallels, for example totemism in Native American culture, animal taboos in Hindu culture and power animals in shamanism.

In ancient Ireland and Britain, clan names were often derived from animals or trees with some claiming descent from animals such as the wolf. In Ireland this connection with the wolf may well be the source of wolf people cursed by saints and the wealth of folklore relating to werewolves (lycanthropy)[14]. Like the Roman twins Romulus and Remus, Cormac mac Art was supposedly suckled by a wolf. Similar cases exist with other mythological or historical figures such as Oisin who was son of a doe and was under *geis* not to eat venison. Cú Chulainn (formerly Sétanta), who took the name after killing Conor McNessa's hound replaced the dog in the role of guardian, hence his new name; thereafter Cú Chulainn was under *geis* to never eat dog meat.

These taboos sometimes extended to whole tribes who might abstain from pig flesh or for example, the ancient Britons who, according to Caesar, were forbidden to eat chickens, hare or goose. The sacredness of the hare is well known as linked with the goddesses of the land, its lore surviving into modern times in the distorted form of the Easter bunny. It is recorded by Dio Cassius that Icini queen Boudicca used the hare to perform divination by sacrificial ceremony. Other animals were held sacred for this purpose or hunted ceremonially at specific occasions such as the wren in Ireland.

Sacramental eating of animals was also widely practised, sometimes in divination, as was the case with dog flesh, and also by association with a particular festival such as the wren in the Isle of Man, France and Ireland, which was eaten despite its diminutive stature. A particularly interesting instance of this is the inauguration ritual of a king in Donegal, Ireland, which was graphically described by Geraldus Cambrensis, perhaps somewhat politically and negatively motivated, given his allegiance to Henry II of England. Similar ceremonies existed in Vedic, Roman and Norse tradition, indicative of the wide reaching sacredness of the horse and clear proof that this was not just some barbaric act confined to 'uncivilised' Ireland. In the ritual (*Banis Rí*) it is said that the king made a sexual union with the mare and thereafter it was slaughtered and the king ate its flesh and also bathed in its broth whilst sat inside a large cauldron. Personally, I believe the sexual union to be symbolic rather than actual, apart from the distastefulness of the act, the Irish most likely saw the mare as a symbol of the goddess of sovereignty and not as an actual avatar (physical embodiment).

The Celts believed it possible for the soul to manifest as small or infant animals, Lleu Llaw Gyffes being a prime example. Magical births occurred where a woman ate a magical animal or being such as the grain of wheat that Cerridwen (in hen form) ate and which grew inside her to become the child Taliesin. Other similar examples of rebirth via eating are Finnebach Ali, Sétanta and Donn Cuailnge. The swineherds from *Táin Bo Cuailgne,* Fruich and Rucht who whilst fighting are transformed into maggots become reborn as bulls after they are consumed by cows, and continue to fight as the bulls Donn Cuailnge and Finnebach Ai until Donn Cuailnge (Fruich) finally kills the other.

Clearly, animals were of great material and religious value to the ancient Celts and it is apparent that the great significance of the animal kingdom survived well into the Christian period, with Christianisation being a gradual process, many of the earlier attitudes and beliefs were retained. In view of the fact that early British Christianity was Arian in nature (supporting the more tolerant views of Arius) and gave rise to the now heretical Pelagian beliefs, the Celtic Church would most probably have accommodated an animistic view of creation that recognised the sacredness in all living things. By the time of the Synod of Whitby in Northumbria (664 AD), the Roman church had gained significant ground in Ireland and most of Britain and was in the process of eradicating the 'heresy' of the Celtic church, which had been predominantly spread by Irish clergy from Iona. Although the illuminated gospels such as those from Iona and Lindisfarne are works dedicated to Jesus, the Celtic influence is obvious – they are filled with illustrations of the natural world and animals in particular, highlighting their continued symbolic importance. I feel that their artistic representation is not merely a matter of style or ornamentation, more likely it is indicative of a holistic view of the natural world, although these depictions were no longer representative of deity as would have been the case in earlier pagan times.

In modern terms, animals are symbols of deity, of certain qualities and also they perform a function in a shamanic sense as allies in other realms. The witch's familiar, often in the form of a cat, is the equivalent of the shamanic power animal, which acts as a guide and helper in the astral realm. The animal transformations of Cerridwen and Gwion in the story of Taliesin can be interpreted in shamanic terms and the Pythagorean/Druidic doctrine of metempsychosis, also espoused in *Barddas* gives rise to the possibility of reincarnation or rebirth in animal states. The relevance of the animal in mythological terms and as a metaphor for the characteristics or power of the gods cannot be underestimated; an understanding of animals and plants and their Celtic context is central to understanding Celtic culture and Celtic religion as a whole.

The Boar

Generally regarded as symbolising courage, strength, fertility and wealth, boars are also associated with warriors and conflict. The swine god, representative of the corn-spirit or vegetation deity was widespread across Europe, the Celtic swine god Moccus in particular also being identified with the Roman god Mercury. The use of the boar/swine imagery was common on coinage, altars and in bronze or stone figurines. Often the swine was linked with fertility as a symbol of the goddess, sometimes with the goddess depicted riding on its back. Many examples of the boar/swine exist in Celtic myth and legend clearly demonstrating its importance. For example, the magical swine of the Tuatha Dé Danann that spring to life again after being eaten; Twrch Trwyth the magical boar hunted by Arthur (from the story

Culhwch and Owen); the death of Fionn after stepping on a boar's bristle; Diarmaid and the great boar Beann Ghulban who kill each other, as prophesised; and the magic swine of the cave of Cruachan that destroy the young crops. Numerous finds of swine bones in Celtic burials and cremations exist and in later times, stories describe how swine led saints to the sites of their churches, thus transferring some of their magical or spiritual significance into the Christian era. And later still, a boar's death appears in a dream to foretell the death of Tristan in the story Tristan and Iseult.

The Bull/Cow

Perhaps the most valued of animals in Celtic culture for its meat, hides and milk, the bull/cow became a symbol of the wealth of a leader or tribe; one of the most famous Irish sagas, *Táin Bo Cuailgne* (Cattle raid of Cooley), is a perfect demonstration of this. In general, cattle represent the fertility and wealth of both the tribe and the land. The goddess of the Boyne valley Bóinn was originally in bovine form, her name thought to have meant 'illuminated cow'. In ancient Ireland, a *tabhfheis,* or a highly ritualized 'feast of the bull', preceded the crowning of a new High King.

The Horse

Similar in many regards to cattle, the horse is highly valued and representative of fertility. Nightmares, were thought by the Celts to be brought by a visiting horse Goddess such as Epona, hence the name. The cult of Epona seems to be pan-Celtic and in Ireland linked with Macha. The horse cut into the chalk ground at Uffington, England illustrates a horse goddess cult reaching far back, perhaps into Neolithic times. Horses were important for transportation and warfare and feature heavily in mythology, particularly in journeys to or from the otherworld for instance Oisin's return from *Tir na nOg.*

The Bear

Evidence of bear cults is distributed across Europe with various names and place names associated with the bear goddess. Into the 19th century Berne, which takes its name from the bear, was still associated with bears. Names such as Artos, Arta, Andarta and Artaois are associated with the bear deities and it is also possible that Arthur of Welsh tradition and various 'Arts' of Irish texts are derived from a link to a bear god or goddess.

The Serpent

In the ancient world, the snake was generally a symbol of wisdom, not evil as has become common in the Christian era. The Gallo-Romans revered the horned snake, which is also associated with the god Cernunnos in his otherworldly aspect. In Greece, the god Dionysus sometimes took the form of a horned serpent. The druids' egg or *balain/ballaun* is described by classical authors as a magical item made from entangled serpents. The world tree is also depicted with a huge snake wrapped around its trunk as guardian, offering a very different view to that depicted in the story of Genesis. Snakes are common in much of Celtic jewellery and are thought to be symbolic of the cycle of death and birth because they shed their skin and are seemingly reborn. In the Christian era it was said that St. Patrick drove the snakes from Ireland. However the adder, although rare, is still to be found in Ireland and Britain; the story is obviously a metaphor for Patrick driving paganism out of Ireland even though the conversion of the whole country took over two hundred years.

The Deer

The cult of the stag was later replaced with that of a god bearing stag's horns, generally regarded as Cernunnos. The stag is associated with the otherworld and was often seen as the manifestation of woodland gods, such as Cernunnos. The giant

Elk, which still lived in Ireland into early Celtic times, was most probably worshipped in Ireland perhaps giving rise to the stag cult. The deer may also have been associated with the corn-spirit, particularly with its emergence from under the ground. The doe was also associated with goddesses such as Saba and Flidais. The theme of the hunt, which usually involves either boars or deer, is often used in Celtic mythology to symbolise a transition into the otherworld or into contact with magical/divine beings. In these cases, the animal often has supernatural qualities such as larger size, fleetness of foot, or unusual colour. White stags were believed to be from the Otherworld and their appearance in myths and sagas was generally considered portentous, a three antlered stag features in a story of the Fianna, the third antler signifying its divinity.

The Salmon

This fish is particularly associated with knowledge. The story of Fionn eating the Salmon of Knowledge that fed from the hazels surrounding the well of Segais at the source of the Boyne River is perhaps the most famous example. Taliesin, the archetypal Welsh seer, was found as a baby in a leather bag caught on a Salmon weir. The Salmon of Llyn Llyw was questioned by Gwyrhr as the last of a succession of beasts, being older and wiser than all of them. The salmon is rather unique in its qualities in that it is born in fresh water and makes its way to the sea, returning to its spawning grounds to breed and most often also to die. In modern day Ireland and Scotland this fish is still a highly valued food.

Birds

Birds are mostly associated with prophecy and otherworldly knowledge. The crow is linked to goddesses of death or war such as Badb or Mór-Ríoghain. The Irish war goddesses called ravens down to the battlefield to feed upon the corpses of the dead. Crows and ravens feeding is something that is still seen today but most usually on the remains of roadkill. Mór-Ríoghain appears as a raven on the shoulder of Cú Chulainn at the moment of his death. The raven has been the otherworldly body for both gods and goddesses and is also associated with the Teutonic god Odin and the Irish/Welsh god Bran. In the Sons of Usna Deidre dreams of three black birds drawing blood, a prophetic vision of the death of her three protectors.

In a less sinister aspect, birds can often be otherworldy messengers, Rhiannon's birds possessed magical qualities such as being able to charm a person or send them into a deep sleep. Birds are often associated with magical speech, Branwen sent a starling to find her brother after having taught it speech and Gwyrhyr (who talks to the ancient salmon) converses with a blackbird, an owl and an eagle along the way. A form of divination was performed using birds sacrificially as well as by observing their flight. The eagle is possibly linked to gods such as Bel and in Greek myth was sometimes linked with Apollo. In Welsh myth, Llew transforms into an eagle in order to escape his murder but shed maggots and rotten flesh from this eagle's body. In a charming story, the eagle (in a contest to find the king of birds) flies the highest of all, only for a tiny wren to pop out from under his plumage to fly just above his head. The wren as detailed earlier, was sacred to the Druids and ceremonially eaten, the custom surviving in a different form into modern times. The heron is referenced in the Druidic stance of standing on one leg, with one arm and one eye used; perhaps this is related to the prohibition of eating heron in Ireland. The crane, often referred to as a heron in the literature, is the source of the Druidic Crane Bag, however the crane has been extinct in Ireland for several centuries[15]. In Scotland especially, the swan was revered and its appearing was regarded as a good omen. To see seven swans was regarded as a sign of peace and prosperity for seven years to come.

The Dragon

This is one of the few animals associated with infertility. Two dragons were heard screaming on each May day and thus causing a blight on both land and water. In the Arthurian legends, the white and red dragons asleep underneath Vortigern's tower cause it to continually collapse each time it was rebuilt. Merlin's prophetic vision of the red dragon fighting and slaying the white is indicative of Vortigern's defeat at the hands of Uther Pendragon (Arthur's father). In Ireland, a dragon laid waste to the land preventing farming; in general, mythological dragons had to be destroyed in order to restore the land to fertility. Generally depicted as fire-breathing and often as evil creatures, dragons are associated with the power within the earth. In shamanic terms, the white and red dragons are associated with the energy of the earth and cosmos respectively, which is more akin to the Chinese view of dragons as auspicious and energetically powerful creatures, as opposed to the generally negative modern European view.

In practical terms, these animals can be experienced in a physical sense by spending time in wild places or in some cases by visiting a zoo, as many animals such as bears are rarely found in the wild and besides are best avoided if possible. This might seem a puerile suggestion, however I believe there is value in experiencing them first hand if at all possible. A person who is interested in dogs would hardly confine themselves to reading about them but never actually see one in the flesh.

As far as their use as power animals is concerned, they can be experienced in your own inner realms or in *Immrama* in the upper or underworlds. Some people experience this contact as verbal communication, others as thoughts, emotions or physical interactions. Whether the power animal is a 'real' entity or a manifested expression of some hidden part of the self is hard to say. Perhaps both are possible. Whatever the case may be, animals can provide assistance and guidance on the inner planes of existence and often prove to be of great value in spiritual and magical development.

X

Cycles of the Sun, Moon and Earth

As was discussed earlier in chapter VI, we know that the Celtic year was divided into the dark and light half, that the month was based on the twelve/thirteen annual lunar cycles of 28 days. The fortnight was the period of fourteen days between new and full moon and vice versa, the week being half that period – seven days. As is well recorded, the Coligny calendar was a way of reconciling the cycles of the moon and the sun into one system. In keeping with the Celtic importance of the sun and the moon, the modern Druidic annual cycle of the year reflects the passage of the seasons and the journey from dark into light and eventual return to darkness again.

There have been various arguments about the 'invention' of the wheel of the year, which can also be found in a slightly different form in Wicca. Some say it is an invention of Gerald Gardner or Ross Nichols or others again. Many argue that instead of eight festivals the ancient Celts only celebrated the four 'Fire Festivals'. What is fairly certain is that whatever system of observances existed was not codified. What we know of the rituals of the ancients is through survivals of folk custom that were recorded by observers in previous centuries, folk customs that are still extant and from archaeological evidence found at sacred sites.

The Lunar Cycle

To begin with, we shall consider the twelve or thirteen lunar cycles and their observances. In Celtic culture, both the new moon and the full moon are of importance. The new moon can be viewed as the beginning and end of the cycle, its relevance for instance, is recorded in folk custom in the *Carmina Gadelica*[16].

A' ghealach úr	The New Moon (extract)
Fáilte dhut a ghealach úr,	Hail to thee, thou new moon,
Ailleagab iúil na báidh!	Guiding jewel of gentleness!
Ta mi lúbadh dhut mo ghlún,	I am bending to thee my knee,
Ta mi curnadh dhut mo ghráidh	I am offering thee my love.

And again...

A' ghealach úr	The New Moon (extract)
Bitheadh gach ní naomh	Holy be each thing
Air an soillsich i;	Which she illumines;
Bitheaddh gach ní caomh	Kindly be each deed
Ta i foillseachadh	Which she reveals

For those unfamiliar with the passage of the moon, it follows clockwise in the path of the sun. After the new moon it begin to wax (grow) from the right hand side across to the left until it appears complete for a period of three days, although the middle day only is truly full. After the full moon it begins to wane (diminish) shrinking from right to left again so that the phases either side of the full moon form a mirror image. The moon's rise and set is not static and changes throughout the year, in fact it often is within view during the daytime but is often very difficult to see except on clear and bright days. In addition, the moon does not set or rise in the same place as the sun, although it's rising and setting is relative to the sun's position and hence can be calculated from the sun's position at rise/set. It is commonly understood in esoteric circles (including Celtic culture) that the properties of the waxing moon are associated with increase and growth and the opposite is true of the waning moon, hence working with lunar energy is largely dictated by the progression through its phases.

Robert Graves, in his book *The White Goddess*, links the cycles of the moon to the Ogham alphabet, trees and the Song of Amergin. Unfortunately, Graves' model was based on the false assumption that there are thirteen consonants to correspond with the thirteen moons. However, it appears that he was not wrong to link the cycle of the moon with the first thirteen lines of Amergin's poem, which has led on to a model for ritual use given in *Celtic Rituals* by Alexei Kondratiev. Interestingly he gives the lines associated with the series of moons in a jumbled order (without explanation) rather than that of the original poem.

Kondratiev's model (which I have summarised) assumes the following interpretation of the Coligny calendar:

Dark half (*giamos/geimhreadh/gaeaf*)	
Samonios (30 days)	October – November
Dvmannios (29 days)	November – December
Rivros (30 days)	December – January
Anagantios (29 days)	January – February
Ogronios (30 days)	February – March
Cvtios (30 days)	March – April
Light half (*samos/samhradh/haf*)	
Giamonios (29 days)	April – May
Simivisonnos (30 days)	May – June
Eqvos (29 days)	June – July
Elembivios (29 days)	July – August
AEdrinios (30 days)	August – September
Cantlos (29 days)	September – October
Antaranos (30 days)	Intercalary month (two per five year cycle)

Note: For the lines from the poem 'Song of Amergin', translation in brackets is that of R.A. Macalister from *Lebor Gabála Érenn* as also given in Robert Graves' *The White Goddess*.

1. The Cliff (full moon 30 Oct – 25 Nov)

Am fuaim mara I am the noise of the sea (I am a sound of the sea) Here relating the edge of the sea as boundary between the otherworld and our world and also connecting with Donn (Irish god of the dead) he relates this moon to the death of the light half of the year and a dark otherworldly journey.

Waxing: approaching boundary of life/death. Full: crossing boundary. Waning: let go and allow otherworld to restore and replenish.

2. The Tide (full moon 26 Nov – 23 Dec)

Am tond trethan I am an ocean wave (I am a wave of the sea) Here relating the wave carrying us beyond the 'ninth wave' into the depths of the otherworld, to the House of Tethra — dismissing/processing the old in preparation for new beginnings.

Waxing: attune to strength of dark tide. Full: enter the house of Tethra. Waning: pulling away of the past to facilitate healing and growth.

3. The Stag (full moon 23 Dec – 20 Jan)

An dam secht ndírend I am a stag of seven tines (I am a bull of seven fights)

Here relating the sacred otherworldy messenger as a herald of the emergent new life that has yet to surface.

Waxing: contemplate the light. Full: focus on the stag as luminous messenger. Waning: see the path of the light, giving hope for the future.

4. The Flood (full moon 21 Jan – 17 Feb)

Am loch i m-maig I am a lake upon a plain (I am a lake on a plain)

Here relating the flood myths and the genesis of Boann to the waters of spring and the awakening of the land.

Waxing: feel the gathering pressure ready to break forth. Full: release of the waters over the land. Waning: restoration of fertility/creativity.

5. The Wind (full moon 18 Feb – 17 Mar)

Am gaeth i m-muir I am a wind over the sea (I am a wind of the sea)
Here relating wind to the breath and the spirit and the Tuatha Dé Danann carried to Ireland on a magical wind.

Waxing: awareness of gathering wind from the otherworld. Full: power and spirit of life given by the fullness of the wind. Waning: gathering strength for cycle of work ahead.

6. The Sun-Tear (full moon 18 Mar – 14 Apr)

Am dér gréne I am a drop of the sun (I am a tear of the sun)
Here relating the growing power of the post-equinox sun to the goddess Brighid and the returning fertility of the land.

Waxing: sensitivity to growing light. Full: illumination of the fire/light and protection of Brighid. Waning: sense emerging thoughts/feeling/ideas that we can choose to manifest.

7. The Hawk (full moon 15 Apr – 12 May)

Am séig i n-aill I am a hawk upon a cliff (I am a hawk/griffon on a cliff)
Here relating the hawk as a catalyst to the fulfilment of growth and its manifestation in the land and ourselves.

Waxing: approaching the cliff upon which lies the fertile land. Full: identifying with the energy of the hawk. Waning: Follow his path into the land as champions of the light.

8. The Flowers (full moon 13 May – 9 Jun)

Am cain lubai I am a beautiful flower (I am fair among flowers)

Here representing the arrival of the summer in the form of the land goddess.

Waxing: awareness of the greening land in growth and increasing abundance. Full: relate to the goddess/flower maiden as source of the beauty and fecundity of nature. Waning: Allow yourself to be carried by and absorb the energy of growth.

9. The Fiery God (full moon 10 Jun – 7 Jul)

Am dé delbas do chind codnu I am a God who sets the head on fire (I am a God who forms fire for a head)
Here relating to the summer solstice and the triumph of samos, also the individual fire of illumination as symbolised by Cernunnos's relationship with the land.

Waxing: focus on the sun's heat and absorbing its energy. Full: attune to Cernunnos at the peak of his achievement yet defeat by the Maponos. Waning: Internalise the fire of illumination.

10. The Spear (full moon 8 Jul – 4 Aug)

Am gaí i fodb feras feochtu I am a keen spear that pours forth battle (I am a battle-waging spear)
Here relating to the opposing needs of the tribe with the continued solar energy threatening the harvest. The spear of Lugh is used here to symbolise focus of energy and creativity.

Waxing: preparation for a change in energy and balance brought about by the spear. Full: perceive Lúgh's wielding of the spear and its use ushering in the *giamos* energy. Waning: focus on the energy stored as we prepare for harvest.

11. The Salmon (full moon 5 Aug – 1 Sep)

Am he i l-lind I am a salmon in a pool (I am a salmon in a pool)
We reap the reward of our work and experiences, here symbolised by the wisdom of the salmon.

Waxing: attune to the gentle otherworld energy that is cooling and contemplative. Full: Enjoy the fruits of labour and experience the benefits of the journey. Waning: treasure and analyse our fruit as we gather in the harvest.

12. The Hill of the Bards (full moon 2 Sep – 30 Sep)

Am brí dánae I am a hill of skilled ones (I am a hill of poetry)
A sharing of creative energy among the tribe as the preparation for winter begins.

Waning: articulate and share the fruits of our creativity. Full: sharing with others of experience and learning. Waning: appreciation of the richness gained by this sharing.

13. The Boar (full moon 1 Oct - 29 Oct)

Am torc ae gail I am a boar in battle-frenzy (I am a boar)
Here the boar becomes the harbinger of death, the decline of the year as the *giamos* energy grows.

Waxing: the hunt of death progresses with the change in the landscape. Full: we face the boar and offer it a prepared gift symbolic of the fertility of the land. Waning: looking inwards to the close of the cycle and new beginnings.

If this model is appealing I would suggest investigating Kondratiev's book which details the meaning and ritual elements in far greater detail. I have presented the above merely to give the bare bones of his ideas. Personally, I feel that like Graves's work, it relies on a number of assumptions and although it is highly creative and poetic I find this section of his work is not strongly rooted; however I leave it to you to make your own assessment.

Niall MacCoitir, author of *Irish Trees — Myths, legends & Folklore* also references Graves but presents a somewhat different model based not on the 'Song of Amergin' but on his own interpretation of Ogham and the Coligny calendar. Like Graves he uses a calendar of thirteen equal months (28 days) with an extra day to mark the year end. He also relates it to the months of the Coligny calendar but in contrast to Kondratiev, the summer and winter half is reversed, based on the belief that *Samonios* means simply 'summer' rather than 'summer's end'. This is backed up by the fact that the Welsh word *Gorffennaf* meaning 'summer's end' refers to July (and not November, which might imply a link between *Samonios* and *Samhain*). MacCoitir's calendar begins after *Samhain* (Halloween), with the trees given according to seasonal attributes:

Month	**Tree**	**Date**	**Gaulish Month**
Idad	Yew	1 Nov – 28 Nov	Antaranos
Ailm	Pine	29 Nov – 26 Dec	Giamonios
Beth	Birch	27 Dec – 23 Jan	Simivisonnos
Luis	Rowan	24 Jan – 20 Feb	Equos
Fern	Alder	21 Feb – 20 Mar	Elembivios
Sail	Willow	21 Mar – 17 Apr	Edrinios
Huath	Hawthorn	18 Apr – 15 May	Cantlos
Onn	Ash	16 May –12 Jun	Samonios
Dair	Oak	13 Jun – 10 Jul	Dumannios
Tinne	Holly	11 Jul – 7 Aug	Rivros
Coll	Hazel	8 Aug – 4 Sep	Anagantios
Cert	Apple	5 Sep – 2 Oct	Ogronios
Ruis	Elder	3 Oct – 30 Oct	Cutios
Bile Buadha	Tree of power	31 Oct	

MacCoitir relates the properties and folklore of the trees to the season and folk tradition, but does not relate it specifically to lunar activity or performance of ritual. Like the models of Graves and Kondratiev it has its appeal but is also subject to criticism.

I've presented these two models by means of illustration of possible guidelines for lunar observances, there is no recorded information I know of as regards Druidic practice, although it is recorded that the lunar cycle was observed and various activities (such as collecting mistletoe) carried out on this basis. Therefore I leave it to you to consider how best to mark the transition of the moon within your own practices. However it is clear that as a Druid one should at least be aware of the moon's cycle and the effects of its waxing and waning on the human psyche, the greater world of nature and upon the practice of magic.

Traces of much older lore exist in Scotland and Ireland and as late as 1900, the elderly still paid their respects to the sun and moon and their actions were often dictated by the phases of the moon as shown by the words of a very old man recorded by Alexander Carmichael in the late 1800s:

> The men of old would not kill a pig nor sheep nor goat nor axe-cow at the wane of the moon. The flesh of an animal is then without taste, without sap, without plumpness, without fat. Neither would they cut withes of hazel or willow for creels or baskets, nor would they cut tree of pine to make a boat, in the black wane of the moon. The sap of the wood goes down into the root, and the wood becomes brittle and crumbly, without pith, without good. The old people did all these things at the waxing or at the full of the moon. The men of old were observant of the facts of nature, as the young folk of today are not. The new moon was propitious [favourable] for clipping hair, for cutting peats, for reaping corn, for shearing sheep, and for many things of that nature.

The Solar Cycle

So now we move to the cycle of the sun, or rather the cycle of the earth's passage around the sun. This cycle is the basis of all life on this planet and its importance is reflected in all ancient religions around the world, not least of all in Celtic culture. The Celtic celebrations mark the transition of the year from the light to the dark half of the year and back again, highlighting the tension in this duality that represents male and female, night and day, permanence and the ephemeral amongst many other things. This division into *giamos/geimhreadh/gaeaf* and *samos/samhradh/haf* can also be seen as the embodying of the divine god/goddess principle, with the shift in dominance between the two played out over the course of the year. There are eight festivals in all. Perhaps the 'fire festivals' were of greater importance as suggested by many writers, however we cannot be sure either way. What is certain though, is that all eight, both fire and solar festivals have been celebrated as part of Celtic tradition for a considerable time. Below is a diagram showing the structure of the wheel and some of the correspondences associated with each festival.

This 'wheel' represents an annual cycle of the seasons of our planet, the cycle of the tribe or human world, the cycle of life and the four elements of western magical tradition. In terms of modern Druidry this is, in my opinion, a core part of the life and activities of a Druid.

The process of celebrating the rituals, preferably outside, over the course of the year and hopefully every year, is a vibrant and powerful way of connecting with the land, making contact with the upper and lower realms and tuning oneself to the rhythms of nature.

In previous centuries, humankind's lifestyle was agrarian and necessarily linked to the land and the cycles of the seasons and the pace of change was very slow, at least until the industrial revolution. People lived their lives rising with the sun and going to bed not long after it got dark unless they were wealthy enough to burn oil lamps and candles for long periods of time. Most people spent the majority of their days outside, usually working on the land or some auxiliary form of work, the working day was much slower, restricted in part by the weather and the limited power available (largely men and horses). Most people did not own watches and concern regarding time was confined usually to townspeople and business people, although even they were not half so obsessed or dominated by the hands of the clock as later and current generations.

The life of previous societies was not dead, stagnant or unchanging though, it was a way of life that ebbed and flowed, that was by necessity in harmony with and dictated by the natural cycles. Technology has enabled us to quicken the pace of everything we do, in our working lives especially, but its effects are so widespread and far-reaching that many of us find ourselves living at a frantic pace, unable to relax or slow down even when we have the opportunity and desire to do so. The increasing detachment from the realities of the natural, physical world seems to be the root of much discontent, spiritual unrest and unhappiness in modern society. One can also mention increasingly poor physical and mental health amongst those who live modern western lifestyles and an ever widening social and financial gap between those who fully embrace consumer capitalism and those who chose not to be, or are not able to be, predatorial in their lifestyle.

Although there appears to be a growing awareness of a more holistic approach to life among modern communities, this is not translating into action quickly enough. In fact, the pace of technological change and its spread throughout the world in both work and domestic living is still outstripping the growing awareness. While most of these laudable ideas about holism remain in the ether and are not manifesting as actions, things will continue to deteriorate due to the increasing proliferation of television, computers, printed media and other impersonal forms of stimulation that increasingly detach us from interpersonal interaction and interaction with the real physical world.

I believe that using a system of spiritual/religious celebration in the real physical world in a way that connects directly with the wider realms of existence, beyond the inner world of the ego and our tendency to anthropomorphise everything, is an effective and necessary antidote to our increasingly unhealthy perspectives. It does not necessarily need to be Druidry — any path that works along these lines will be of great benefit in attempting to regain some sense of balance. However, for those looking for such a system that is based on or linked to the indigenous practices of Europe, Druidry is perhaps the most obvious choice.

The main concepts embodied in the cycle of the year are represented through the god and goddess and the transition of their states through the year is indicative of the transition of the earth and life upon it as it travels around the sun. The god represents the active (solar) principle that grows and diminishes until death and rebirth. The goddess represents the passive (lunar) principle, although seemingly weaker, in fact is the constant and irrepressible wellspring that endures so that life may continue. The two forces or principles are intertwined, interdependent and fail to function successfully if divided from one another, unlike some other religious/spiritual models. The seemingly dominant transition of the god is only possible within the framework created by the goddess that underpins and maintains existence.

Likewise, the year is divided into the light and dark half, symbolising these principles in the same way as the Chinese *yin* and *yang* — it is through the interchange and union of these divine opposites that *Tao* exists and that *Ch'i* is able to flow. Although expressed in a different way, the core concept of two forces interacting to create a third is central to Druidry, Alchemy and Taoism.

In the Celtic model, the god and goddess symbolise the power of the sun and the moon but also the tribe and the land. As is often the case in many religious/spiritual systems the divine is represented as celestial objects, as animals and also in human form, which has been discussed earlier in the chapter on Gods and Goddesses. In general, the goddess in animal or human form represents the land, the external celestial powers are often either gender (e.g. the sun — Belenus, Gráinne) and the tribe is usually represented through the male.

In the Celtic year the male representation is transient, travelling from birth to death and rebirth in synchronisation with the state of the changing land, brought about by the eternal and nurturing presence of the goddess. The primary images of the god in this transition in the modern Druid tradition are that of Maccan/Mabon/Maponos — the 'child of light' and the antlered god Cernunnos. Distinct from a horned god, Cernunnos may grow or lose his antlers depending upon whereabouts in the cycle between the dark and light halves of the year he is (*giamos/geimhreadh/Gaeaf* and *samo/samhradh/Haf*). The Irish story 'Tochmarc Emire' records the division of the year into these two halves — summer from *Bealtaine* to *Samhain* and winter from *Samhain* to *Bealtaine*.

The motif of conflict between the old and young male for the favour of the female is carried throughout Celtic lore and ritual as is evident in the stories of Oengus Mac Og, Myrddin Wyllt, Dairmuid and Gráinne, Rhiannon and so forth and even into the modern Mummers Plays. Ultimately this is a sexual drama, which anthropomorphises the transition from *Giamos* to *Samos* and back again — a simple enough concept that has been discussed and analysed to such a great extent that it might appear to be a complex and intellectually challenging philosophy. However, I believe that if children are able to comprehend and emotionally absorb the core of this belief (which they are), then there is no real need to complicate matters. Unnecessary complexity usually over-intellectualises what in essence is a simple emotional experience and thereby creates emotional distance and lack of empathy or understanding. Therefore, for that reason I have chosen not to explore the esoteric meaning of this concept in greater depth. For spiritual experience to be 'real' it needs to be felt more than understood, therefore I believe anything that goes beyond the necessary level of understanding is often best omitted, at least until a strong spiritual/emotional connection has been established.

In terms of ritual, I shall now give brief outlines of possible themes for inclusion in a rite, specific to each of the eight parts of the cycle. This is preceded by an explanation of the significance of each festival and the customs that are connected with Druidic practice.

Before performing the appropriate rite, you may wish to verbally or mentally create a sacred space, cast a circle, acknowledge the three realms, call upon the elements and invoke deity or spirits and such as required. Once the preliminaries are complete you may wish to incorporate the themes/ideas discussed — although specific wording or structures are not discussed here I hope that this will be sufficient for you to create your own rite to suit your own preferences. One should remember that the energy, focus and intention put into the rite is of more importance than slavishly following some particular form of words; also it is better to use a rite that has meaning for you/your group than one from a third party that you do not easily relate to. On completion of the rite, it is wise to give thanks to deity/spirits, the elements and realms and close the circle/sacred space before ending the ceremony.

On a practical note, one should remember that the solar year applies to the northern hemisphere; the cycle is a mirror image in the southern hemisphere. For those who live between the tropics of Cancer and Capricorn the changes in the sun's path are less pronounced, and at the equator there is virtually no change in the length of the days and nights and it is effectively summer all year, with a short rainy season.

For those unfamiliar with the sun's journey (northern hemisphere) – the sun rises in the southeast and sets in the south west at the winter solstice (i.e. a short day) with the sun passing low in the sky. At the equinoxes the day and night are of equal length with sun rise and set from east to west and the sun is midway in height between where it passes at either solstice. At the summer solstice the sun rises in the northeast and sets in the northwest (i.e. a long day) and passes across the sky at its highest, almost directly overhead at midday. Given time, this cycle becomes familiar and one can roughly tell the time of day and find one's direction by looking at the position of the sun.

Samhain — Samhuinn, Calan Gaeaf, 31st October

This time is traditionally given as the Celtic New Year. *Samhain* is thought to be derived from *sam-fuin*, meaning end of summer. The month of November in *Gaeilge* is *Samhain* and is mentioned in 9th century ecclesiastical *Gaeilge* texts referring to All Souls Day – 'the saints of the teeming world ennoble stormy Samhain'.

It might seem sensible to start the year at the winter solstice, the modern calendar starts approx ten days displaced from this time, although the date has been moved around several times in the last millennium. In the old Gaelic calendar the year, like the day was divided into dark and light halves, with the dark half preceding the light. The pivotal points of *Samhain* and *Bealtaine* are the threshold between the two or *Tráth na Táirsí*, although in astronomical terms this transition point is actually the two equinoxes. In practice though, the end of October (in the northern hemisphere) is generally when a noticeable change in light levels and coldness occurs. Most modern pagans celebrate Samhain on 31st October, although some celebrate it at the new moon or when the first signs of winter approach.

With the return of the darkness, growth ceases and the natural world largely appears to die or go into hibernation. In light of this the Celts believed that the forces of life retired into the underworld, into the womb if you will, symbolised by the image of the cauldron. It is within the darkness, the womb of the goddess that the New Year gestates, in preparation to re-emerge in the spring at *Imbolc*.

It was also widely held that the boundary between the other-world and everyday reality became thinner and that super-natural powers and the dead had the ability to break through or return to this world. The *sidhé* or Tuatha Dé Danann were able to run amok if they were not placated. It was believed that they had power over the fertility of the land and could cause harvests to fail or succeed, kill livestock, cause disease or increase prosperity if they wished. For this reason, it was common to offer libations of milk and oaten cakes on the ground to please the *sidhé*, also people commonly wore iron pins, or carried a black handled knife and used various blessings or protective plants to ward off malign intentions or the possibility of being taken by the fairies.

Sacrificial offerings were made to ensure the return of the vital forces after winter. Animals were slaughtered at this time, especially those that might not survive the winter, some of which would be offered as payment to the spirits of the land to ward off blight and famine. Sacrifice of a pig was common in ancient times and in still earlier times, human sacrifice was probably practised as evidenced by the remains of ritually slain people found preserved in peat bogs. This custom of sacrifice has survived in Ireland into the modern era in the form of 'bleeding for St Martin', although this takes place on St. Martin's Day (11th November). A chicken would be killed in honour of St. Martin and its blood sprayed on the wall (or walls) of the house, this practice still exists today in some rural parts of western Ireland. This practice was recorded in the 1830s — but in this case inside the house, the four corners were sprayed with the blood of a cockerel.

Being also a time of the dead, families would set a place at the table (with food also) for returning ancestors and also light candles in the window, sometimes inside a hollowed out turnip. Doors and windows might be left open or unfastened to allow the spirits of ancestors to enter the home. It was generally held that the spirits of the dead inhabited megalithic tombs and ancient burial sites at this time and offerings were made to these and to the ancestral dead, a belief that echoes into the current era albeit in a somewhat distorted form.

Respecting the dead was so much a part of the culture that failure to observe the expected honouring could end in disaster — for example a person foolish enough to eat the food left for the ancestors would be said to be barred from enjoying this tradition after their own death. In addition, people who did not take precautions to throw out dirty water or damp down the fire correctly could be vulnerable to attack from unwanted spirits of the dead.

Throughout the Celtic world it was common to light great bonfires at *Samhain,* a tradition that continues to this day (displaced in UK to 5th November). In Tlachtga (Hill of Ward) in Ireland, a great fire was lit at the sacred site, visible from Tara some twelve miles away. Tlachtga, in Irish myth, was the daughter a blind Druid Mogh Ruith, who died there giving birth to triplets. Their names in English mean 'Earth Spear' and 'Devotee of the Wheel' respectively. It is possible that both were ancient gods in earlier times, who have been somewhat demonised in the legend written down in the Christian era.

At Tara, the *Ard Rí* or High King feasted together with and surrounded by the *Rí Tuaithe* (provincial kings) and *flatha* (nobility), symbolically demonstrating the unity and stability of the people at this time of growing darkness, chaos and threatening forces within nature. Interestingly the Mound of the Hostages (at Tara) is illuminated by the sunrise at *Samhain*.

After the lighting of the sacred fire at Tlachtga the fire would be lit at Tara and then all over the country, offering warmth and protection from evil influences that might be abroad and a symbolic re-kindling of the sacred heath fires for the period of renewal and rest over the winter months. All kinds of trickery might take place at the hands of the *sidhé* and also in more recent times the young. Removal of gates and door, turning signs the wrong way round etc. originates from the removal of gates and barriers to signify the suspension of ordinary boundaries that separate us from the otherworld.

An abundance of lore and myths exist throughout the British Isles in relation to the *sidhé* riding out, the Wild Hunt, The King of the Faeries and so forth gallivanting across the land at *Samhain* and sometimes leaving chaos and even death in their wake. A fine example of this is the story Eachtra Nera, wherein Nera a warrior of Connacht actually returns with the Tuatha Dé Danann into their *ráth*.

Another aspect of *Samhain* is funeral games, dancing and celebration, linked to traditions of earlier times. In Ireland the *buachaillí tuí* were a group of masked revellers with straw mask, supposedly the spirits of the lands free to run riot and cause mayhem, in some cases the festivities involved cross dressing (also in Wales and Scotland). If households gave generously to the groups calling they would be blessed with prosperity, otherwise they might be cursed with evil luck. In Munster young men led by a man dressed in a fake horse's head and billowing sheets would march through the countryside blowing horns and causing a ruckus, upon reaching a house the woman of the house would come to the door with cakes or money in exchange for a song from the group. The horse (*Láir Bhán*, or white mare) represented the land goddess abroad and the entourage represented the spirits of the dead. Again, to show them discourtesy was to invite disaster into your home.

The apple bobbing tradition which is now common, is quite old but was formerly also included in a far more dangerous addition, involving trying to grab an apple on a stick that bore a lit candle again with just the teeth. Apples are in abundance at this time either just picked or being stored from earlier in the season – apples had a particular otherworld significance which is evident in mythology for example the land of apples *Eamhain Abhlach* which evidently connects them with this otherworldly time of the year.

Divination is also an aspect of *Samhain*, the *Báirín Breac* (fruit loaf), that is still commonly eaten at this time, contains a ring – whoever finds the ring is said to become married in the near future. All manner of strange forms of predicting the future existed, particularly pertaining to marriage – for instance watching nuts jumping out of the fire, placing a charm under the pillow so that you dream of your future spouse and so on. In fact, it was generally considered that any form of divination performed at this time was more likely to meet with success.

Many divinatory customs are localised or pertain to a particular site and stories of *Samhain* divination are common in folklore. In the story Eachtra Nera, Nera is shown a vision foretelling the *sidhé* attacking the king's *dún* at the *Samhain* to come, he then uses this knowledge to avert this disaster.

Rite

In terms of ritual, themes of importance are as follows:

Death and renewal – at this point the natural world is dying the *Mabon*/Child of Light has gone beyond maturity into death, enabling the Cernunnos/Green Man archetype, who has shed his antlers, to retake his place as consort to the goddess of the land. The sacred fire is an essential symbol of the renewal of the land ahead of us – like a seed that is planted in darkness seemingly dormant until shoots appear above ground in spring. If at all possible a bonfire should be central to the celebrations, if it is not possible to do this either a skillet pot/cauldron could be used in a small outside setting or a large candle for inside.

Games, tricks, divination – for a large gathering, particularly if children are involved it is nice to include a divinatory game such as apple bobbing, create a chaotic performance that turns the usual order on its head, or act a 'trick or treat' type ritualised bit of mischief, this may involve dressing up, masks or perhaps even the *Láir Bhán*.

Welcoming of the dead – in addition to private participation in this act, it may be appropriate to include this aspect in ritual by invoking (requesting) their presence and making a suitable offering of traditional foods such as *Kornigoú* (Brittany) or *Bonnach Samhuinn* (Scotland), *Báirín Breac* (Ireland) or soul cakes of some form. This could take place prior to your/the group's feasting. If you feel the presence of the dead, you may wish to spend some time in meditating, journeying, or communing with the spirits, afterwards giving thanks for their participation. It may be appropriate to involve the dead in divination/revelation (I suggest this with caution), it was by this method that the *Táin Bó Cúailnge* was recovered from Fergus Mac Roy. Even if there is no apparent involvement of the deceased, it is still important to remember and honour them at this time.

Sacrifice – in modern terms it is not necessary to make a sacrificial killing, however that does not mean that it might not be appropriate to slaughter a chicken (humanely I might add) as a blood sacrifice if this is in keeping with your moral values and social circle. For most people it is sufficient to make a symbolic sacrifice, perhaps by casting objects or foodstuffs into the fire – the most important thing is the making of an offering that is meaningful, sincere and encapsulates our intentions.

With this rite and any others that involve fire and use of implements, it is essential that safety and responsible behaviour is paramount, especially if other people are involved in your ceremony.

Winter Solstice — Alban Arthan, Grianstad an Gheimhridh Deuoriuos(?), 21st/22nd December

The celebration of the winter solstice is perhaps one of the oldest known human spiritual celebrations – it marks the shortest day of the year, the sun rises in the south east, passes at its lowest in the sky across to the south west where it sets. The sun also appears to remain in the same lateral position (sun standing) for three days, moving one degree northwards after the third day (on 24/25th December). At this time, the three stars of the belt of Orion and the Dog Star (star in the east) point in a straight line directly to the point of the sunrise on the solstice. It is no coincidence that Christmas was chosen to fall at this time, like many other gods, such as Horus, Mithra or Krisha, born on the same day, of a virgin, with twelve disciples (the Zodiac), foretold by a star in the east and resurrected – Jesus can be interpreted as representative of the reborn sun or Child of Light. The Roman Saturnalia was also celebrated at this time, as was the Norse Yule, along with the aforementioned and other solar deities. The existence of a multitude of stone circles and tumuli throughout Europe (such as Newgrange or Stonehenge) which are unquestionably aligned to the winter solstice demonstrates the significance of the winter solstice as far back as the Neolithic period. The significance of this festival continued into the Bronze Age, very clearly in Celtic culture, which is often recorded in the allegorical myths that survive. Some of the customs associated with this pre-Christian solar/earth worship have survived, perhaps somewhat separated from their meaning, into current times.

In the case of the temple of Brugh na Bóinne (Newgrange) in Co. Meath, Ireland which is believed to be at least five thousand years old, the Celtic (Tuatha dé Danann) myth relating to its religious significance is still with us – demonstrating that the Druids, if not actually using the temple, were at least aware of its function. Daghdha, who is associated with the sun, is thought to have built it although he did not live in it. He tricked Elcmar who lived there, sending him away for one day so that he could lie with his wife Bóinn. Daghdha magically held the sun at a standstill for nine months during Elcmar's absence until Bóinn gave birth to Aonghus, the child of light, before Elcmar returned. Later Aonghus claimed the temple as his own, ejecting Elcmar (in some versions with Daghdha's assistance).

This ancient story is an allegorical version of the displacement of the old sun by a new reborn sun, born of the earth. In Brugh na Bóinne (Newgrange)[17] the light of the rising sun on the 21st, penetrates to the sepulchre at the rear of the temple through the portal above the door that once held two translucent quartz stones (now in Dublin). The story associated with Newgrange and the solstice existed in different forms throughout the ancient pagan world and indeed, it still exists in a disguised form in the story of Jesus – born in miraculous and precarious circumstances, forced to flee in infancy to escape Herod, returning in triumph. In earlier times it was necessary for the Christian church (which marked Jesus's birth from 4th Century onwards as 25th December) to remind the public that they were worshipping Jesus and not the birth of a solar god! Regardless of the image – Jesus, Lúgh, Maponos/Mabon, Mithra and so forth, the Child of Light is basically the same in relation to the solstice. In Wales the equivalent to Aonghus is Mabon ab Modron who is 'Great Son of the Great Mother', detailed in the story *Culhwch ac Olwen*, who is stolen at the age of three nights old and freed in adulthood to rescue Olwen from her father. In the story of Rhiannon (*Peder Keinc*) he appears as Pryderi, again stolen at birth, leading to Rhiannon's punishment. Lúgh also fulfils this role – born of Eithne (daughter of Balor) and Cian he is fostered by Tailltiu and Manannán Mac Lir. By his birth he unites the Tuatha Dé Danann and Fomorion blood lines and on his return from hiding goes on to slay Balor, his grandfather, so ending the war.

Non-Christian practises related to this solstice have survived in Europe into the modern day – in the Celtic countries these are most notably activities performed communally over the 'twelve days of Christmas' involving feasting as well as customs. Traditions such as the Yule log, of Norse/Germanic origin, became naturalised in the British Isles, perhaps combined with native elements such as practised in Scotland. The *Cailleach Nollag* was a log carved into the shape of a woman and burnt over a peat fire, perhaps symbolising the demise of the destructive and sterile aspects of the goddess, strongest in the depths of winter. In Wales this was known as *Y Bloccyn Gwlian*, it would be decorated with ivy. It was common to pour a libation (e.g. cider) on it prior to lighting with a piece of last year's log as kindling, symbolizing the continuity of light and life. Decoration of houses with evergreen boughs is still common as is use of candles. in Ireland the *coinneal mór na Nollaig*, was a large candle lit for the whole period.

Mistletoe (*Drualus* in Irish) is very much associated with both Druids and Christmas. It appears in treetops mysteriously (it is a parasite), producing sticky white berries in mid winter whilst in full leaf, a potent symbol of fertility it was regarded as a 'heal-all' herb. Mistletoe is in fact poisonous and extremely dangerous. However with extreme care it can be used in herbal medicine to treat various nervous disorders. The tradition was widespread in Britain but was brought to Ireland some time after the Norman conquest, it is not native to Ireland but has become naturalised, as have some of the traditions surrounding it. It is thought that it was originally used to protect the home during winter, gaining its romantic custom at a later time. Various exotic beliefs related to fertility and marriage existed perhaps leading to it being banned from churches until recent times. It is widely regarded that mistletoe was sacred to Druids, largely due to Pliny's account of Gaulish Druids ceremonially cutting it from an oak. In fact, mistletoe rarely grows on oak but seeing as mistletoe is linked to Jupiter it may well have significance appearing on oak, which is also sacred to Zeus/Jupiter and Daghdha. Ovid referred to Druids singing under the mistletoe and Bronze Age burial remains in England have revealed large quantities of mistletoe in the graves.

Interestingly a Norse myth perhaps sheds clearer light on its significance – Baldur the Norse solar deity, son of Odin and god of love, was protected from death by his mother Frigg who asked all creatures and plants in the world not to harm him. However she forgot to ask mistletoe, believing it to be too insignificant to be considered. Using this unfortunate fact Loki creates a spear from a mistletoe stem picked from an oak and then tricks Baldur's Brother Hod into killing him with it. Perhaps mistletoe was a symbol of the young solar god Baldur who is symbolically reborn at midwinter, due to its otherworldly evergreen foliage and its significance of growing on an oak – Odin's tree. Perhaps this connection with rebirth and its flowering at the time of the winter solstice gave it significance to the Druids, which has in part been retained into the modern era.

Mummers Plays, dramatisations of the invocation of the spirits/goddess of sovereignty or fertility of the land in the form of a horse or semi-equine creature, were common throughout Europe and are still to be found in parts of Ireland, Wales, Scotland and England. In Wales, the *Mari Lwyd* (Grey Mary) is still brought around towns and villages in procession and brought into homes. In earlier times, an artificial bird on a decorated pole (*Aderyn Pica Llwyd* or grey magpie) was also included in the procession. In a ritualised exchange, the leader asks for entry and the householder demands assurances of good behaviour, culminating in the group entering and the *Mari* snapping at people, women especially. The horse is placated by feeding it, and is usually fed by a small child. This can be seen as the child of light subduing the negative aspects of the land-goddess so that the land may become fruitful again in the year to come. Sometimes a communal drink 'wassail' was passed around in a circle, consisting of a spiced alcoholic beverage, in much the same way that the ancient Celts passed around a communal cup at meals (always clockwise) as recorded by the Greek writer Athenaeus. Perhaps this is the origin of the spiced mulled wine, which is popular today in the British Isles.

Another ritualised play the Hunting of the Wren, which I have mentioned earlier, is a pan-Celtic tradition still in existence, particularly in the west of Ireland. On St. Stephen's Day (26th Dec) a wren ('King of the birds' linked with the solar deity Lugh) is caught and killed and placed in a decorated cage or box (also sometimes attached to a pole) and paraded around the village/town from house to house. The wren is accompanied by *An Dreoilín* (the wren boys) consisting of musicians and dancers. The wren's retinue often wear masks and in Ireland this usually includes the *Cailleach* (a man dressed as a hag) and the *Láir Bhán* (white mare, hobby horse character). It is often conceived that the wren is a substitute for man, who has to die in order that the land will prosper and his sacrifice is the price paid for life. The retinue accept money or gifts from each house supposedly for the wren's burial but it was considered bad luck for the wren to be buried on your land. Hence the wren boys would often bury the wren on the land of the least generous household. More usually it would be left on a sea shore – at the cusp of sea and land where its negative powers would have least effect.

These traditions are an exchange or sacrifice associated with solar energy to ensure the vitality of the land at the darkest point of the year where the sun is at its weakest. The light is reborn at this point, this powerful image giving an obvious reason for the placing of the birth of Jesus to coincide with the re-emergence of the sun on the first day of its ascension upwards in the sky. Paralleling the view of Christ as the redeemer or saviour of the world, a light in the darkness, the divine child as the Maponos/Mabon/Maccan who is pure arrives to renew the land (and later become consort to the land-goddess). Likewise, the prosperity of the land, especially in Ireland and Wales, was linked to the purity and honesty of the king, with the success or failure of the king inextricably linked to the success or failure of the land, the king mirroring the role of the maponos in his connection to the land. This theme is explored in the context of advent in detail by Sean Ó Duinn in his book *Where Three Streams Meet*.

Rite

In terms of ritual, themes of importance are as follows:

The Child of Light/Maponos/Mabon/Maccan — the child born in tenuous circumstances representing the spark of light born at the time of greatest darkness. This child must survive to grow into maturity as consort to the land goddess before diminishing. At this time of the triumph of the dark, we celebrate the birth. Perhaps night-time is convenient to symbolically act this out, with the lighting of a single candle in absolute darkness. It may also be preferable to begin a ceremony before dawn so that the rising sun of the solstice performs this function. Some form of meditation or journey on the triumph of the dark and the rebirth of the light might be appropriate.

The stilted energy of the land goddess — the goddess in the form of the hag or Cailleach, represents the negative aspects of the land in the time of coldness, death and infertility. The powers of fecundity are still present but unable to manifest themselves, only the negative aspects of the land are evident. Through the

Mabon's eventual rise (as with successful sacred kingship), the negative aspects of goddess are overcome and the marriage to the goddess of sovereignty bears fruit. At this barren time, the first glimmer of hope of this return to fertility arrives. This may be acted out in the form of a play for example with the hobby horse/wren representing the power of the land and the hag attacking being representative of its negative aspect. Instead, it might be appropriate to read or tell the story of Aonghus Mac Og, Lugh, Mabon and Modron or Pryderi and Rhiannon – all versions of the birth of the child of light against a backdrop of danger and/or the suffering of his mother.

Renewal of the solar energy – the passing around of a 'wassail' bowl or cup, clockwise or sunwise to everyone in the group may also be incorporated as a symbol of the newly created solar energy that will now begin to grow. It may also be possible to incorporate mistletoe in some way – perhaps as a symbol of protection and regeneration. It is also appropriate to dance, sing and eat (as we may do at Christmas) to celebrate the beginning of the return of the light.

Imbolc — Lá Fhíle Bríde, Oímealg, Gwyl Mair Dechrau'r, Oímelc 1st February

The festival of Imbolc is the beginning of spring in Celtic tradition and it is also irrevocably linked with Brighid (Bríde, St Brigit, Brig, Brigantia, Bridie). Perhaps it is the tradition that has been changed least of all by its absorption into Christianity. It is generally celebrated on 1st February; however some may wish to mark it at the first signs of spring, such as the first snowdrop appearing or ewes producing milk for their lambs.

A celebration of this type is by no means unique to the Celtic world – the Greeks celebrated the return of Persephone (daughter of Demeter) from the underworld, Romans worshiped Februa by processing through the streets with lighted candles. At this time the Aztecs celebrated their new year, as did the

Tibetans. In Christian tradition, Candlemas is celebrated and in Ireland and Scotland in particular St. Brighid's Day. The lighting of candles or a bonfire was very much part of *Imbolc* celebration, Brighid being linked intimately with the hearth, prosperity and health of the home.

The name *Imbolc* has several interpretations, the most common being 'ewe's milk' from the older form *Oímelc* supposedly derived from *Oui-melko*. Another etymology is *imbolg* or 'in the belly' referring to pregnancy, as if the earth is about to give birth to the summer. Although spring can hardly be said to be in full swing at this usually cold and bleak time, the first signs are there and a great deal of activity is taking place just under the ground. This time was the end of *Dubhluachair* (in Ireland) or the darkest part of the year, which in actual fact ended at the winter solstice but only becomes easily noticeable now. In some parts, it was considered lucky for snow to fall at *Imbolc* as if the diminishing powers of winter would finally exhaust themselves, ushering in better weather.

Imbolc also marked the beginning of the agricultural year, at this time the ground may be soft enough to plough in some areas. Ritual cleansing in preparation for the new year of work was part of *Imbolc* with people lathing the head, hands and feet with water and perhaps also their tools, this gives rise to another etymology – *imb-fholc* meaning 'to wash oneself'.

In Scotland the Cailleach (hag) transforms into Bride by drinking of a sacred stream or in other folklore Bride is released from imprisonment within Ben Nevis at the hands of the Cailleach by the hag's own son (or Aonghus) who rescues her despite a deluge of storms sent to prevent it.

Also in Scotland, Ireland and the Isle of Man an image of Brighid in the form of a straw doll was made, often clothed, this was known as a *brídeóg*. The format varied from place to place but generally involved a procession of the doll accompanied from house to house by young people, girls especially, who sang and recited. The household would honour Bride with gifts of food or money. As late as 1942, this custom was recorded in Co, Kerry in which masked boys and girls brought the 'Biddy' to houses and money was collected after a short dance. A dance called the 'Biddy Ball' was held using the money collected at which the whole community could join in.

In some parts of Ireland, a young woman *An Bhrídeóg* was chosen as a living substitute to represent Brighid/Bride. Another form of the procession included a *crios Bríde* which was a belt or hoop containing four rush crosses, that was carried by the men whilst the women carried the *Brídeóg*. At each house, the household would pass through the *crios Bríde* in order to receive her blessings. At night, the *brídeóg* would be given a place of honour in a specially prepared bed or chair being present at the feast the next day. In some parts, families made their own *brídeóg* and put it to bed, or a bed was made up and candles lit before Brighid was invoked three times at the open door of the house.

Other forms of doorstep ritual took place to invite Brighid into the home, these threshold rites or *Gnás na Tairsí* involved the *Brídeóg, Brat Bhríde* (Brighid's cloak) or the *Crois Bhríde* (Brighid's cross) in various ceremonies that invoked her arrival and blessing of the home.

In some areas, work such as that involving the turning of wheels was forbidden and a day's holiday taken in order to celebrate and visit holy wells dedicated to Brighid. Some form of feast was a usual part of the celebrations in the evening and this might include a place set and a meal left for Brighid or cakes left overnight for her outside the house. The water brought back from a Brighid's well would be later used to ritually wash and in some places to bless the house by sprinkling on the walls.

Two particular items are associated with receiving and retaining the blessings of Brighid, they were/are believed to harness her power, acting as a talisman to provide her protection or healing properties, these are the *crois Bhríde/bogha Bríde/crosóg*

(Brighid's cross) and *Brat Bhríde* (Brighid's cloak) which are still with us today. The *crois Bhríde* is found throughout Ireland in the four-legged form and in some of the northern counties in its three legged form, in both cases they are usually made from rushes. The four-legged form is considered as a symbol of the cycle of the seasons, of the four fire festivals and also as a sun wheel as well as a symbol of Brighid herself. A large variety of designs exist, especially in Ireland, being particular to local communities or distinct areas. This symbol bears similarities to the hindu 'swastika' and is found throughout Europe in megalithic art and figurines of fertility goddesses, implying that the cult of Brighid may be the remnant of a pan-European fertility/agrarian goddess worship that survived intact only in the Celtic fringes.

The cross is a protection against storms and bad weather; they were often put into the thatch of houses to protect it from storms and also from catching fire. The rushes for making them were often ritually gathered by the oldest daughter or failing that the mother of the house and she would be welcomed on her return to the house with the rushes. After placing the rushes before the household for everyone to make crosses, she would bless the house and all inside it, especially the hearth or fireplace. Another function of the cross was to prevent bad luck and to preserve milk and ensure plentiful food. One story of the origin of the cross relates to how Brighid purified some poisoned milk that was given to her by use of the cross to bless it. Another story tells how a penniless Brighid prayed and placed crosses in the empty cupboards, later to find them filled up with cheese.

Brighid's crosses are often to be found over or near the door, sometimes with last year's under the doormat and they are still regarded as a talisman for good health and protection from harm.

The *Brat Bhríde*, Brighid's cloak/mantle is less common today, this being a piece of cloth which one leaves outside the house or on the outside windowsill during the night of St. Brighid's Eve while Brighid is said to be passing throughout the land. Sometimes the cloth was tied onto a tree or bush or onto the front door handle; often a prayer would be said during doing this. The purpose of the *brat* is to absorb the energy, blessings or power of the goddess as she passes by, once impregnated it can be used by the members of the house as a protection and also to aid healing. In general, the same piece of cloth would be used each year, achieving full potency after a period of seven years. It was thought the *brat* could cure toothaches and headaches as well as other pains and aches for both people and animals.

Rite

In terms of ritual, themes of importance are as follows:

Ritual purification – if at all possible collect water from a known Brighid's well or failing that any holy well/spring. If this is not possible and bottled/tap water is all that is available then the water should be blessed in Brighid's name before being used for washing the body or blessing the house. If used in a group setting each person may bathe themselves or be sprinkled by a female chosen to represent Brighid. At this time it may also be appropriate to ask for her blessings (e.g. while bathing forehead ask that your thoughts be blessed).

Welcoming Brighid – using traditional invocations (such as in the 'Carmina Gadelica') or your own chosen words the goddess can be invited into the house/ritual space. A candle or fire may also be used during this as a symbol of the re-emergent energy in the land and the increasing solar heat.

Receipt of blessings – in addition to asking to receive her blessings personally and for the home and so forth the *Brat Bhríde* and/or *crois Bhríde* can be used as a talisman or receptacle for Brighid's power and blessings. Perhaps you might hold up the *crois/brat* and invoke Brighid's blessings on the circle and within the *crois/brat*. A more elaborate process might be to use the belt (*crios Bhríde*) with all members of the group passing through it while other members chant or sing an invocation to Brighid.

Feasting – perhaps towards the close of the ritual eat/share food or a meal, this might well include milk products. It would also be appropriate to leave an offering of bread, cakes or butter behind or otherwise outside the doorstep at home or even at a place set at the table for Brighid.

Vernal Equinox — Alban Eilir, Cónocht an Earraigh 21st/22nd March

The relatively sparse evidence of ancient Celtic celebration of either equinox has led many to deny the importance of the astronomical festivals and reject them as genuinely Celtic. However, evidence shows that they were celebrated in Celtic countries well over a thousand years ago in a Christianised framework but incorporating some rather bizarre customs that have little or nothing to do with Christianity.

In addition to the multitude of customs that survived into the Christian era, megalithic sites such as Loughcrew (Slieve na Calliagh/Sliabh na Cailligħe) in Ireland, Llananno in Wales, the ruined Duntreath Stones at Blanefield, Scotland or Stonehenge in England are aligned with the equinoxes. Interestingly, at Newgrange 'site U' less than half a mile due east of the main tumulus appears to be a ruined mound with a several large stones at the site. Archaeologists have suggested that this site may well have been aligned to the equinoxes but it has been destroyed, being rather small, unlike Newgrange, which although ruined, was far too large to be completely destroyed. Stonehenge, perhaps the most famous megalithic site, is now most associated with the summer solstice, although clearly it served a wider purpose through the year being also aligned to both solstices and both equinoxes. Loughcrew is perhaps the best example of a solar site specifically aligned to the equinoxes.

On either equinox, the sun rises in the same place, at which time the passageway of Cairn T (at Loughcrew) is illuminated and the back stone, marked with a series of notches is lit up. This site was built in 3200 BC approximately, long before the Celts arrived in Western Europe.

The spring equinox has had religious significance throughout the world, in Egypt Sham El Nessim was celebrated as far back as 2700 BC, although the modern date is now Easter Monday. In places as far away as Persia and Mexico, the equinox was highly significant and in some cultures marked the beginning of the year.

A multitude of customs still exist in Europe related to the spring equinox and/or Easter and the placement of many Saints' days (e.g. St Patrick, St. Piran, St. David, St. Mary) around this time may well have been an attempt to replace earlier pagan rites with Christian celebrations. The name Easter itself is derived from the Teutonic goddess of Spring Eostre, with the 'Easter Bunny' being her sacred animal the hare. Obviously, this does not indicate that the same significance was common to Celtic culture, however similar customs seem to exist throughout Europe that long predate the proliferation of Anglo/American culture.

Cakes marked with a cross predate Christianity and may be linked to the solar year or possibly the moon as evidenced by the tradition of burying them at crossroads as a sacrificial offering to Diana (Greek moon goddess). In Ireland, these cakes were perhaps originally indicative of the splitting the year into quarters rather than a symbol of resurrection. In Wales these were shared out after Good Friday services and kept (not eaten) as talismans. Several writers have suggested that the equal arm cross found on cakes and which was also worn in the past on St. Patrick's Day (*crois Pádraig*) is of pre-Christian origin and is actually a symbol of the quartered year, for instance the four seasons or perhaps the solstices and equinoxes. This cannot be proven either way but this theory does fit well enough with existing records of Celtic custom referring to the quarters and the well-known fact that the equal arm cross is an ancient pagan symbol.

Easter eggs are a pan-European tradition and are thought to be a symbol of the sun's passage through the heavens (i.e. rolling them along). The egg is sacred to the Druids (the serpents egg will be discussed later) and is referred to in classical accounts, linked with the origin of the world. It was common until fairly recently for children to paint eggs with bright colours and roll them down hills, also they were used empty as decorations, perhaps the origin of the Faberge egg. Pancakes, which are now associated with Shrove Tuesday may well have a solar significance as a solar disc although this is a rather tenuous argument. One genuine Shrovetide tradition found in Wales is that of a game of football that took place across entire villages and could last all day. The object of each team was to try to kick the ball (made from a bull's bladder) to the opposite end of the village. This was generally confined to the men, who ate pancakes during the course of the day. Rather than a simple game of football, this was symbolic of the transition from darkness to light at this time of balance, with the ball being symbolic of the sun.

Although in some cases, the first turn of the sod might have been at *Imbolc* it is around the time of the equinox that agriculture begins in earnest. Ploughing and planting would begin, perhaps on a Friday for good luck, in a sunwise (*deiseal*) direction. In Ireland, it is still customary to begin agriculture after St. Patrick's Day, in some places, Good Friday was auspicious and in Wales it was tradition to go to the fields on Easter Sunday to invoke the blessings of the Corn Spirit and offer libations, cakes and prayers.

Sir James Frazer recorded a rite for Auvergne, Bavaria that

involved the construction and burning of an 'Easter Man', which was in fact a wooden cross padded with straw to look like a man. This usually took place on Holy Saturday with the ashes being spread on the fields on Easter Monday to bring fertility to the land. In some cases, any charred remains were kept for next year's burning. Likewise, old palm leaves from the previous Palm Sunday would be burned with the Easter Man having been kept from last year.

Interestingly Frazer also refers to a similar custom in Ireland (placed at *Bealtaine*) where a person who draws a blackened piece of cake from a bag is to be burned as a sacrifice to Bel, although he/she was not actually burned in the *Bealtaine* fires. The person was referred to as dead and sometimes was subjected to a fake (acted) dismemberment. Frazer seems to imply that in earlier times, a live person was burned to placate the gods and ensure a productive year, and that later offerings and rituals are an echo of this. Classical authors refer to a similar ritual in Gaul involving a wickerwork man filled with animals and on occasion people, used for the same purpose. Modern day Christianity retains this notion of sacrifice at this same time of year in a different form with the self-sacrifice of Christ for forgiveness of humanity's sins and his resurrection three days later.

Rite

In terms of ritual, themes of importance are as follows:

Passage from dark to light – this could be enacted in a game perhaps for example football or tug of war as part of festivities if there is a large group. In ritual, this transition could be symbolised by passing through some form of gateway, perhaps between two people.

Re-awakening of the fertile earth – at this time the sun, which began its return at the solstice is now in the ascendancy and the natural world begins springing to life, the ritual area might be decorated with daffodils or painted eggs. A ceremony might include the scattering of seeds or the ritualised planting of a tree/shrub whilst invoking the elements and the blessing of the sun and earth.

The return of the Mabon/Maponos/Maccan – in the cycle of the year he now is no longer the fragile child but has come of age, ready to begin his ascent to become consort to the goddess. The sun child in his ascendancy is symbolised by Arthur or Fionn who was portrayed as not dead but asleep and thereby ready to return when needed. At this stage, he is re-awoken and empowered to be united with the land as king/chieftain.

Bealtaine - Beltane, Beltine, Boldyn, Bealtuinn, 1st May

Following on from the re-emergence of the sun at the balance point of the equinox, the light half of the year gains dominance and summer begins. It is the culmination of a process of awakening that began at *Imbolc* that sees the energy of growth and fertility in nature reaching its peak.

Bealtaine is the Irish word for the month of May and is thought to mean good fire or fire of Bel/Belenus, the solar deity that was found throughout the Celtic world; he was the god of light and fire, associated with the sun god Apollo by Greco-Roman writers. Fires in honour of Bel were lit on hilltops all over to celebrate the return of summer and renewed fertility in the land. Celebrated on May Day, now a Europe wide day of celebration, it might equally be marked when the first hawthorn blossoms emerge.

In Irish lore, the first *Bealtaine* fires were lit at Uisnech (Co. Meath) which was visible from Tara. Uisnech was sacred to the Druids of Ireland and it is said that the Druid Mide (meaning centre) lit the first fire. It is from his name that this central province (now county) Meath takes its name. Mide's fire burned for seven years and could be seen from all the four provinces of

Ireland. Interestingly the story of St. Patrick tells that the High King lit the first fire of *Bealtaine* (Easter in some versions) at Tara but Patrick usurped his spiritual power by lighting a fire first at Slane. Whatever the origin in Ireland, the bonfire is central to this festival and was to be found in Scotland, Wales and England also.

In Scotland and Wales wood from nine sacred trees was used to make the fire, constructed and lit using friction, by nine men or a multiple of nine, these had to be honourable men otherwise it was thought the fire would not light. The fire was usually lit at dawn (not dusk) in contrast to *Samhain* fires. It was also common in Scotland and Ireland to have two fires, between which all of the livestock were driven as a form of purification. In Scotland it was also common to take a long hair from each cow and tie them into a rope with red string and drag it through the morning dew on *Bealtaine* whilst chanting, 'The milk of the one below, the milk of the one above, into my own big pail' (*Bainne an té seo shios, bainne an té seo shuas,'nam ghogan mhór fhein*). This supposedly would ensure the abundance of milk from each cow.

As well as purification of beasts, people used the *Bealtaine* fires for celebration and also for luck by jumping over them once they had died down. Younger people leapt through the fire, perhaps three times, for good luck for themselves and their livestock, whilst old people would walk sunwise (*deiseal*) around the fire saying prayers. Young women jumped the fire to obtain luck in love, pregnant women stepped over the ashes for an easy birth and mothers would carry their young children over the ashes for their protection and good health. Embers were often brought home to relight the hearth fires and finally the ashes were scattered on the fields for luck and fertility of the land.

Fertility was a central theme to *Bealtaine,* which is exhibited in the symbolic sacred marriage of the land-goddess here depicted as a flower maiden and the Maponos/Mabon/Maccan who has reached sexual maturity. This union is captured in Celtic myth in a variety of stories – Blodeuwedd and Lleu (from the

'Mabinogion'), Culhwch and Olwen, Diarmaid and Grainne, Cú Chulainn and Bláthnat and Gawain and the Green Knight. In all these stories, the young hero has to overcome the hostile aspects of the land in order to avail of the goddess' blessings in the form of fertility and fruitfulness. Often this dark and hostile aspect is portrayed as a father/older man/husband who the hero must kill/overcome for example the Hawthorn Giant, Fionn, great boar, Cú Roí etc. In some cases, the Cailleach or Hag is seen as being overcome and killed or transformed into a young maiden who then bestows her favours on the hero. This fruitful marriage of the solar god/hero with the land goddess was acted out literally with marriages at *Bealtaine* being fairly common. On the eve of *Bealtaine* young people would collect boughs of flowering hawthorn and flowers (e.g. *lus buí Bealtaine* – Marsh Marigolds) in the woods, also taking the opportunity to indulge in sexual union. In continental Europe, it was common for young men to 'sneak' hawthorn branches into the houses of young ladies they liked, referred to as Planting the May. The young lady might respond by keeping the man company during the festivities and no-doubt participate in sexual union if she so wished. Those returning before the dawn bringing branches of hawthorn and rowan and flowers would decorate the village and sing to wake those still asleep; it was usual to repay the singers with food or money.

In parts of Wales, the conflict between the emerging powers of the summer and the sterile aspect of the land was acted out in a mock battle between two teams of men representing winter and summer. The leader of the winter team was covered in tufts of wool (as snow) carrying a blackthorn staff while the leader of summer wore white with garlands of flowers and a willow staff, also decorated with flowers. Of course the summer team eventually won and the leader chose a May King to be consort to the May Queen chosen earlier by the people.

The custom of the Maypole, an obvious phallic symbol, is an

English custom of probable Saxon derivation. Although it is not Celtic, it shares a clear reference to fertility in common with more clearly Celtic customs. This custom seems to have become integrated or combined with Celtic practices in Wales, Cornwall and northern England and survives to this day as a pagan 'leftover' despite attempts by clergy to stamp it out. It is now something of a quaint curiosity and dancing around the maypole is much more of a cultural/traditional celebration than a religious event.

Rite

In terms of ritual, themes of importance are as follows:

Purifying fire – ideally you would have two fires representing polar opposites, male and female deities, sun and moon and so forth. The passing between the two fires ritually cleanses the participant, burning away the energy of the dark half of the year as we enter the summer. If you can obtain agaric (a fungus on birch trees) this is the traditional way to kindle the fire. The jumping of the fire/ashes (be careful) also brings fertility and good luck. If two bonfires are not possible use fires in two skillets/cauldrons or even two candles. You may wish to dance or walk three times around the fire(s) clockwise (*deiseal*).

The Divine marriage – the joyous union of the mature maponos with the goddess of the land brings the abundance of summer and autumn. This can be ritually enacted with a 'Queen' or 'Flower Maiden' and a 'King' or 'Champion'. This can also be symbolically represented with a cup/cauldron/chalice and a wand/rod, held by a female and male participant. Internally this is about the union of the female and male qualities in each of us – the child of the alchemical marriage is our own creativity and insight blossoming and manifesting in the external world.

Decline of the Cernunnos archetype and Cailleach – if you have enough participants this can be acted out in a procession or play in which Cernunnos or Hawthorn Giant is defeated by his younger foe, the hag (Cailleach) is banished or transformed into the comely maiden. Otherwise, this can be visualised or told as one of several suitable mythological stories (e.g. Culhwch ac Olwen).

Celebration – feasting and dancing was always an important part of *Bealtaine,* perhaps bring special food and drink to share (e.g. *an Bonnach Bealtaine* cake). Perhaps select a person who has the blackened piece as the symbolic sacrifice to Baal/Bile/Belanus and enact mourning for him/her and 'pretend' wake celebrations in their honour. This is also a popular time for handfastings, which you might wish to include in the celebrations. This also might include jumping the fire but I know of at least one instance where this was substituted by a ring of flowers (perhaps for safety reasons).

Summer Solstice — Sun Standing, Grianstad an t-SamhraidhAlban Hefin, Lá Fhíle Eoin, 21st/22nd June

There is no recorded Celtic name from antiquity that relates to this festival, although various names for June refer to mid-summer perhaps indicative of its importance – *Meitheamh* (Irish), *Mehefin* (Welsh), *Metheven* (Cornish) and *Mezheven* (Breton). In the modern calendar, the feast of John the Baptist is observed on 24th of June with celebrations beginning the night before. The folk practices relating to the summer solstice seem to have long ago been transferred to this date, which like the other festivals seems to be an appropriation of older pre-Christian rites.

Great bonfires were lit on hilltops to celebrate the triumph of the light, which also marks the beginning of its descent. Celebrations included feasting, song and dance and prayers for a good harvest and that the blessings of the sun would continue until the harvest begins in earnest at *Lúghnasadh*. In some cases, a special person presided over the building, lighting and maintaining of the fire. In Breton custom *Furze* (Gorse) was used to light the fire, itself being a solar oriented plant with bright yellow flowers around this time. Fire games would also take place, including rolling of fire wheels down hills. The highly risky act of casting embers (or ashes) into the fields was common or a torch was carried through the fields to bring the sun's power of growth and fruition onwards. Like *Bealtaine* it was also common for people to jump the fire for good luck and retention of the solar or *samos* energy onwards into the dark half of the year.

This was also the time of a special pre-harvest if you will – the picking of sacred herbs (linked to the power of the sun and thereby the solar deities) such as St. Johns Wort (especially), Henbane, Vervain, Stonecrop and Yarrow took place at this time. It was thought that this was the most beneficial time to collect them and they are all in flower at this time, the power of the sun at its height was supposedly captured. This was to be undertaken in a ritual manner as befitting plants of magical properties and prayers might be said during the picking such as recorded in Scotland in the 'Carmina Gadelica'.

The summer solstice was also considered one of the three times at which the veil between worlds grew thin, falling exactly half way between the two others – *Bealtaine* and *Samhain*. It was also believed that magical powers in certain plants were high at this time – elderberries picked now could ward off evil and malignant charms, fern seeds had the power to make one invisible. St John's Wort was cast into fires and used to garland both the doors of houses and the farm for its protective powers.

Interestingly the Irish land goddess Áine (meaning brightness) is most associated with this time. Although depicted as a Tuatha Dé Danann lady in the literature, the folklore surrounding her, particularly from Knockainey (Cnoc Áine

Cliach) associates her with the sovereignty of the land. Such was her reputation in Munster that the Fitzgeralds exploited her as a means of legitimising their rule by claiming ancestry from her line. Various legends associated with Áine and the solstice tell of her appearing on the hilltop with an entourage of the *sidhé,* her appearing as a beggar woman to poor families and rewarding any kindness with prosperous harvests and livestock. The fact that a pre-Christian goddess link to the summer solstice survived into the 19th century indicates that not only was Áine an important deity in earlier times but also that this solstice was of significance to the early Celts, which has often been dismissed by pagans and scholars alike. Further evidence of the summer solstice in pre-Christian Celtic lands is clearly found in the Neolithic monuments of the British Isles such as Stonehenge, Callanish, Dombeg and Brodgar or Carnac in France. Some of these solar temples are around five thousand years old and were of considerable religious and social importance. It seems unlikely that times of such significance as the solstices would have been forgotten or discarded by peoples of the late Bronze Age and early Iron Age – the surviving folklore and myths of the Celtic peoples suggest that this is not the case.

Rite

In terms of ritual, themes of importance are as follows:

Fire ritual – a bonfire preferably prepared and lit in a ritual manner perhaps using a gorse branch. It would be customary to do this on the night preceding the solstice or on St. John's Eve. You may wish to stay up to watch the dawn and keep the fire burning until the sunrise. It would also be traditional to jump the fire and to use ashes or embers to gain a solar blessing on land (perhaps your garden if you don't have fields). If a fire is not possible or appropriate then a contained fire in a cauldron or even a candle can act as a symbolic substitute.

Thanksgiving and recognition of the sun's power – an invocation of the sun such as in the *Carmina Gadelica* would be appropriate. You may wish to create your own words in praise of the sun to be read out, recited or sung. We should also acknowledge the zenith is also the point of decline and pray for the continued benign solar influence as we slowly head towards the dark half of the year.

Magical/otherworldy presence – this is a time to acknowledge the magical power imbued in the natural world by the sun, this is recognised in the ritual harvesting of solar associated plants. It would be appropriate to pick St. John's Wort and burn some of it in the fire. This is also a time of the *sidhé* and the solar/land deities such as Áine and Bel who we hope join us in our celebrations – seen or unseen. Their presence should be requested and recognised. Above all this should be a joyous celebration of the peak of solar power that keeps this planet and all its inhabitants alive.

Lúghnasadh — Lúnasa, Lughnasa, Domhnach Chrom Dubh, Calan Awst, Laa Luanys, 1st August

This festival is most obviously linked with the god Lugh and his role in defeating the Fomorians (*Fomhóraigh*), however it is also associated strongly with his foster-mother Tailtiu, who gave her name to Teltown (*Tailteann*), the place in Ireland most associated with *Lúghnasadh*. The word itself means 'the commemoration of Lugh' and it is also the Irish word for the month of August.

Tailtu was wife to the *Fir Bholg* king Eochaidh Mac Eirc and also foster mother to Lugh. She cleared the central plain of Ireland (Breagha) so that it could be cultivated for crops, although this huge effort resulted in her death. She was buried at Teltown and the great assembly and funeral games were instituted by Lugh in honour of her at her request. She prophesied that Ireland would always be rich in corn, milk and good weather so long as the celebrations in her honour continued every year. This was known as *Aonach Tailteann* (assembly of Teltown) and was held every year at this place by the Irish High Kings at this time. The *Aonach* in general was of great social importance to the Irish Celts at which kings, nobles, druids and clan members gathered. This particular gathering brought together the usual social aspects with games, sales of goods, passing of new laws and of course the celebration of the beginning of the harvest. The last recored official celebration at Teltown, celebrated by the High King, Rory O'Connor (*Ard Rí,* Ruari Ó Conchúir) took place in 1169, just prior to the Norman invasion of Leinster, although the practice was carried on unofficially by local people, on a smaller scale until 1770.

There were also numerous sites throughout Ireland particularly where *Lughnasadh* was celebrated, most often on a height but also at holy wells. Similar festivities took place in Britain and France, Lugh being widely acknowledged as is demonstrated by the reference to him in many place names. Various survivals of celebrations carry on mostly in Ireland but also in Cornwall in the form of plays featuring 'Jack the Tinkard' at Morvah Fair, although the explicit reference has been lost.

Although the remembrance of Tailtiu is an important part of this festival, the core myth associated with this time is that of the second battle of *Maigh Tuireadh* which symbolically represents the triumph of the gods of light and prosperity (leading to a successful harvest) over the dark divinities that bring blight, poverty and starvation. More explicitly the gods of the people (Tuatha Dé Danann) led by Lugh triumph over the gods of the land in its darkest aspect (Fomhóraigh/Fomorians) led by Balor.

The Leinster version of this story from *Aonach Carman* ties the two aspects together: Carmain (synonymous with Tailtiu) invades Ireland with her three sons and begins to destroy the land and the harvest. The *Tuatha Dé Danann,* led by Lugh, drive them out but take Carmain hostage until she eventually dies at the oak-grove that became the site of the assembly in Leinster. In this variant she is not Lugh's foster-mother but allied to the Fomorian powers, her benign land-goddess aspect only being released upon her death.

In the battle of *Maigh Tuireadh* story, we gain further insights into Lugh's role and the conflict between the powers of growth and prosperity and those of blight and destruction. The Tuatha Dé Danann are subjugated and half starved under the regime of King Breas whose loyalty is to the Fomorians. Finally, unable to stand their servitude they rise up against the Fomorians in a terrible battle that sees much slaughter on both sides. The deadlock is resolved by single combat between Lugh and Balor, interestingly Lugh, the Tuatha Dé Danann champion, is the son of Eithne and grandson of Fomorian champion Balor, the only person (by birth) who could possibly defeat Balor. Balor's evil eye brings death to all who gaze upon it and it took four men to lift the lid on the third terrible eye, which was used to great effect against the Tuatha Dé Danann. Lugh Lámhfhada (of the long arm) used his sling to aim a stone at Balor's eye which was so powerfully and accurately thrown that it took out the eye and killed Balor and twenty-seven of his followers behind him. Thus Lugh brings victory but decides not to kill Breas as he possesses knowledge of agriculture from the Fomhóraigh/Fomorians. Breas imparted his knowledge to the Tuatha Dé Danann in exchange for his life, evil as they are the Fomhóraigh represent the sometimes necessary destructive aspects of the land and still have a part to play in life.

Lugh undertook a victory march to Teltown together with his people and upon his arrival he was declared king as Nuadha had already been killed in the battle with the Fomhóraigh. The ritual marriage to the land goddess, *Bainis Rí* took place as has taken place subsequently with kings well into recorded history. This marriage was said to have taken place at *Samhain,* with their child being born at *Lúghnasadh* — nine months later, the new harvest.

Hence, we can now see the significance of the battle – the forces of light and dark, culminating in victory of the light and impregnation of the earth which yields a bountiful harvest.

It is interesting to compare this myth with that of St. Patrick and Crom Dubh: this is celebrated at Croagh Patrick (formerly *Cruachán Aigle* or Eagle Mountain) at the time of *Lúghnasadh*. In various versions Crom and his followers are defeated, killed or converted to Christianity, however in one version Patrick's adversaries appear as crows or ravens, which he dispels by throwing a black bell at them, in much the same manner as Lugh used his sling. The last Sunday of July, *Domhnach Chrom Dubh* (Black Crom's Sunday) is the most popular time for the Croagh Patrick pilgrimage and represented an important process of purification and the triumph over the forces of darkness in the Celtic Church. It is also interesting to note the discovery of an ancient pagan site at Bohea by Gerry Bracken. From this rock outcrop a 'rolling sunset' can be observed on Croagh Patrick on the 18th of April and the 24th of August each year, clearly demonstating the pre-Christian significance of this mountain[18]. I think that it is quite clear that the pagan *Lúghnasadh* was supplanted by the Croagh Patrick pilgrimage (that takes place to this day) because it was considered necessary to replace this ancient festival with something Christian of similar importance.

Similar festivities took place in Brittany around the same time, such as *Le Grande Troménie* at Locronan, it has been suggested that some of the practices here derive from worship of pagan deities[19] and have survived, out of context, into the modern era. It has also been suggested that the myth central to *Lúghnasadh* is also embodied in tales like St. George and the Dragon and various other dragon fights.

Returning now to the festival itself, it would usually take place over a number of days, with people convening at high ground. Plays or parades dramatising the myth were common as was enjoyment of the first fruits of the harvest and also competitions and games. In the times of the High Kings great entertainments were performed, pageants, music, poetry and storytelling. Some of the pageantry survived and in Ireland, ritualised battles between young men continued until recently, with the victors proclaiming that they would receive better luck and a better harvest next year. In ancient times, feasting was of great importance at this time at all the *Aonach*, especially Teltown, which involved tributes of fruit, fish, and meat for the High King from the chieftains around Ireland. Bread was not included in this feast, produced from the corn. One of the most important elements of the celebrations was the offering of the first sheaf of ripened corn, which was left on the hill or buried in the ground.

In later times, in Ireland and Scotland, the head of the clan or household would cut the first sheaf and hold it up to the sun turning *deiseal* three times and chanting a prayer. The wheat from this first sheaf was made into cakes that were brought up onto the hill for consumption by all the celebrants. In an echo of the earlier sheaf ritual, flowers worn by people on the way to the festivities were buried in the earth.

Various games and contests took place, including horseracing and feats of athleticism. Fertility games took place between young men and women, harmless offering of flower garlands and the 'Teltown Marriages' in which young men and women were randomly paired for a year and a day, which they could choose to end the following *Lúghnasadh* by simply turning their backs to each other and walking away. These and other fun activities are most likely echoes of a more explicit sexual enactment of fertility rituals, perhaps representative of the divine ritual marriage Bainis Rí.

These annual celebrations continued throughout Britain and Ireland, most notably in Teltown, Silbury Hill, Morvah until the last century. It was common for towers to be built on hilltops as well as great bonfires, feasting and drinking and revelry took place, perhaps somewhat divorced from its roots, but still in celebration of the harvest. Even now, Puck Fair in Killorglin, Ireland, featuring a wild male goat on a tower as a crowned king, continues amidst celebrations and a commercial fair. The goat is crowned by a twelve-year-old girl (the Puck Queen), kept on the tower for the three days and released into the wild at the end.

Rite

In terms of ritual, themes of importance are as follows:

Reaping of the first sheaf — this is highly significant and should be done if at all possible. If it is not possible for you to obtain wheat, barley and such, I would suggest that long grass that has run to seed will suffice. The grain sheaf should be cut ceremonially with a sickle or knife whilst reciting an appropriate quote from the 'Carmina Gadelica' or a prayer of your own making in thanks for the first fruits. It would also be appropriate to raise it overhead towards the sun and turn three times *deiseal* (sunwise).

Again, only if possible, you may wish to use some of the grain to make cakes or bread for use later and the rest of the sheaf can be buried at the site of celebration.

Gathering on a hill — if possible a hillside is the best place to perform a *Lúghnasadh* ceremony, bringing all the necessaries with you, including the sheaf or flowers to be buried in the earth. Here is where all the other elements of the festival should take place, usually now on one day, but also if you wish to spread it over several days.

Feasting — the pre-prepared cakes/bread may be consumed and also offered to the gods, perhaps cast into the fire if you have one. Failing homemade cakes, fruit you have grown or collected can be shared and failing that food that you have prepared yourself (not bought in packs) should be shared and offered.

Fun and games – fertility games in the form of harmless flirting, dancing and so forth can be enjoyable, particularly if young people are participating in the ritual. A pageant or enactment of the battle between Lugh and Balor would be appropriate or even a simple mock 'fight' with sticks as took place in 19th century Ireland. For the more athletic, you may wish to have races and for the more creative you may wish to have music, poetry and story-telling.

Thanksgiving – through ritual offering of food, recitations or meditation you can give thanks for the bounty of nature, the fruits or a successful summer and the triumph of growth over decay. At this time though we become aware of the transition towards decay, destruction and darkness, the sun is in decline even now as the fruits are becoming abundant. This is a time to be aware of the continual cycle of the seasons, which culminates in the harvest, ensuring our survival. Although modernity has minimised the apparent reliance of many humans on this harvest, without its continuation all over the planet, we and all creatures that depend on it, would have no future.

Autumn Equinox — Alban Elfed, Cónocht an fhómhair' La Fhéile Mícheal, Gwyl Fihangel 21st/22nd September

This is the second balance point of the year, the vernal equinox being the first, once again the day and night are of equal length, the sun rises due east and sets due west. On this occasion, the sun is in decline, growing ever lower in the sky and its transit from east to west grows noticeably shorter, this is the entry point to the dark half of the year in the *samos/giamos, samhradh/geimhreadh* cycle.

Although the harvest is not totally complete until *Samhain*, this represents the close of the main harvest, particular that of grain crops; this is the culmination of the year's agricultural work and the reaping of the rewards of that work. This has been celebrated in more recent times as Michaelmas, the feast of St. Michael or *La Fhéile Mícheal* in Ireland and Scotland around 29th September. It has been suggested that St. Michael is a direct substitution for the pagan god Lugh[20], thus making ancient traditions acceptable to the Christian Church. Michaelmas was particularly important in Scotland, as the harvest is always later than in other Celtic countries due to its more northerly latitude, hence the grain crop might only be ready at this time. As with the ancient Irish, the Scots into the late 19th century made ceremony of the cutting of the first sheaf with the patriarch lifting the first handful overhead towards the sun and turning three times whilst chanting the *Iolach Buana*[21]. The whole family would witness this in their Sunday best and join in the chant before the harvest began in earnest. This is basically an ancient *Lúghnasadh* practice transferred to September due to the climate.

In ancient Greece, a significant celebration of the Eleusian mysteries also took place in late September, particularly at Eleusis in SE Greece (Attica). This cult, which lasted into the 4th century AD, was centred around the agrarian cycle and the veneration of Demeter, her daughter Persephone and also the god Dionysus. The myth relating to Persephone and Hades relates closely to Celtic myths that explore the cycle of nature. Initiates were given a single grain of wheat and told 'In silence is the seed of wisdom gained', which parallels the Taliesin myth wherein he is ingested by Cerridwen as a grain of wheat.

In general, the main activities at this time (in Celtic countries) surrounded the end of the harvest and the cutting of the last sheaf was of great significance. The person to perform this task was usually selected in some game of chance, as this was a solemn duty that had to be performed in order to assure the continuance of the cycle. The last sheaf was known as the neck, mare, *penn-yar* (Cornish for hen's head), maiden, *Gobhar Bhacach* (lame goat) or kern baby. It was thought that the corn spirit, conceived by the union of the land goddess and her consort, resided in this last sheaf. In cutting the last sheaf, the spirit of the harvest would be slain and pains had to be taken to ensure that the spirit would return to the bosom of the land and the fertility not be lost. This unlucky task of cutting the last sheaf was often performed at a distance by throwing the sickle and the sheaf was then collected and made into a representative of the goddess – an appropriate means of transference of this energy of life.

This symbol of the goddess' fertility was a 'corn dolly' made from the last sheaf. In Wales, it was known as the *caseg fedi* (harvest mare) and could take many different shapes, a tradition that survives in Wales and England to this day. In Ireland and Scotland, this dolly was either the Harvest Queen or the Hag, a differentiation being made depending on the quality of the harvest. This doll was kept for the duration of the year with last year's doll being burned now that a new one had been made. If there was a good harvest then the doll might be stored with the grain to impart its energy into the seeds for next year, it might equally have been kept in the house (usually the kitchen) or in a church (Christian era). If the harvest had been poor, the doll in this case known as the Cailleach, was kept by the person who cut the last sheaf. This was not a popular task, however it was said that the guardian (*babban*) of the Cailleach was able to receive otherworldly blessings in return for this role. In due course, the Cailleach was buried in a place where its infertility could be disposed of harmlessly. In the case of unkind or mean landowners they were sometimes cursed by the secret burial of the Cailleach upon their land thereby rendering it less fertile.

In the Hebrides (northern Scotland) the last sheaf itself was known as the Cailleach and was unwanted due to it being unlucky. It was common for farmers to throw this last sheaf into a neighbour's field, thus transferring the bad luck, this went on like a game of pass the parcel until the last farmer to finish reaping was left with the poor luck, likened to having to care for and feed an elderly woman through the harsh winter months.

A communal feast was celebrated at the end of harvesting, which is the ancestor of the 'harvest festival' or 'harvest home', which often sees goods and produce being distributed to the poor or elderly. In Cornwall, this feast was known as Goeldheys, in Scotland this was the time for ritual carrot gathering by the women and eating of *struan Mícheal* (Michael's bannock). An interesting prelude to the feasting called *clabhsúr* (closure) took place in southwest Ireland. The men threatened to ruin all of their farming tools if they were not given a feast by the women of the community; the tools would be thrown into a smouldering fire and quickly fetched out by the women so that the feast could then be prepared.

In the highlands of Scotland, an interesting ritual dance took place between a man and a woman: the man holding a druid wand (*slachdan Druidheach*) waved it over his own head and then that of the woman, which caused her to fall down as if dead. He would perform as if in mourning for her (perhaps keening) before touching her hands, arms, feet etc one by one as he danced about so that they became alive again (the lady moving them as appropriate) until finally he breathed life into her mouth and touched her heart with the wand. She would then spring up again and join the man in the dance, thus re-enacting the cycle of agriculture that has sustained us for thousands of years.

This cycle is represented mythologically in the story of Daimuid and Gráinne a symbolic slaying of the Mabon/ Maponos/Maccan type (Dairmuid) which occurs at the entry to the dark half of the year, with Grainne returning to being the consort of the Cernunnos type (Fionn) like Persephone entering Tartarus (the underworld) to reside with Hades for the winter.

Rite

In terms of ritual, themes of importance are as follows:

Reaping of the last sheaf – this represents the killing of the corn spirit and thus must be performed with due care and ceremony to ensure the preservation of the fertility of the land. If you are able to do this, a 'dolly' can be constructed from the stalks of wheat, barley or even grass. If you have a dolly from the previous year, you may wish to burn this or bury it in the earth. If this is not possible, you may wish to ceremonially collect the last item of fruit or vegetable that you have grown and give thanks for the fertility of the land.

Feasting – it has long been a tradition to partake of the full fruits of the harvest whilst also giving thanks, this abundance should be shared, perhaps with family or friends. You may wish to give produce to neighbours, elderly relatives and so forth or perhaps if this is not possible make a charitable donation instead.

Preparation for the dark half of the year – now is the time of passing through the gateway into the dark half of the year, symbolised by the death of the Maponos and the disappearance of the land goddess' fertile (youthful) aspect. Although this theme of death and exploration of *giamos/geimhreadh* energy is more fully embraced at *Samhain* its beginnings are here at the equinox and it is an apt time to meditate on or ritually acknowledge the end of a cycle and prepare spiritually for the approaching darkness.

Conclusion

These festivals have been discussed in outline only, this is intentional. Specific ceremonies can be found in individual groups, groves and orders and they can vary greatly. I have attempted to cover the main elements of past and current practice in broad terms without over-intellectualising them. One must remember that these festivals, although originally led by Druids, were for the people to participate in and were spiritual not intellectual affairs. This cycle has been discussed in philosophical and intellectual terms ad infinitum but the core themes are simple enough and can be understood by children; I believe that it was supposed to be that way and should not be unnecessarily convoluted.

The purpose of these festivals is to foster a connection with the land, to give thanks and to acknowledge the eternal cycles of nature and our part within that. We must take part in this process in a way that is meaningful to us; otherwise it is a pointless exercise. I would not be overly concerned with correct performance of ritual or observance of exact dates and times, there is an argument that certain festivals were moveable anyway for example *Bealtaine* being celebrated on the arrival of the hawthorn blossom. What is most important is that we participate in the cycle and find a meaningful way to express our gratitude, emotions, hopes, fears and connection with deity and the spirit that flows through creation.

XI

Tools of the Trade

By now, if you have read the preceding chapters, you should have a fair understanding of the role of Druids in a historical perspective and some of the work that they undertook. Most people would have some impression of the Druid, perhaps holding a staff or wand, dressed in a white robe, possibly possessing a long beard – a vision not so different from the medieval enchanter, alchemist or magus, but these preconceptions are most likely wrong or only partially correct.

One of my former teachers, a well-known Wiccan High Priestess, once asked me a question about magic and magical tools; this was 'Which tool is the most important?' This question relates not just to Wicca but to Druidry and all magical paths, the answer to this question being simply 'None of them.' What is most important is in fact yourself and your ability to focus your will and energy. Any of the tools of magic, the clothes, wands and so on, may assist you in the process of mental preparation, focusing your energy etc., but they are all useless without the power of the mind that utilises them. In fact, I am of the opinion that over-dependence on tools is a great mistake, although they can be helpful – like training wheels on a bicycle, but one ultimately has to learn to do the pedalling and balancing. It is quite possible to use magic with just a finger and one's own concentration and those who are truly adept in this art are able to work with or without the accoutrement of the magician.

None-the-less, tools were/are used by Druids, obviously they are useful otherwise they would not have been employed. So here, we shall take a look at the tools of the Druid and their uses:

Clothing

This an area that causes much discussion and disagreement. The ideas of the Druid Revival of the 18th and 19th century are largely based on romanticism and some descriptions given by classical scholars. The general image is that which I described at the opening of this chapter, a billowing white robe, perhaps with a ring/crown of ivy, oak or laurel on the head. This is not entirely wrong, in so far as the white robes, however, this is dependent on location and also function as other clothing was worn and certainly romantic ideas about style of clothing leave a lot to be desired.

In the account (Tirechan) of the Irish Druids' conflict with St. Patrick and their attempt to kill him, Rechrad and his eight followers were dressed in white. Pliny also described a Druid of Gaul as robed in white. Irish historian Eugene O'Curry described the Druid Tulchinne, from the reign of Conaire, as dressed in a speckled white cloak with gold clasps on his ears (earrings?). He also describes the dress of *Fili* as 'three speckled cloaks...shirts with red interweavings of gold...and three brooches of gold.' He also gives an extract from the Book of Ballymote regarding clothes:

> Mottled to simpletons,
> Blue to women,
> Crimson to the kings of every host,
> Green and black to noble laymen
> White to clerics of proper devotion.

This source of course was from the mid medieval period and refers to Christian clerics, but it is highly likely that the colour code changed little or not at all from pagan times.

O'Curry provided another interesting insight in his translation of 'The Seige of Drom Damhghairé', which refers to the Druid Mogh Ruith: 'Then Mogh Ruith called for his dark-grey hornless bull-hide and his white-speckled bird headpiece, with its fluttering wings and also his Druidic instruments.

Another reference from 'The Intoxication of the Ultonians' (Ulstermen) describes the Druid Sencha: 'A fair bright garment about him, with borders of all-white silver. A beautiful white shirt...a white-silver belt around his waist, a bronze branch at the summit of his shoulder.'

The Roman Strabo also gives this account of Gaulish Bards, *Uatis* (*Vates*/Ovates) and Druids: 'Around their necks they wear gold collars, on their arms and wrists they have bracelets, and those of good position among them clothe themselves with dyed garments, worked with gold.'

Also from the 'Colloquy of the Two Sages', the Munster Lord Bricriu gave 'a purple tunic, with gold and silver' to Nede, who aspired to become an *Ollamh* (chief Druid). Nede was also wearing a three-coloured robe which was gold at the top, covered in brightly coloured bird feathers in the middle and speckled with gold, silver and brass at the bottom.

Obviously white was one of the important colours for Druids to wear but it appears that different clothing was worn depending on the occasion and status. It would appear that the bull-hide and bird headdress was used for battle, the white robes for ceremony and multicoloured robes for important social and royal occasions. Jewellery featured in Druidic clothing, as it did for all the upper echelons of Celtic society. The *lunulae* was worn by Druids in Ireland, Gaul and Britain, this being a crescent moon shape made of gold. There are various excellent examples at The National Museum of Ireland or The British Museum, which are often intricately marked in crosshatch patterns. The *torc* (around the neck) may also have been worn as well as the items described above. Gold and silver was clearly a symbol of high status and would have been worn by royalty, nobles and the druidic classes, the lower classes using bronze, brass or copper.

In Ireland a long shirt that could be hitched up with a belt was worn, called a *Léine*, under which was worn trousers (*Bracae*). Over this a *Brat* was worn, which was a cloak, held at the neck by a metal clasp or brooch, those who could not afford metal probably used a wooden peg, cloth or twine. It appears that clothing changed very little in style until the arrival of the Normans, after which English fashion was very gradually introduced.

In both Scotland and Ireland, there was a rigid colour system that applied to clothing. Stripes and multiple colours were reserved for people of high status, the lowest classes wore dull colours and slaves wore saffron yellow. According to the *Lebor Gabála Erin*, the Milesian King Tighernmas introduced the colour system in around 900 BC.

The kings or queens wore red or crimson and their offspring could wear scarlet, blue or purple. Nobles could wear green or brown. It is said that royalty might wear up to seven colours, the *Ollamh* or Bard six colours, chieftains five, great warriors four and so on down to the commoners and slaves who wore one colour only. In Scotland, the royal tartan had seven colours and only the king or queen could wear purple in their tartan. This colour system is the basis of the system employed for the tartans of Scottish Clans, used in kilts and cloaks today.

According to some sources, these colours were not only indicative of status but also had a symbolic meaning for example white — truth, red — strength (commonly associated with warriors and royalty). Seán O'Tuathail gives the following correspondences:

Blue — protection
Black — purity and power
Brown — strength
Gold — wealth, status
Silver — authority (spiritual)
Red — war, authority (political/secular)

White – emptiness
Yellow – gratefulness

Given the use of colour that is clearly recorded in many ancient manuscripts I find one or two interpretations to be troublesome. I can't imagine that slaves (wearing yellow) were particularly thankful or grateful for their lowly status, however these were often prisoners of war and hence they may have been grateful to have been left alive!

It was immediately obvious who was who in ancient Celtic society; it was not necessary to speak as one's appearance was sufficient. Up until the modern age (in Europe) certain classes of people wore particular types of clothing for example doctors, priests, nobles etc that indicated their function in society, however it seems that the Celtic system was considerably stricter than that of later times.

Sickles

This tool is an agricultural implement but many examples of these implements have been found in Ireland, Britain and Europe that are rather small and made of soft metals such as gold or silver. Farming implements were of bronze or iron in later times, it would have been pointless to ornament or decorate them like these small sickles (called *Searr* or *Carrán*) which are obviously quite impractical for agriculture. It is most likely that these would have been used for ceremonial reaping of crops or herbs, perhaps the most famous example of this is given by Pliny: '...the priest ascends the tree and cuts the mistletoe with a golden sickle.'

Rods, Wands & Staffs

Various myths describe Druids making use of the above to direct their energy and to perform magic such as shape shifting or curses. The hazel or alder wand is commonly referred to, yew sticks were used in divination and interestingly an aspen rod was used in association with burials. It has been suggested that the staff or wand is symbolic of the male energy and the active forces in life; also it has been compared to the world tree, - symbolically connecting the Druid in the middle world with the upper and lower realms.

Druid's Egg

Known by many names *balain/ballaun, anguinum, glain neidre, gleini na Droedh,* the Druid's Egg was a roughly circular object, depicted in two dimensions as an ellipse, which was said to be constructed from congealed serpent spittle or (by Pliny) the foam produced by serpents motion while intertwined in a ball. The serpents threw their 'egg' up into the air and the prospective owner would have to catch it in a cloak or blanket and run away with it, making sure to cross a river or stream so that the serpents could not recover it. Pliny stated that it was thought to possess healing qualities, bring good fortune in legal matters and gain audiences with kings, in the Scottish Highlands they were thought to protect from serpent bites. Pliny also claimed to have been shown one by a Gaulish Druid who stated that they were among a Druid's most valued possessions. Elliptical, egg shaped crystals and stones that have been found are thought to be these Druid's eggs. It is also said that they were made of glass, perhaps sea urchins or ammonite fossil. Some suggest that this is a symbol of the soul, that it symbolises the primordial egg from which the universe hatched, an idea that is common to both Chinese and Sumerian mythology. Helen Benigni likens it to a 'cosmic egg of thought' and she believes that the elliptical shapes found in Newgrange and Knowth (in Ireland) are in fact representations of the balain. It is also suggested that the balain represents the lunar cycle, which takes the form of an ellipse, various elliptical engravings and the Coligny calendar being used to back up this claim.

'Eggs' have been found in Gaulish, Welsh, Cornish, Irish and Scottish tumuli, which would indicate their widespread use, they were often fossils, old spindle-whorls, stones or glass. Pliny's account is highly implausible and was either a Druid's joke at his expense or a mythological account of their formation relating to a serpent cult that they originate from.

To most modern Druids it is most likely linked with the serpent, many of the various names meaning adder-stone, serpent-stone or serpent's egg. Serpents were associated with wisdom, so as the egg of a serpent they might have been thought to incubate wisdom or have regenerative power, like snakes that regenerate by shedding of the skin. Some use the egg as a means of grounding energy and it has also been used as a means of absorbing negative energy from the sick, wherein it is transformed and 'hatched' as positive energy. Unfortunately, there are no ancient accounts of how they are made (if that is the case) or how they should be used.

Cauldron/Chalice/Grail

Both Daghdha and Cerridwen possessed magical cauldrons. Daghdha's cauldron could revive dead warriors that were put into it and Cerridwen's cauldron was used to brew the three drops of wisdom that Gwion unwittingly received. Other properties such as infinite supply of food were also connected with the cauldron, which is often cited as the feminine equivalent of the rod/wand. Cauldrons were certainly of great ritual and social significance in Celtic society and many fine examples have been found in burials, perhaps the most famous being the impressive silver Gundestrup cauldron which must have been stolen from Ireland by Vikings, it now resides in the National Museum of Ireland. The sacred cauldron is the source of the Holy Grail Arthurian legends, a Christianisation of the magical healing properties associated with the cauldron. This concept of the regenerative cup or cauldron is not unique to Celtic culture and can be found around the world. It is thought to be associated with the land/mother goddess and the womb in the same way that the wand can be associated with the god and the phallus. The cauldron is also connected with cosmology - the three realms and the microcosmic world within humans i.e. the three cauldrons of vitality, vocation and wisdom.

In modern terms, the cauldron is used in performing spells, for the making of offerings, as a symbol of the divine feminine and also used shamanically regarding the inner energy flows (three cauldrons). The cup takes on the aspects of the divine feminine but it was also an important social item. The common cup was used at the *Aonach* (assembly) when kings and their entourage would dine together. The higher status people drank wine from silver cups and the lower ranks drank wheaten beer (called *corma* in Ireland), in both cases, a server would bring the cup around to all but passing it only in a sunwise direction. There are so many examples of the cauldron or cup in mythology and such a wealth of symbolism that a huge quantity of books have been written on this item alone; John and Caitlin Matthews have explored this area exhaustively in recent years and I would direct the reader towards their works for further investigation of this hallowed object.

Magical Branch

There are numerous accounts of magical branches being used in mythology, particularly from Ireland. Typically, the branch was silver with golden bells, usually carried by an otherworldy figure and on occasion given to heroes, sometimes it might be gold or bronze but most often silver. King Cormac received a silver branch with which he was able to heal his subjects. These branches usually had some magical property for example the music of the bells might lull all but the bearer to sleep. Sometimes the branch might have golden apples or blossom on them, an obvious link to the otherworld Tír na nÓg (land of the young) and various synonyms such as region of apples (Eamhain Abhlach), land of wonders pleasant plain, land of promise etc. Often the giving of the branch is a prelude to the hero entering the otherworld. It is said that the branch (*craebh ciuil*) was used by bards in mediations as a symbol of their authority. In modern Druidry and Celtic Shamanism the magical branch is used to call to the *sidhé* and deities invoked. It may also be used in the blessing of magical circles, their opening and closing and also in spiritual purification by waving it around the person in question.

Musical Instruments

The harp and the *bodhrán* are two instruments used in a modern context; however various horns and pipes were also availed of in ancient times. The harp is particularly associated with Irish Druidry and magical qualities; its function survives in European tales such as Jack and the Beanstalk. The *bodhrán* may originally have also doubled as a tray for sifting soil and that is certainly the case of 'frame drums' in some other ancient cultures. Although mainly used as a musical accompaniment in the usual manner it was also to be found in religious/cultural festivals: a perfect example being the hunting of the wren, in which the wren boys are accompanied by various musicians including *bodhrán* players. In modern Druidry and Celtic Shamanism the *bodhrán* is mostly used in *Immrama* to facilitate a trance state, although it is also common to see them played in processions or ritual celebrations as a means of raising energy, to accompany song or enliven the participants. For a full exploration of ancient Celtic music, I refer the reader to O'Curry's *Manners and Customs of the Ancient Irish* in three volumes, which covers this subject very extensively.

Crane Bag

The crane bag originates from a legend of Manannán Mac Lír, the magical bag literally being made from a crane's skin. Within this bag Manannán kept the blacksmith god Goibniu's hook, the King of Alba's shears, a fish-skin belt, the King of Lochlann's helmet, bones of Asal's boar and his knife although the bag was said to be empty at low tide and full again at high tide. The bag was given to Cumhall (father of Fionn), which Fionn had to recover after it was stolen. In the epic poem 'the Hostile Confederacy' Taliesin mentions his 'well-filled Crane bag', seemingly similar in concept to that possessed by Cumhall.

In modern terms, the crane bag is equated with the Native American 'medicine bag' and it is now a common tool of the Druid or Celtic Shaman. In most cases, one would make it, perhaps from leather or cloth and use it to hold herbs, ritual tools or any other useful magical items.

Sword

Druids did not generally use the sword in their Druidic functions. However, some warriors such as Cú Chulainn or Lugh, were also trained in magic (Druidry) and would hence possess a sword with which to fight. In general, Druids were involved in battle (e.g. Mogh Ruith) but they used magic such as curses, the elements (e.g. wind) and did not use physical weapons to procure a victory or advantage for their own side. We are all familiar with the sword of Arthur — Excalibur and perhaps also the sword of Tuatha Dé Danann King Nuada and the magical infallibility of these swords, not to mention their symbolic properties of protection, justice, strength and so on.

In modern Druidry, the sword is used as a ritual implement or as a Shamanic weapon in otherworldly encounters with entities. In Druid rituals a sword may be used as a symbolic link between the earth and sky, particularly at the Summer Solstice. Some Druidic orders have a sword bearer who carries it at their rituals.

Treasures

The four treasures of the Tuatha Dé Danann may be used in a ritual sense, although there is no evidence of them or representations of them being used by the ancient Druids. The four treasures of the Tuatha Dé Danann are the Spear of Lugh (from the city Gorias), the Sword of Nuada (from the city Findias), the Lia Fail (stone of destiny from the city Falias) and the cauldron of Daghdha (from the city Murias).

The treasures of Britain, referred to in the Welsh triads are: Dyrnwyn (white hilt), sword of Rhydderch, hamper of Bwyddno Garanhir, horn of Bran, chariot of Morgan, halter of Clydno Eiddyn, knife of Llawfronedd, cauldron of the giant Dyrnwch, whetstone of Tudwal Tydglyd, coat of Padaen, crock and dish of Rhygenydd, chessboard of Gwenddolau and the mantle of Arthur.

It is not uncommon for representations of the four treasures to be used in ritual, most often associated with the elements or directions. I do not know of any instance of representations of the thirteen treasures being used in Druid ritual, although that is not to say they have not or could not be used.

As I mentioned at the beginning of this chapter, all of the tools are only there to assist. The tools should be selected based on the purpose or symbolism in the performance of magic or ritual, use them with care and responsibility.

One last comment I might add is that it is infinitely preferable to find or make tools rather than to buy them. With use all tools take on the energy of the user although those that have been found by chance, are already in your possession or you have made specifically for use are going to be immediately more powerful in focusing your will.

XII

Divination

The art of foretelling the future, prophesy or divination has been an area of interest to humanity perhaps since the beginnings of civilisation, certainly since recorded history and it remains a preoccupation of many people around the world to this day. The Druids were well known for the practice of divination, this is corroborated by the accounts of classical authors, the extant Celtic texts and the mythology and folklore that has been handed down orally.

The classical authors mentioned various forms of divination, which includes the use of sacrificial human and animal victims. Some modern pagans and historians scoff at these descriptions, dismissing them as no more than political propaganda to aid the Roman suppression of the Druidic 'cult' in Gaul and Britain. Unfortunately, these accounts are so widespread, largely consistent with each other and also to some extent corroborated by later native descriptions of the use of animals and symbolic use of humans. It is most likely that in the earliest times both humans and animals were used for divination purposes and that use of the former ended under pressure from outside influences. I find it not so shocking a thing to accept this, as other cultures such as the Israelites, Japanese, Romans and Greeks practised similar activities in their infancy, as did the peoples of South America long after the ancient Druids had become a distant memory.

> The Druids consult the gods in the palpitating entrails of men
> Tacitus

Through auguries and animal sacrifice, these seers predict the future and no one dare to scoff at them. They have an especially odd and unbelievable method of divination for the most important matters. Having anointed a human victim, they stab him with a small knife in the area above the diaphragm. When the man has collapsed from the wound, they interpret the future by observing the nature of his fall, the convulsions of his limbs and especially from the pattern of his spurting blood.
Diodorus

Strabo described the Druids striking men down with a sword and watching their convulsions in order to predict the future. Human sacrifice was put down by the Romans in Galatia and then Gaul and according to Roman records it had ended completely (in Gaul) by 40 AD. Human sacrifice prevailed in Britain, which of course was invaded later than Gaul, however it was suppressed by the start of the 2nd century AD. There is no classical evidence pertaining to human sacrifice in Ireland, but this is no surprise as the Romans had very little contact with the Irish. The *Dindsenchas* (metrical poems) very clearly attest to the use of human sacrifice in Ireland, which would lead one to suppose that divination was also performed from the death throes of the victims. Again, one can claim that Christian monks undertook a propaganda campaign against their pagan predecessors, but however incredible these accounts are, it seems unlikely that the monks had sufficient ingenuity to forge whole passages convincingly in the same style and quality as the genuinely ancient passages.

In reference to Cromm Cruaich:

Milk and corn They would ask from him speedily,
In return for one third of their healthy issue.

In Welsh legend, Vortigern's Druids foretell that a child born with no father has to be sacrificed and his blood be sprinkled at the site of Vortigern's castle in order to prevent it falling again. This child grew up to be the Druid Merlin, who demonstrates his superior power of prophecy and hence is not slaughtered, although the story clearly illustrates human sacrifice.

An example of animal sacrifice is given in the Irish story of 'Da Derga's Hostel': whilst at the hostel King Conari/Conaire and his entourage notice various ominous portents (signs) such as the king's juggler dropping his balls for the first time ever or the howling of the king's dog Oscar. These portents were considered a warning of impending disaster which led Conari to tell his Druid Fer-Caillé 'Sacrifice your pig now and find out who is about to attack the hostel'. The Druid duly did as requested and from his observations foretold the attack on the hostel by Ingcel and his pirates and its subsequent destruction.

The technique *Imbas Forosnai,* which means 'illumination between the hands' was begun with the chewing of raw flesh from a freshly slaughtered animal (sometimes a dog). Raw flesh was placed as an offering to the gods of whom help was desired and the Druid then waited for inspiration. If no illumination was received by the next day incantations were recited over the palms of the hands and the Druid slept with his/her hand pressed against the cheeks. The information sought would then be received in the form of a dream or upon the Druid awakening.

Another ancient practice was the slaughter of a bull and the wearing of its hide whilst sleeping on a burial mound. The Druid would receive enlightenment in the form of a dream. A similar process (called *taghairm*) survived among the Scottish Highlanders, who slept in a desolate place whist wrapped in a cowhide. It was supposed that the seer would be visited by spirits or the gods whilst sleeping and the inspiration received in dreams. In Ireland sheep were sacrificed and the skin worn, not for divination but for the healing of the (sick) wearer.

In both Scotland and Ireland, looking into a sheep's shoulder blade was used to discover events in the distant future. In Britain, observing the path taken by a hare was used to foretell events. Birds were a common source of prophesy. In Ireland two birds in particular were significant – the crow/raven and the wren. Just prior to Cú Chulainn's death a crow lands on his shoulder, a symbol of his imminent demise. A bas-relief found at Compiegne in France shows two crows 'speaking' into the ears of a man. An account of crows being used to end a dispute is given by Artemidorus: two piles of food were left by each disputant, if the birds scattered one pile rather than eating it then he whose pile was eaten lost the dispute.

The Irish Druids listened to the sound of birds as a way of divining and this was commonly practised. The chirping of the wren or croak of the raven was particularly auspicious and a key to interpreting the sounds in book form was said to exist. The wren (as discussed earlier) had particular significance symbolically and as an oracular bird, one of its old names *drean* is possibly derived from *drui-én* which means 'druid of birds'.

> ...they have soothsayers too of great renown who tell the future by watching the flight of birds and the entrails of victims; and everyone waits upon their word.
> Diodorus Siculus

Calling upon the dead was a popular Celtic method of divination, the most famous example (discussed earlier) being Murgan's recovery of the *Táin Bo Cuailgne*. Sleeping upon a burial mound was one way of consulting the dead and to this day it is said that one can receive wisdom from the spirits of the dead by sleeping upon the Mound of the Hostages at Tara. An example of such practice, from the second century BC, is given by Nicander of Colophon:

> It is often said because of visions in dreams that the dead truly live. The Nasamones receive special oracles by staying at the tombs of their parents, as Heraclides — or Nymphodorus or Herodotus — writes. The Celts also for the same reason spend the night near tombs of their famous men.

Other forms of observational divination existed such as the direction of movement of smoke, flames of sacred fires, stars and planets or clouds or even people sneezing. Observation of clouds was a common form of augury: the chief Druid Doghra used this technique at *Samhain* to foretell the year ahead for High King Dathi. Doghra spent the night on top of *Dumha na n-Druadh* (Druid's mound) near *Rath Archaill* looking at the clouds. At sunrise he returned to the king and said to him 'Art thou asleep, O king of Erin and Alba?' He went on to explain that Dathi would successfully conquer Scotland (Alba), Britain (Wales and England) and Gaul (France), which he supposedly did with the aid of the armies of all the provinces of Ireland. It is said that Dathi reached the Alps, defeating all before him but was killed by a bolt of lightning, after which the Irish returned home bringing Dathi with them to lie with his ancestors at *Rath Cruachain*.

The old Irish (*gaeilge*) *néladóir* means 'diviner' or 'astrologer' and *néladóracht* means 'cloud divination', also the words *nél, néul* and *néll* mean 'cloud' in modern Irish, which lends weight to the belief that this was indeed a common form of divination.

It is undoubted that the Celts practised astrology — reading the stars. A legend of St. Columcille (Columba) states that his foster father consulted a Druid with regard to the beginning of his education; the Druid scanned the heavens before pronouncing that the boy's lessons should start immediately. Unfortunately, whatever method of astrology the Druids used is now lost which leaves the modern Druid astrologer with the sole option of using Ptolemic (Greek/Egyptian) astrology, which has survived into the modern age.

Another Irish method was *Teinm Laegha*. After performing a sacrifice the Druid or *Filé* would repeat a verse (like a mantra) over the person or thing that was the object of the knowledge sought, he/she might also touch the person's body, thereby obtaining the required knowledge. A form of singing was also used. The Druid sang a *Cétnad* through the loosely clenched fist in order to discover the whereabouts of a stolen item or the thief. Another *Cétnad* was sung to the 'seven daughters of the sea' in order to find out how long a person was to live. One can only assume several forms of this incantation existed, varying depending on the type of information that was to be discovered.

Another method, reminiscent of that used at the Delphic oracle, involved the *filé* being lulled into a deep sleep during which he/she would receive illumination and speak out whilst apparently still asleep. The Druid would seemingly be in an ecstatic trance, something akin to a sleepwalker and mixed in with random shouts, roars and moans would be the information sought. These utterances were believed to be caused by spirits who would leave at the Druid's awakening, leaving them with no apparent memory of what had passed. This method, common to Wales and Ireland was called 'illumination by rhymes'.

The gaelic word *baile* meaning 'ecstasy' refers to such methods whereby the Druid achieved a suitable trance state, perhaps through dancing, vigorous and frenzied movements or meditations. It is also stated that the crane posture – one eye covered, whilst standing on one leg with one arm free, was often used whilst prophesising, whether in a trance state or otherwise is not clear.

The Druid in a trance state was often unintelligible; the Delphic oracles who would inhale vapours produced a similar verbal deluge, which was then interpreted by priests. A similar method of prophecy exists today, in which the same ecstatic state is brought about, usually through meditation, drumming, staring into a pool of water (scrying), staring into flames or singing. I have witnessed this 'trance-utterance' form of prophesy myself and it appears to be quite popular among Druids, Wiccans and mediums in general.

The eating of acorns or hazel nuts from the tree surrounding Connla's sacred well was meant to provide prophetic inspiration. It is also thought that certain hallucinogenic herbs and mushrooms were used as a means of divination.

Perhaps the most famous form of Druidic divination is the use of wooden rods/sticks. In the story of Queen Etain's abduction by fairy king Midir the Druid Dallan used four yew rods with Ogham writing on them to divine where she was. The first known reference to Ogham is that from 'Gallic War' by Julius Caesar, describing Druids in Gaul writing on wooden staves. What we know of Ogham comes primarily from two main sources — the 'Ogham Tract' and *The Scholar's Primer* (*Auraicept na n-Éces*) and secondary information comes from mentions in mythology.

Ogham divination has been 'reinvented' in the 20th century, largely inspired by the work of Robert Graves. There are various methods suggested for use of the Ogham alphabet as a divination tool. Some use sticks of hazel, each carved with a different Ogham, some use yew wands with four or five Oghams (one per side) and others use wood of each respective tree to represent each Ogham letter. Generally, the divination technique involves throwing them on the ground or onto a sheet. Some also recommend use of 'Fionn's window/wheel' based on an illustration in the *Book of Ballymote*. This set of concentric circles featuring Ogham symbols is used in conjunction with the staves/sticks however there is no ancient method extant to enable one to use it correctly and besides there is no proof that it originates from the Druidic era. Some authors, such as Searles O'Dubhain have worked out methods of utilising this wheel, although it is not possible to ascertain the correctness of these methods due to the lack of empirical evidence. There are various interpretations of the medieval glosses referring to Ogham, which adds further confusion to what is already a complex area to begin with. I shall explore this subject in depth in the next chapter and make no further mention of it here.

Mention of Fionn's Wheel brings me to the next method of divination — 'wheel divination'. The best example of this is that of ancient Munster Druid Mogh Ruith (from Daibre or Valentia Island in Kerry) who was famed for his skill in the use of this method. Of him it was written 'Mogh Ruith signifies Magus rotatum, the wizard (or devotee) of the wheel, for it is by the wheels he used to make his *taiscéladh druidh-echata* or "magical observation"'. Interestingly his name actually translates as 'devotee of the wheel'. His daughter, who gives her name to Tlachta (Hill of Ward) the pre-eminent place of *Samhain*, was said to have learnt magic with him in the East (the Levant?). She made a *roth ramhach* or 'rowing wheel' which among other uses could be used for divination. It is also interesting to note that the ancient solar god of the Gauls is sometimes depicted holding a wheel — perhaps the source of this divinatory power? In addition, it is perhaps not mere chance that Tlachta, a prophetess and wheel diviner, is associated with *Samhain* — the most auspicious time for divination.

Another Irish form of divination, that bears similarity to Ogham or Runes is the 'Leary Stones', also known as Kerry Stones or Gypsy Runes, which are supposedly derived from the sea god Lír. Use of the stones is a bit like playing the French game Boule. An eye stone (painted with an eye) is thrown and the remaining nine stones thrown together towards it. If the stones land with the image down they are ignored, otherwise their distance from the eye stone relates to the relevance or distance in time. If a stone lands image up right on the eye stone it is of great significance.

There is a special method of making a set of stones: they

should be collected (ten stones) from the sea just after high tide, preferably on a full moon. The stones must be soaked in salt water for one night and thereafter in fresh water for one night. After this, they can be dried, blessed and consecrated and painted/varnished with the symbols as so desired. The symbols are available from some Druid orders and can also be found on the internet. I have used this very simple method myself and can confirm its efficacy – whether or not this is genuinely Druidic remains to be seen, I have not found any evidence to support it being a survival from ancient times.

A modern form of divination that is very popular among Druids and pagans generally is oracle cards, although these have no history in Celtic culture. These are in essence the same as Tarot cards, which are proven to originate from no later than the 14th century in Italy, although it has been suggested that they are far older. This is a system that has served magi and spiritual practitioners for centuries and has a proven track record, hence its continued popularity. In the last decade especially, a plethora of new decks have appeared; some alternative visualisations of Tarot and others Oracle Decks with completely different correspondences and imagery from traditional Tarot cards.

Personally, I learnt the basics of Tarot long before I had ever seen a 'Green Man' deck or other such new innovations and I feel quite happy to use my traditional Tarot deck as a general divination tool. I do not consider it to be a Druidic divination tool nor do I consider its offshoots to be so either. Attractive and interesting as these new decks may be I find them superfluous when, for me, the tried and tested traditional Tarot is perfectly good. This is a highly subjective and personal opinion, so I would encourage you to explore both Tarot and its Oracle variants if you are drawn to the use of cards. Ultimately, each of us needs to find methods that work for us and that we feel comfortable with, I suggest that you experiment and form your own judgement.

This concludes my investigation of divination methods; however, I feel that a few points should be discussed. Firstly, the majority of original Druidic methods of divination are sadly lost to us or we are left with only a vague description of the method, which is of no practical use. The methods, which we can employ such as Ogham, trance-utterance and scrying, are approximations, although perhaps equally valid. I have come across people touting their methods as archaic and original where clearly this is an impossibility, so beware of such charlatans – many methods of divination do work but do not be fooled into thinking that modern reinventions of ancient practices are faithful to the original methods.

Secondly, I would like to warn against the over reliance on divination, I have met people who seem reluctant to get out of bed without consulting their cards first. An Arabic tale of a merchant who receives a fortune predicting his death in the city he inhabits leads to him fleeing. On reaching the gates of the city, he is attacked by robbers and killed, thus fulfilling the prophecy. This story is a valuable lesson in the need for caution, sometimes when we know our own future it changes the outcome. Sometimes we are better off not knowing what is ahead of us, particularly if the future is ominous.

I do not use divination on a regular basis, I choose to make my own luck and steer my own ship, only when I am confused or have a particularly difficult decision to make do I consult my divination tools. Of greater importance than use for oneself is the responsibility of performing divination for others. I cannot stress enough the huge responsibility one bears in taking on such a task, although it is a person's own choice to consult a seer, one must be careful to provide this service in a way that is beneficial to them. Some practitioners will refuse to pass on bad news, others will refuse to read for people that they consider unstable or incapable of coping with divinatory revelations. This is, of course, a personal judgement call and I can only suggest that one talk to prospective clients before agreeing to engage in divination on their behalf.

Decisions of this nature are ethical and these decisions can often be coloured by money — there is nothing at all wrong with a financial charge or exchange for this service, however it is not always easy to turn away custom when it is your main or sole income. I have never charged anyone for divination, but I am fortunate in that my income from other employment is sufficient to enable me to provide my services free. I would advise the diviner to follow one's instincts, be true to one's principles and always tell the truth. Some though have difficulties with being the bearer of ill news, even despite the fact that often divulgence may later on turn out to be for the best. If you feel it is necessary to omit certain details it is at least better to do this than to tell an outright lie.

XIII

Ogham

The Ogham alphabet and its uses is an area that has been covered extensively in modern esoteric literature, particularly since the publication of Robert Graves's *The White Goddess* (first edition 1948), it was also an area of interest to Celtic scholars in the preceding century following translations by O'Curry, Calder Joyce and so forth.

In recent years, it has been critically re-examined by Celtic scholars such as Damien McManus, Niall MacCoitir and Druids such as Searles O'Dubhain, which I believe throws new light on the subject and provides a more viable interpretation of the alphabet than what has become the accepted norm in pagan circles. I shall come to this in due course, but first let us look at the origins of Ogham and its development.

As I stated in the previous chapter, the first mention of anything resembling Ogham is that of Julius Caesar in Gaul over two thousand years ago, although no actual examples of Ogham Stones exist in France or Belgium. If indeed it is the case that Ogham or similar symbols were carved only on wood by the Gauls that would easily explain the absence of archaeological evidence. Pliny also describes the use of yew rods cast upon the ground (again in Gaul) which may or may not be equivalent to the Irish method of divination that uses Ogham. Examples of Ogham itself can be found on stones in Scotland, Wales, Isle of Man, Cornwall and Ireland although the vast majority of Ogham stones are to be found in south west Ireland.

It is considered that the original Ogham list was of just eight letters[22], which hardly constitutes an alphabet, however it would have been sufficient to convey simple messages or act as a divination set. When we consider that the ancient Greeks inherited their alphabet from the Phoenicians, which possessed no vowels and hence was limited in terms of expression, perhaps this is not dissimilar to Ireland. The Greeks added the vowel, which gave rise to a massive increase in written vocabulary, poetry and the first creative flowering of classical literature. It is believed that the Phoenicians had contact with Britain and Ireland and it is quite possible that they had influence on the development of writing in these countries too.

In Wales a similar system to Ogham may have existed — *Coelbren y Beirdd* as described in *Barddas* and attributed to LLywelyn Sion. Apparently, the ancient Druids cut letters upon staves of wood that were then held in a wooden frame, thus creating a 'book' of sorts. *Barddas* gives the exact method of construction of this frame and the staves and also the sixteen 'primitive letters' and the later 26 letter alphabet, which appears somewhat similar to Norse Runes. Scant evidence exists to corroborate the claims of *Barddas*, which is known to contain a fair amount of forged material, although that does not mean that the *Coelbren y Beirdd* did not exist.

Whatever, the case may be regarding the origin of early alphabets in the British Isles and Gaul, the Irish Ogham list increased from eight to fourteen, then twenty and finally twenty-five with the addition of what is called *Forfeda* or supplementary letters at a relatively recent (medieval) period. This may have occurred due to outside influence as these extra letters made it easier to render foreign words into *Gaeilge*. It is highly likely that Ogham originated in Ireland, and Irish accounts and stories attest to that being the case; the existence of Ogham in Wales and Scotland is most likely due to Irish settlements in those countries and in the case of Scotland, the gradual process of *Gaeilge* becoming the predominant language.

In modern terms, Ogham has several uses — a form of writing *Gaeilge* (note Ogham does not make any sense if used in any other language as it does not contain all of the Roman alphabet). Secondly, it is used as a divination tool. Thirdly, it is a system of tree knowledge, the Ogham symbols acting as mnemonics. Fourthly, Ogham represents a tree calendar to modern Druids, however its existence in ancient times is still hotly debated. I shall take each of these uses in turn and do my best to elucidate them.

Ogham — The Gaelic Tree Alphabet

The Ogham's origin is attributed primarily to the Irish God Ogma Grianaineach (meaning either youthful or sunface) or Ogma Mac Elathan – the god of knowledge and eloquence, who is thought to be equivalent to the Gaulish Ogmios. This form of letters and also speech was certainly in use up until the Norman conquest and was learned exclusively among the learned classes, '...this speech should belong to the learned apart, to the exclusion of rustics and herdsmen'.[23] There are various ideas about Ogham as a form of sign language using the hands to represent the lines on the stave. However, as with the theory about speech, I could find no substantial evidence to corroborate this, although Ogham speech and variant forms such as 'Cow Ogham and 'Bird Ogham' are mentioned in some ancient sources.

The other source of origins of Ogham is from the 'Ogham Tract' and *The Scholar's Primer* (*Auraicept na n-Éces*) which describes the adventures of Fenius, supposed progenitor of the Irish language who brought *Gaeilge* back from the Tower of Nimrod in the far East, one of 72 languages existing from the 72 'counsellors' present at the building of the tower. This is an interesting tale but clearly pure fabrication, based on the biblical tale of the Tower of Babel. Considering this book (which is a capitulation and compilation of earlier sources) was produced by Christian monks, it should be no surprise that its contents be in some way connected to the Judeo-Christian tradition rather than its more likely pagan origin.

Indigestible, repetitious and convoluted as this volume of

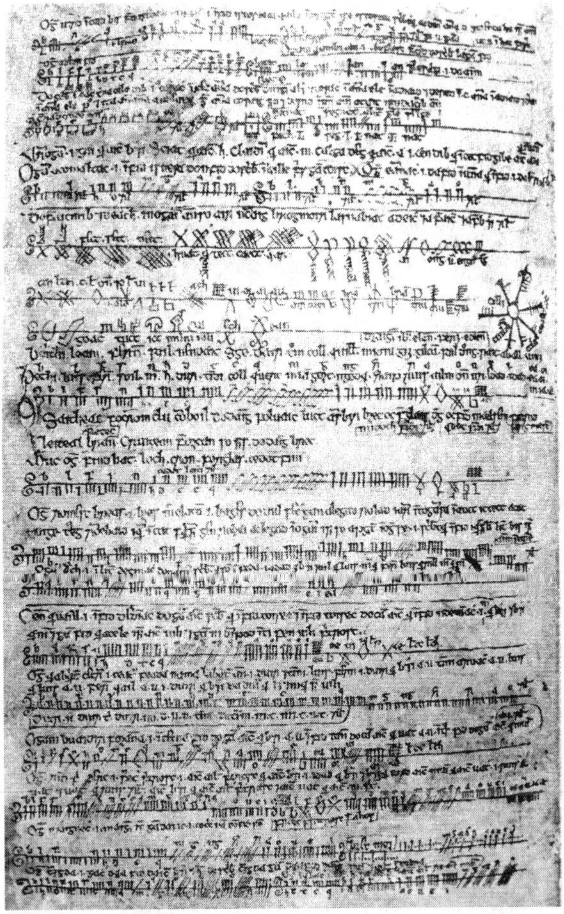

work is, it does throw considerable light on how Ogham was written, the meanings of the various symbols and their correspondences and in fact also gives Ogma as the source of Ogham writing itself, describing him as a man rather than a God. Although Ogham writing was generally found on stones, written from bottom to top using the corner/edge (*druim*) as the vertical divide, Ogham was also carved on wood and written on paper in later times. The *Scholar's Primer*, translated by Calder, gives examples including reproductions of pages from earlier books in *Gaeilge* and *Beth-Luis-Nin* which is the Irish name for Ogham script, meaning 'birch, rowan letter' (*Beith* and *Luis* being the first letters in Irish as alpha and beta are in the Greek alphabet). An example of a plate from *The Scholar's Primer* (showing original source material of *Beith-Luis-Nin*, together with Gaeilge in the romanised Irish alphabet) is given opposite. It is interesting to note that the Irish version of the Roman alphabet still only contained twenty Roman letters until the 1960s after which more were introduced, the traditional shapes of letters dropped and accents, such as the *bualte* on aspirated words, were largely abandoned in favour of the sounded letter (e.g. h) to create a modern European form of *Gaeilge*. Examples of the older Irish alphabet can occasionally still be seen on old street and shop signs all over Ireland. The process of *béarlochas* or 'Englishisation' of *Gaeilge* continues today with the addition of letters V, W, X, Y and Z and blatantly gaelicised English words. However, in the case of Ogham, which has a mere 20 proper letters, it is not possible to render all modern European words into Ogham and one should not even think of doing so, it was created for *Gaeilge* and is non transferable to other languages.

Moving on to the writing of Ogham itself: in general the *druim* is vertical, certainly in the case of stones, however for the purpose of writing on paper, as the example page demonstrates, the *druim* was usually horizontal, running from left to right. Although roughly half the names of the letters are actual tree names, the remainder refer to some attribute of the tree or poetic names that are of an arboreal theme. I believe that the reason for this is that there were not sufficient native tree names (beginning with appropriate letters) to cover all of the necessary Ogham letters and hence other appropriate words were chosen.

The terminology pertaining to the alphabet itself is all related to trees: the name *Beith-Luis-Nin*, letters collectively are called *feda* (meaning woods) and individual letters are called *fid* (meaning tree). The term *nin* also has the dual meaning of letter and 'branch fork'. The term *feda* is also used to refer to just the vowels and the consonants are called *tábomnai* (meaning side of a tree-trunk); lastly the single lines or scores of each letter are referred to as *flesc* (meaning twig), all of which should leave us in no doubt as to the arboreal nature of this alphabet. *The Scholar's Primer* also states that Ogham is read as a tree is climbed – from the bottom to the top.

The 25 letters of the *Beith-Luis-Nin* are as follows, given in correct order (bottom to top) given in their five groupings of five, together with their Roman equivalents.

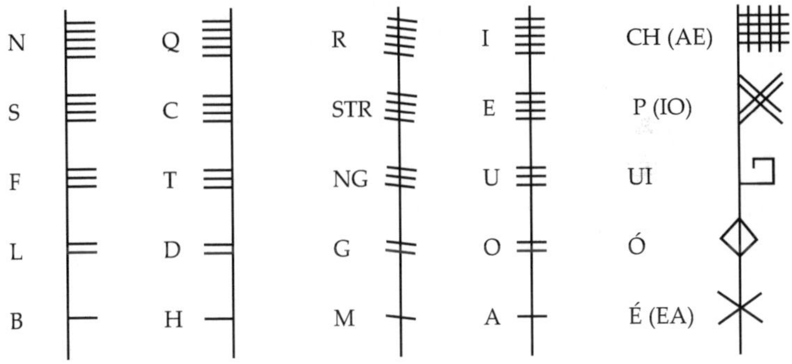

The word-oghams (*briatharogaim*), which are short poetical descriptions associated with each letter, are derived from the *Scholar's Primer* and the *Ogham Tract*, giving three sets of 'glosses'. These are in old Irish rather than the medieval Irish of the time of compiling these works. These three lists are called *Briatharogaim: Morainn mic Moín, Maic ind Óc, Cú Chulainn* and the three do not concur with one another, plus further confusion exists due to the difficulty of correctly translating the Old Irish into modern English.

There are a variety of interpretations of the three glosses given by modern writers, however I am only aware of two writers who have seriously endeavoured to return to the original source texts and re-translate the Old Irish into modern English, these being Damian McManus and Niall MacCoitir, both of whom are well versed in the Irish language. Hence, I have chosen, after reading their works, to rely on their interpretations and dispense with the earlier and generally accepted translations of the glosses and the names of trees associated with them. I believe that in time these two gentlemen will be proved to be correct, as is often the case in both history and science, what is held for truth is eventually superseded by new and more rigorous investigations.

Therefore, from here onwards I will refer to the tree list given by MacCoitir and the glosses as translated by McManus and MacCoitir. The table on the next page gives this information in English, although the Irish text together with an in-depth discussion of his research is also available in 'Irish Trees: Myths, Legends and Folklore' by Niall MacCoitir.

Ogham	**Letter**	**Tree**	**List A**	**List B**	**List C**
Beith	B	Birch	Withered foot with fine hair	Greyest skin	Beauty of eyebrow
Luis	L	Rowan	Lustre of Eye	Friend of cattle	Sustenance of cattle
Fern	F	Alder	Vanguard of warriors	Milk container	Protection of the heart
Sail	S	Willow	Pallor of a lifeless one	Sustenance of bees	Beginning of honey
Nin	N	Cherry	Otherworld sustenance	Boast of women	Boast of beauty
Huath	H	Hawthorn	Assembly of hounds	Blanching of faces	Most difficult at night

Ogham	Letter	Tree	List A	List B	List C
Dair	D	Oak	Most exalted of trees	Work of craftsman	Most carved of craftmanship
Tinne	T	Holly	Third part of a wheel	Marrow of charcoal	Third part of a weapon
Coll	C	Hazel	Fairest tree, edible nutty	Friends of nutshells	Sweetest tree
Qert	Q	Apple	Shelter of the wounded	Power of the weak	Dregs of clothing
Muin	M	Buckthorn	Strongest in action, most noble goodliness	Proverb of slaughter	Path of the voice
Gort	G	Gorse	Sweetest grass, greenest pasture	Suitable place for cows	Satisfaction of all
NGétal	NG	Broom	Sustenance of a leech	Raiment/ strength of physicians	Beginning of slaying
STRaif	STR	Blackthorn	Strongest reddening dye, chief of streams, dam of a river, hedge/dam of blackthorn	Increase of secrets	Seeking of clouds, arrow of the clouds

Ogham	Letter	Tree	List A	List B	List C
Ruis	R	Elder	Most intense blushing Hue of the eye	Reddening of faces	Glow of anger
Ailm	A	Pine	Loudest groan	Beginning of an answer	Beginning of calling
Onn	O	Ash	Wounder/ Helper of horses	Smoothest of craftmanship	Sustenance of warriors
Ur	U	Elm	In cold dwellings, most devoted sharing	Propagation/ dripping of plants	Shroud of a lifeless one
Edad	E	Aspen	Discerning/ satirising tree	Exchange of friends	Brother of birch
Idad	I	Yew	Oldest Tree	Fairest of ancients, most beautiful in age	Sustenance of a leper
Édad	É (EA)	Aspen	Fair swimming letter Water letter (?)	Prevention of leper	Fairest fish

Ogham	Letter	Tree	List A	List B	List C
Ór	Ó	Spindle	Most venerable	Splendour of form	-
Ullen	UI	Juniper	Fragrant tree	Great elbow/ cubit	-
Pín	P (IO)	Gooseberry	Sweetest Tree	Most wonderful taste	-
CHoll	CH (AE)	Hazel	Groan of the sick	Groan of the ill	-

Note that list C does not give a single *briathurogaim* for the supplementary letters (*Forfeda*), one can only presume that list C pre-dates the introduction of these five letters. These were mainly used for rendering Greek and Roman words into Irish and hence there are relatively few examples of their use.

The order of the *Forfeda* is seemingly arbitrary, however Mac-Coitir posits an interesting theory regarding their association with the five senses:

Ebad/Aspen	noted for the rustling/whispering sound of its leaves
Ór/Spindle	noted for the visually impressive sight of its fruit in autumn
Uilen/Juniper	noted for the aromatic smell of its leaves and also the wood when burned
Pín/Gooseberry	noted for the sweetness of its berries
Emancholl/Hazel	noted for the nourishing quality of its nuts

Although the last tree relates to sustenance or strength, Mac-Coitir explains that the *Forfeda* relates more to the five organs:

ears, eyes, nose mouth and heart. In folklore, the nut is often linked to the heart, hence the expression 'O nut of my heart' (*a chnó mo chroíse*).

The first instance of Ogham writing (according to legend) was a message left on a single birch rod for the God Lugh. The message was seven single strokes representing the letter B seven times. Lugh interpreted this message as meaning that the *Sidhé* would carry off his wife into their *Dún* seven times unless she was protected with birch.

Ogham appears again, used by Cú Chulainn in the *Táin Bo Cuailgne*. Firstly, he left a message via an oak sapling, also bending it into a hoop, secured with a wooden peg on which the message was cut. Apparently, this was all done whilst in the Druidic pose of standing on one leg, with one eye closed and using just one arm. The hoop was left around a standing stone for the Munster men to find, which was duly found by Fergus Mac Roich (leading the forces of Queen Maebh). The message translates thus: 'Come no further, unless you have a man who can make a hoop such as this with one hand out of one piece. I exclude my friend Fergus.'

Fergus showed the Munster Druids the hoop, being somewhat bemused by it, and it was explained that a great hero had done this alone and that they could not progress further until the feat had been equalled by one among their party. In doing this, Cú Chulainn was able to delay the Munster men by a day, buying him valuable time in his single-handed defence of Ulster. This message disproves the commonly touted theory that Ogham was only used for the briefest of messages, the equivalent of signposts, clearly it was possible to write complex sentences and the sentence of Cú Chulainn is a perfect example of this.

Ogham as a Divination Tool

The list of meanings/glosses given is rather cryptic but it is from this information that modern Druids attempt to interpret the divinatory meaning of the oghams. In the Irish tale 'The Wooing of Etain' or *Tochmarc Etaine* the Druid Dalan uses Ogham divination to locate Etain who has been kidnapped by the fairy (*sidhé*) king Midir. To do this he cut four wands of yew and cut three oghams on each and cast them (termed *eochra ecsi*, perhaps translating as 'keys of divination'). There is no record of how the oghams were interpreted; most probably the Druid had this committed to memory. One can only hope that the glosses given in the *Ogham Tract* and *The Scholar's Primer* are derived from the Druids themselves for that purpose, the use of old Irish lends itself to the possibility that the glosses had survived from antiquity into the medieval period.

If you look at the three lists, one can see that they are not easily interpreted; we must assume they would have made greater sense to the Druids of fifteen hundred or more years ago. It is of course entirely possible that they relate only to the trees and are not meant to be used for divination at all. Despite the obvious difficulty of ascertaining the meaning, authors such as Caitlin Matthews have made brave attempts to unravel the meanings of the glosses in terms of divination; her guide to Ogham accompanying her set of Ogham rods might be useful for those wishing to attempt this method of divination. There are various other Druids and Shamans who have attempted this labyrinthine task, although some of them were inspired by the largely erroneous *The White Goddess* by Robert Graves. Graves was not a Celtic scholar; he was a Classical scholar, poet and novelist. Unfortunately he failed to consult either his father of grandfather in the writing of *The White Goddess*, both of whom were respected Celtic scholars, which unfortunately led to them severely criticising the inaccuracies and assumptions when this work was published.

Searles O'Dubhain is another Druid who has done much research into Ogham as a divinatory tool and gives a method that utilises Fionn's Wheel, which is a circular diagram drawn on a cloth, the Ogham rods are thrown all at once over it. O'Dubhain gives his own method of interpreting where the sticks land and also makes use of the glosses. Interesting as his theory is, this is his own invention or reconstruction and sadly, there is no archaic method available for either reading the Oghams or using Fionn's Wheel/Window.

Ogham as a System of Tree Knowledge

The importance of trees in ancient Celtic culture can hardly be overstated. We know from classical accounts, early Welsh and Irish literature, and Celtic folklore that trees were reverenced by the Druids and highly valued by the Celts in general. Some of the Gaulish tribes took their names from trees, and of the Gaulish Druids' veneration of trees, oak especially is well recorded. In Ireland, the *bile/craebh* or sacred tree was common and tribes possessed one or more *Bile Buadha* or 'tree of power'. Ironically, it was not uncommon for enemy tribes to attempt to destroy the *Bile Buadha* of other tribes during conflict. Such an act was a terrible desecration and humiliation – the 'Annals of the Four Masters' describes such events for example the uprooting of the bile of the *Magh Adhair* or destruction of the O'Neill's *bile* in Co. Tyrone. In some cases, the same event occurred again in the same location, so obviously new trees had been planted to replace those destroyed. Being a spiritual symbol of the tribe, linked in most cases with otherworldly power it was considered essential that they were replaced if disaster struck.

In Ireland, there were five particular *Bile Buadha* considered to be sacred above all others, these corresponding with the five ancient provinces – Leinster, Munster, Connaught, Ulster and the now redundant Meath (now two counties). All five of these stood near sacred sites or sites of royal importance for example *Bile Tortan* stood near Tara; further details of these sacred trees and place name origins for the whole of Ireland appear in the metrical *Dindshenchus* (poems) that have survived into modern times.

An immense amount of tree lore exists in Ireland, Britain and France to this day and fortunately much that has been forgotten has been written down long ago so that it may be rediscovered. We shall come to some of this in the next few pages, although what I have provided, in summary form, is as insignificant in content as a drop is to the sea and thus merits further investigation elsewhere if the reader wishes to fully explore this subject.

Before I present the tree knowledge in summary I should also mention the importance of trees in early Celtic law – unwarranted destruction of trees was punishable and the Celts generally lived a far more nomadic and naturalistic life than other civilisations such as the Greeks, Romans or Persians. Gaul, Cisapline Gaul, northern Iberia, Britain and Ireland were all heavily wooded with towns and villages of relatively small size, usually constructed from wood, mud and thatch. In Ireland and Britain particularly people lived in small semi-nomadic communities that were separated from each other by sometimes huge stretched of woodland. It was said that the red squirrel could travel from Donegal to Kerry (in Ireland) without having to touch the ground; such was the extent of woodland. Human reliance on woodland for food, fuel, for livestock, plus raw materials for weaponry, chariots, housing, medicines and metalworking (furnaces) was extremely high, hence it was preserved and protected as much as possible. It is therefore no surprise that the Druids enforced reverence and respect for trees through the laws.

In Ireland, these laws were codified at an early stage (eighth century or possibly earlier) in the *Bretha Comaithchesa* or 'Neighbourhood Laws'. It is thought that an earlier form of tree law existed – *Fidbretha* or 'Tree Judgements', which was mentioned in other texts. The tree laws of Ireland classify trees into four classes of tree and bush – noble (*airig fedo*), commoner (*aithig fedo*), lower division (*fodla fedo*) and bushes (*losa fedo*). There are seven native species in each class and the class attributed to a tree depends on its economic value for example quality and volume of timber, food value, suitability as fuel or weaponry and so forth. The penalties for unwarranted damage or destruction of trees varied according to the class of the tree, with the fine for felling a noble tree being the value of two and one half milk cows. This may not appear so great a sum to the modern reader, however this would represent a small fortune to the average Irishman of the late Iron Age or early medieval period. It has been suggested that in Gaul that the ultimate price – execution, was paid by those who felled an oak tree, although I have not found any texts that corroborate this claim.

In Wales, a system very similar to the Irish laws existed, with fines on a sliding scale dependent upon the perceived value of the tree or trees felled or damaged. Laws instituted by King Howel Dda in or around 950 AD gave fines for up to one pound for a sacred (saint's) yew, which was an enormous sum of money at the time.

Trees also feature heavily in folklore, poetry and in place names in addition to what I have already discussed, however those areas could constitute a book in themselves. So now having discussed some aspects of tree knowledge let us move on to the trees of the Ogham alphabet (*Beith-Luis-Nin*) and the knowledge relating to each of them.

Beith, Beithe (Birch) B ⊢

First consonant of the *Beith-Luis-Nin*
Third month of the Ogham Tree Calendar 27th Dec – 23rd Jan
COMMONER OF THE WOOD (*Aithig Fedo*)

Renowned for beauty, fast growing, used in brooms and brushes and also for beating, the Birch was used for corporal punishment in Scotland up until the 1980s. Birch symbolises birth, rebirth, youth, love and purity.

It is one of the first trees to colonise new ground and one of the first to come into leaf in spring. It is best suited to a cooler climate and is native to northerly countries such as Finland, Russia and Mongolia as well as the British Isles and France. Some arboriculturists believe that if average global temperatures continue to rise that Birch may disappear from the most southern areas of England and Ireland.

Folklore: Birch is put over cradles to protect children and is thought to promote fertility. It is a symbol of love in mythology, of maidenhood and it is often compared to a beautiful young woman. Birch features in summer festivals, particularly the maypole at Bealtaine.

Interestingly the silver Birch was associated with maidens, virginity and purity whilst the weeping Birch was associated with wisdom, experience and the crone/old woman.

Birch offers purity and protection against evil. The sidhé or fairies do not like this tree, for example, Birch was used to protect Lugh's wife Eriu.

Burials took place with Birch branches placed into the grave – a symbol of rebirth after death.

The Birch was associated with Angus Og (god of love) and Cú Chulainn. It was also associated with Brigid and the end of winter in addition to the beginning of summer (*Bealtaine*).

Practical uses: Brooms, dyes, tanning, preserving fishing line. It was used in saunas and sweat lodges for the purpose of purification. It was used for corporal punishment and also as a teacher's staff. Birch bark was also an ancient and excellent form of kindling for lighting fires.

Therapeutic uses: Tar from the bark treats eczema, an infusion treats cystitis. It can be used in saunas to stimulate circulation and eases arthritic and rheumatic pain. The sweet sap of Birch can be used to make wine. Used in the treatment of ear, nose and throat infections. Said to cure impotence, exhaustion and fatigue by calming the adrenal glands and said to be beneficial for stress or disharmony related ailments. Birch oil (from *Betula alba*) is used as analgesic, antiseptic, astringent, depurative, disinfectant, diuretic, febrifuge, insecticide and as a tonic.

It is advisable for pregnant women to avoid ingestion.

Luis **(Rowan) L ╞**

Second consonant of the *Beith-Luis-Nin*
Fourth month of the Ogham Tree Calendar 24th Jan – 20th Feb
COMMONER OF THE WOOD (*Aithig Fedo*)

Also known as *Caorthann* and commonly as Mountain Ash or the Quicken Tree it has formidable powers of protection. It is a fast growing tree which prospers on high ground, producing early buds in Spring and bright red/orange berries from late Summer onwards.

Folklore: It was hung over doorways and in houses as protection. It protects milk from the fairies and malign spellcraft. Trees were often planted near the house, especially near the front door to ward off evil. The branches wrapped in a red thread or the berries were thought to be especially protective. In the story of Mogh Ruith's defence of Munster the rowan is burnt to great effect in aiding him to drive a Druidic wind and clouds of fire and blood northwards towards the forces of Cormac Mac Airt. There is also an ancient Irish legend 'The Fairy Palace of the Quicken Trees' which again features High King Cormac mac Airt.

Rowan is associated with fire, *Bealtaine,* protection of both livestock and the home. The berries have magical properties and are also edible but have a poor taste. Rowan is a druids' tree '*Fid na nDruad'*. It is associated with early spring, *Imbolc* and the goddess Brighid. In myth, the first woman is said to have sprung from a Rowan tree.

Practical uses: The berries were used in jam making and also to make a drink. Berries for jam should be stored in vinegar overnight and blanched before addition to other fruits. A valuable magical protection, divining rods: especially for metal divining.

Therapeutic uses: Used in gemotherapy and divination. It can be used as a lymphatic drainer. It is a mild diuretic and purgative and is also used for menstrual or kidney pain.

Fearn **(Alder) F ᚃ**

Third consonant of the *Beith-Luis-Nin*
Fifth month of the Ogham Tree Calendar 21st Feb – 20th Mar
COMMONER OF THE WOOD (*Aithig Fedo*)

Also known as *Fearnóg*, or *Fern* this is the tree of war or death. The wood turns red, a symbol of blood, a colour also associated with warriors in ancient times and royalty in later periods. This tree is associated with fire (red) and also water as it grows particularly fast in marshes or on bog land. The wood does not rot easily as it is extremely resistant to water.

Folklore: It is said that the first man sprang from an Alder tree. It is an unlucky tree, associated with death. It is often mentioned in myth with reference to battles and is associated with the cult of the severed head. It is beloved of water spirits and also linked with Donn, the Irish god of death and the otherworld. Alder is also a symbol of resurrection.

Practical uses: It was traditionally used for making shields, in Welsh poem 'The Battle of the Trees' or Cad Goddeu, Alder fought 'at the head of the line', indicative of its military value. The wood was also used for charcoal and the catkins and bark were used to make red dye, the flowers were used for green dye and the twigs for brown dye. Druidic whistles, said to control the four winds were made of Alder wood and it was often used for pipes and whistles generally. In the case of magical pipes, it was common to beat the pipe with a willow switch whilst reciting incantations, presumably just before or just after playing them. Druid wands were sometimes made of Alder (e.g Druid Seancha (of King Connor MacNessa) uses an Alder wand in the Irish legend Deidre and the Sons of Usnach).

Therapeutic uses: clearing and unblocking, it is traditionally associated with the blood. An infusion made from the dried bark removed from two to three-year-old branches is said to aid a sore throat. An alder infusion is a good astringent and soothes inflamed or burnt skin if washed/bathed with it. It was used for relief of congestion and headaches and also as a thickener of the blood. It is said to be used by expert herbal practitioners for coronary/angina treatment.

***Saille* (Willow) S ᚄ**

Fourth consonant of the *Beith-Luis-Nin*
Sixth month of the Ogham Tree Calendar 21st Mar – 17th Apr
COMMONER OF THE WOOD (*Aithig Fedo*)

Also known as *Sail, Saileach* or Sally. Willow is a fast growing tree that grows exceptionally well near water, it is common to find them on riverbanks. Willow is a symbol of fertility and life. It is regarded as a lucky tree, sally rods were said to bring good luck on a journey.

Folklore: It was thought to bring good luck if branches were brought into the house on May Day. It is linked with the moon, a feminine tree. It is particularly associated with the goddess of rivers Bóinn, who was often depicted as a great cow from whose milk the River Boyne was formed. The willow was sacred in Greece in relation to the death aspect of the triple goddess and was used by Helenic witches. Willow is also linked with enchantment and can be used as a tool to aid manifestation of wishes.

Practical uses: Most widely used for wickerwork – baskets, fences and bronze and iron age homes as part of the construction of the circular walls. The Irish harp was traditionally made from willow. It is also useful in the propagation of plants, placing willow rods into water, along with cuttings encourages the formation of new roots.

Therapeutic uses: An excellent treatment for fevers and headaches, willow bark contains salicylic acid, which is the active ingredient of aspirin. It is also good for colds and neuralgia. Willow can be applied externally in a compress or poultice to aid the healing of wounds; it also has natural fungicidal properties.

***Nin* (Cherry) N ╞**

Fifth consonant of the *Beith-Luis-Nin*
Associated with late spring
COMMONER OF THE WOOD (*Aithig Fedo*)

Also known as *Nuin* or *Silín, Fidach* or *Idath*. Cherry has beautiful blossoms appearing in early spring, hence, there are now many modern sterile hybrid varieties that are popular with gardeners. The native cherry produces a sweet fruit and grows to a considerable height. The cherry is a symbol of youth, beauty and love. This tree is associated with the Cuckoo and forbidden love (i.e. out of wedlock/extra-marital etc).

Folklore: The old Irish *Idath* or *Fidach* meaning 'cherry' appears in legend and is associated with tales of youth overcoming age in romance tales for example Dairmaid and Gráinne. The cherry is also linked with Aonghus Mac Óg, god of love who also as Maccan/Mabon/Maponos replaces his old and spent rival. The fruit is thought to possess an otherworldly quality not unlike the apple.

Practical use: The fruit is a valued food. The strong hard wood of this tree is sometimes used for furniture.

Therapeutic use: The gum/resin is said to be good for the complexion. I was unable to find any further therapeutic uses.

Note: reassignment of tree from Ash to Cherry

The word *nin* means 'branch fork' and also 'letter', as does the more common *fid*, its plural being *feda*. There is no ancient record of the Ash being referred to as *nin*, the more accepted translation. The medieval glosses do not always specify the actual name of trees so it is left for us to guess based on the meanings of the ogham and the three glosses. I am in agreement with MacCoitir's argument in favour of Cherry which I have summarised below:

The original names of letter are in three categories, given in order of preference:

1. Actual tree names
2. Names relating to some attribute of the tree
3. Poetic names based on an arboreal theme e.g. *nin*, *cert* and *muin*.

In the case of nin the word itself gives no clues but the glosses are more enlightening:

Gloss A	**Gloss B**	**Gloss C**
Costud Síde	*Bág ban*	*Bág maise*
Staple food of the otherworld	Boast of women	Boast of beauty

From the above glosses we can expect this tree to bear edible fruit, to be linked with the gods or fairies and the otherworld and to be a symbol of beauty. Clearly, this could not possibly be Ash but Cherry fits perfectly well with these attributes.

Huath **(Hawthorn) H ᚆ**

Sixth consonant of the *Beith-Luis-Nin*
Seventh month of the Ogham Tree Calendar 18th Apr – 15th May
COMMONER OF THE WOOD (*Aithig Fedo*)

Also known as *Scé,* Whitethorn or Maybush, it is a symbol of *Bealtaine.* It is the male fairy bush that is both feared and respected – the wood is rarely used. It is said that harm comes to those who destroy hawthorn, which is no easy task due to the multitude of long thorns that run the length of its branches. To this day, many Irish farmers will leave hawthorn bushes, especially if in a ring, and plough around them. This traditional respect of hawthorn can also be found in Scotland and England and the hawthorn is strongly linked with Glastonbury and Joseph of Arimathea. The hawthorn at Glastonbury Abbey is indeed ancient but is not in fact the original Glastonbury Thorn, which was cut down by Puritans in the 17th century. I have seen both the new Glastonbury Thorn and some considerably larger ones at stone circles in Co. Wicklow, Ireland, which I would estimate to be over a thousand years old.

Folklore: Generally regarded as unlucky but can be lucky if given the proper respect. The blossoms of this tree were considered especially unlucky and thought to bring death. It is interesting to note that the smell of the flowers is very similar to that given off by the body of a two to three day deceased person, perhaps the source of this belief. To keep a stick of hawthorn was considered to be bad luck. Jesus of Nazareth's crown of thorns was said to be of hawthorn.

Hawthorn, despite its unlucky reputation, also protects from evil and lightning and was thought to aid fertility, particularly at *Bealtaine*. The Maybush was decorated sometimes with candles and offerings were made to it. Hawthorn is associated with holy wells and with the Druid Merlin/Myrddin and the solar God Belenus. Hawthorn is associated with male potency and fertility in general.

Practical use: It is commonly used in hedges and to form a barrier on ditches to prevent livestock escaping from fields, as their dense thorny growth discourages attempts to penetrate it.

Therapeutic use: It can be used as a cardiac sedative (by an expert practitioner) and also to reduce blood pressure. It is said to strengthen the heart and regulate blood pressure and palpitations. It can be used in the treatment of various heart conditions but with the utmost of care.

Duir, Daur (Oak) D ᚇ

Seventh consonant of the *Beith-Luis-Nin*
Ninth month of the Ogham Tree Calendar 13th Jun – 10th Jul
NOBLE OF THE WOOD (*Airig Fedo*)

A symbol of strength, fertility, endurance and kingship. Oak is a great provider of quality wood and acorns for animals. The oak provides habitat and sustenance in one form or another to hundreds of organisms from fungi to wild pigs. There are some 450 species of the *Quercus* (oak) genus. Oak was traditionally used to start the *Bealtaine* fires and was also used for summer solstice fires. Daghdha is associated with the oak tree (as was the Helenic Zeus), he owned a harp of oak '*Daur Da Blás*' oak of two meadows.

Folklore: Oak was sacred to the ancient Druids (in Gaul particularly) as was the mistletoe which was found, albeit rarely to grow on them. Interestingly, mistletoe is not native to Ireland and probably became naturalised in the Christian period. The Irish names *Drualus*, 'Druid's Herb' *and Sú Darach*, (Juice of the Oak) imply that the sacred connection between the oak and mistletoe was known in Ireland even though it did not grow there. Oak was said to be sacred to the otherworld god Donn, often regarded as an aspect of Daghdha, also linked to the oak. According to Pliny, Gaulish Druids often performed rites in oak groves and a branch of oak was always present in all rites. Worship of Daghdha was embodied by veneration of the oak and it was considered portentous if Dadga's axe for instance lightning struck an oak tree. In old Irish and Welsh, the word for Chief also means Oak. The link between the land and kingship is thought to be symbolised by the oak. If acorns fall prematurely or are rotten, this was seen as symbolic of this relationship between king and the land souring. In the Book of Leinster: the slaughter of nobles and children by King Caibre Cinnchait led to famine and every oak producing just one acorn until he was deposed, upon which fertility was restored to the land. The oak is also connected with the stag, bull, pig and eagle.

The oak of Mugna (*Eo Mugna*) was one of Ireland's five sacred trees and was said to have three crops: acorns, hazel nuts and apples, it was also of enormous age and height (300 cubits). From the Dindshenchus:

Three hundred high, tree without stain,
A thousand could gather in its shade.
In the Northeast hidden from sight,
Until Conn of the Hundred fights.

Practical use: The timber is of the highest quality and was used in constructing palaces and halls and also shipbuilding. Much of the great oaks of the British Isles were felled by the monarchs of

England to build their navies. The acorns are a source of food to livestock and they can also be made into a drink similar in taste to coffee.

Therapeutic use: Buds produce a tonic for chronic fatigue and for impotence/decreased libido in men. It is a strong astringent and a compress is used for inflamed eyes. A decoction (extraction by boiling) can be used for piles. A douche treats genital infections and ingested it is said to discourage alcoholics from drinking.

Tinne (Holly) D ⫣

Eighth consonant of the *Beith-Luis-Nin*
Tenth month of the Ogham Tree Calendar 11th Jul – 7th Aug
NOBLE OF THE WOOD (*Airig Fedo*)

Also known as *Cuilenn/Cuileann,* holly is an evergreen tree that bears red berries (female tree only) and it has a very tough wood that is symbolic of strength and championship. It is also representative of protection, magic and purification.

Folklore: It was thought to possess magical properties of benefit in conflicts. It is associated with the god Lugh. It is a male warrior tree only and has no associations with fertility. It was thought to be bad luck to chop down a holly tree. It was considered to be an unlucky tree except at Christmas — the time of year it is still associated with. To Christians the berries are a symbol of the blood of Jesus of Nazareth and his suffering. However the symbolic use of holly at this time predates the Christian era, its evergreen appearance and winter fruit perhaps being a symbol of rebirth and endurance.

Practical use: It was traditionally used to make chariot axles, spears and darts. The berries were used to make dye.

Therapeutic use: Young leaves can be used to treat influenza, bronchitis and rheumatism. The berries are mildly poisonous to humans having a violent emetic effect (causing vomiting), they may have been used for this purpose in the past. Holly is used by professional herbal practitioners to treat dropsy and haemorrhages. It is said that in tiny quantities that the berries act as an aphrodisiac.

Coll (Hazel) C ᚉ

Ninth consonant of the *Beith-Luis-Nin*
Eleventh month of the Ogham Tree Calendar 8th Aug – 4th Sep
NOBLE OF THE WOOD (*Airig Fedo*)

Its nourishing nuts are a good source of protein. Hazel often grows close to water and is a symbol of wisdom, fertility, kingship, poetic inspiration and mystical knowledge.

Folklore: Hazel offers powerful protection against evil; the wood is also often used to make magic wands. It is said that the *sidhé* cannot harm any person or animal bearing hazel. Hazel is a favourite of diviners for locating water or metals. The hazelnut is a symbol of the heart and the life giving qualities of the land as well as a symbol of wisdom. The sacred well/pool of segais was surrounded by the nine hazels of wisdom, the great salmon of knowledge was said to eat the nuts as they fell into the water.

Of wisdom, inspiration and knowledge it is said that all three arrived at once in the form of leaves, blossoms and nuts that fall from the tree together. Fionn MacCumhaill is linked to the hazel tree via the Salmon of Knowledge that fed upon the sacred hazel nuts. It was said that it was highly valued by the Gods, hence the triad: 'Three things most valued by the Tuatha Dé Danann: the plough, the sun and the hazel tree'.

Practical use: Shields were often made of hazel. The nuts were a highly prized food. It was also used in furniture, for fencing and wickerwork, for wands and for divining rods.

Therapeutic use: It can be used to treat bronchitis. It is a good stimulant of the circulation and also stimulates bile production.

Quert (Apple) Q ᚊ

Tenth consonant of the *Beith-Luis-Nin*
Twelfth month of the Ogham Tree Calendar 5th Sep – 2nd Oct
NOBLE OF THE WOOD (*Airig Fedo*)

Also known as *Qert, Aball* or *Úll,* the apple tree with its beautiful blossoms and delicious fruit symbolises delights of the other-world, fertility, replenishment and healing. The use of apples in Halloween/*Samhain* games is perhaps more than due to their availability at that time — a link with the *sidhé* and otherworldly experience. The apple still features in modern day Halloween celebrations in the 'apple bobbing game' and the still popular treat — toffee-apples.

Folklore: Apples feature extensively in Celtic mythology, particularly with reference to the land of promise (Tír Taingire), the Island of Apples (Eamhan Abhlach) and Avalon, in which trees grew that bore golden apples. Mananan Mac Lir's branch of nine gold-red apples when shaken produced a music so sweet that it would sooth all torments and weariness. The apple was regarded to have health giving and sustaining magical properties for example a person might survive for weeks on one magic apple. St. Brigid (Christian form of Brighid) is said to have blessed an alder tree and it magically bore a harvest of two-thirds apples and one-third sweet sloes. Like the hazelnut, the apple has royal associations. The apple is also linked with the divine feminine and fertility, coincidentally the apple is in horticultural terms a 'false fruit' being technically in fact an ovum (the plant equivalent of a womb), within which the fruit and seed is contained. The apple also features extensively in Greek mythology.

Practical use: Apple wood is rarely used. The fruit is extremely popular, not least because it can be stored for a long period of time although modern varieties are much larger than the native apple of the British Isles. Apple juice is a popular drink as is cider, which is brewed from the juice of apples. In England, it was a custom to drink to the health of the apple tree with some cider to help ensure a good crop of apples; this is most likely a throwback to the pagan era. The bark of apple trees can be used to make a yellow dye.

Therapeutic use: They are rich in vitamin C but do not have many particular therapeutic uses, although they are associated with good health hence the saying 'an apple a day keeps the doctor away'. Apple cider vinegar is used for treatment of arthritis, neuralgia, pleurisy, pneumonia and also help reduce cholesterol.

Apples are also good for intestinal infections, constipation, strain, fatigue, hypertension, urine retention, gastric and kidney conditions, coughs, hoarseness, bronchial diseases and anaemia. A poultice of raw apple is beneficial for sore eyes.

Muin **(Buckthorn) M** ᚋ

Eleventh consonant of the *Beith-Luis-Nin*
Associated with autumn (when it fruits)
LOWER DIVISION OF THE WOOD (*Fodla Fedo*)

Also known as *Draigen* or *Ramh-dhraighean,* with its purgative berries and bark it is an important medicinal tree. This tree propagates itself very easily although it is not particularly common in Europe. In USA/Canada, where it spreads rapidly to the detriment of smaller plants and shrubs, it has come to be regarded as a weed. Buckhorn is sometimes called 'rotten cherry' or 'rotten apple' due to its sharp taste and its purgative properties if eaten in any quantity.

Folklore: Like blackthorn it is considered a malignant plant yet also has protective powers.
Therapeutic use: It clears toxins from tissues and is also a diuretic, laxative and strong purgative. It is an effective treatment for severe constipation. Buckthorn causes softening of the stool hence it might be used to lessen pressure on the bowel subsequent to surgery. In folk medicine, it was considered to be a blood purifier. In minute quantities, buckthorn can be used for skin problems as well as the treatment of intestinal parasites and gallstones.

Note: reassignment of tree from Vine to Buckthorn
The word *muin* translates as 'neck', 'deceit', 'love' and 'thicket' hence leading to some confusion regarding the correct interpretation.

The glosses give the following correspondences:

Conar gotha	*path of the voice,* which might relate to 'neck.
Ardammiase	*most noble goodliness,* which might relate to 'love'
Tressam Fedmae	*strongest in action* might relate to purgative qualities
Árusc n-airlig	*proverb of slaughter/rottenness* might relate to the rotten taste of the berries.

The common interpretation 'vine' does not seem to bare any of these qualities, buckthorn at least easily relates to two of the above. Another factor here is the fact that buckthorn is a genuinely native tree of Ireland. Vines are not only not classified as trees, they are not native to the British Isles, only being introduced to what is now England some time after 55BC.

I have to agree with MacCoitir in his belief that inclusion of non-native species and non-trees does not fit with the overall scheme of the Ogham knowledge system and is hence most likely erroneous. It is quite likely that medieval and later compilers, unsure of which tree *muin* referred to took a guess based on their own judgement, perhaps not relating their choices to the context of Druidry and the Druids' particular knowledge and veneration of trees.

***Gort* (Gorse) G ᚌ**

Twelfth consonant of the *Beith-Luis-Nin*
Associated with autumn (when cut for fodder)
BUSHES OF THE WOOD (*Losa Fedo*)

Also known as Furze or *Aiteann*, it is usually called Furze in Ireland and even just 'bushes' in some areas, in Britain it is more commonly known as Gorse. It is an evergreen bush, often in bloom with bright yellow flowers. It is fast growing reaching as much as ten feet in height.

Folklore: It is a symbol of the wealth and fertility of the land hence the saying: 'Gold under furze, silver under rushes, famine under heather'. Many *Bealtaine* fires were made with gorse. It was said to be unlucky to bring the flowers into the house. Gorse was linked with the land goddess and its presence on your land was said to increase its value. Today gorse is common enough in hedgerows but it is regarded more as a weed than anything else.

Practical use: The flowers of gorse make a yellow dye, which was often used to colour eggs at Easter. It was also used for fodder despite being spiny the new growth is actually quite soft. The soft growth was also used in bedding, the older more woody growth was used for firewood and dried out gorse makes excellent kindling. It regenerates very quickly hence, it can provide multiple harvests of both soft and woody branches. The ash of burnt gorse is alkaline and was used in soap making.

Therapeutic use: The flowers were used as a cure for jaundice. An infusion of the flowers was used to treat scarlet fever. Gorse has alkaloid properties similar to that of Broom and can be used in the treatment of heart conditions. It should only be administered by expert practitioners as it can increase blood pressure and is potentially very dangerous if misused.

Note: reassignment of tree from Ivy to Gorse

The word *gort* translates as 'field'. Although the medieval glossators mention Ivy (*edeand*) or Honeysuckle (*edlenn*) the actual glosses themselves fit better with Gorse:

Milsiu férai, glaisem gelta — sweetest grass, greenest pasture
Ined erc — suitable place for cows
Sásad ile — satisfaction of all

Neither honeysuckle or ivy are trees, in fact they are both tree climbers and are not associated with either fields or the abundance of the land, gorse is a small tree associated with fertile land. A possible source of this mistake is the pronunciation of *aiteann* (furze) and *edeand* (ivy) which is almost the same; this could possibly have led to accidental substitution of ivy for gorse/furze.

***nGetal* (Broom) NG ᚍ**

Thirteenth consonant of the *Beith-Luis-Nin*
Associated with autumn (when harvested)
BUSHES OF THE WOOD (*Losa Fedo*)

Also known as *Giolcach*, it is a small tree with several uses. It grows well coastally and the root system helps to hold soil together on banks/dunes thereby helping to prevent landslides.

Folklore: The yellow flowers (usually in May) symbolise female beauty, purity and maidenhood. It was a custom for wedding guests to carry or wear a sprig of broom. It is much associated with weddings and conception giving rise to the expression 'broomstick wedding' meaning pre-marital union and 'born over the brush' meaning a child is illegitimate. This tree is associated with witches, astral travel and flight (the witch's broom) however, it was also considered to offer protection against witches.

Practical use: Broom branches were commonly used for brushes and brooms, hence the name. The long thin branches were used in thatching and the bark fibre was used to make paper. Tannin was also extracted from the bark, which was used in tanning leather. In medieval times, the flowers were eaten and considered a delicacy. It can be used as a disinfectant (especially the seeds) or the ash produced after burning has the same effect.

Therapeutic use: It was used as a diuretic and cathartic medicine, considered especially good for blood disorders. A salve or ointment was made from the flowers for the treatment of gout. A decoction of the tips and twigs can be used for liver and kidney complaints. It was given to the severely wounded or those who had lost blood to aid in their recovery. Culpeper considered broom to be effective against sciatica, dropsy and joint pain. Small doses of broom can slow the heart while larger doses can induce sleep, lowering of blood pressure or even coma. It should be used with care by a professional practitioner.

Note: reassignment of tree from Reed/Fern to Broom

The word *gétal* translates as 'act of wounding'. Glossators mention broom, reed, bog-myrtle and fern as possibilities but also specifically mention healing properties. McManus and MacCoitir both cite Broom as the correct choice and the glosses would lean in this direction:

Lúth lego — sustenance of a leech
Étiud midach — raiment/strength of physicians
Tosach n-échto — beginning of slaying

Of the plants mentioned, broom is the only tree and the only one with any significant healing properties. Although not prickly like gorse, broom has long spear like branches, the other plants mentioned are relatively soft and not capable of wounding. On balance, I would have to agree with MacManus and MacCoitir that broom is the only likely candidate of the four mentioned.

***Straif* (Blackthorn) STR** ᚎ

Fourteenth consonant of the *Beith-Luis-Nin*
Associated with late autumn (when berries are harvested)
LOWER DIVISION OF THE WOOD (*Fodla Fedo*)

Also known as *Draighean* or sloe it has a bitter dark berry, hard dark wood and long thorns. This small tree is associated with malevolence, fierceness, strength and protection. It is actually a member of the Cherry family and produces a beautiful white blossom.

Folklore: Blackthorn is a female tree associated with fairies. It is considered an unlucky tree but also is said to protect against the *sidhé*/fairies. Fairy lovers — *Leanán Sídhe* were associated with this tree as is divination in matters relating to love.

Practical use: Shillelaghs (traditional walking sticks) were often made from mature blackthorn. The berries (sloes) are used to make sloe gin, a drink that was traditionally consumed at

Samhain/Halloween. Blackthorn is also a popular hedging plant (like hawthorn) as its thorns make a very effective natural barrier for animals.

Therapeutic use: It can be used as an astringent, laxative and also to reduce fever. Blackthorn is also considered to be a detoxifier. A gargle can be used for treating sore throats and bronchitis and as a general immune system booster.

Note: it is advisable to avoid if: pregnant/breastfeeding, prone to allergies or prone to high blood pressure and cardiac problems.

***Ruis* (Elder) R ᚏ**

Fifteenth consonant of the *Beith-Luis-Nin*
Associated with late autumn (when berries are harvested)
LOWER DIVISION OF THE WOOD (*Fodla Fedo*)

Also known as *Trom* or Bore Tree, it is an untidy looking tree with gnarled bark and it can give off a slightly unpleasant smell. It grows very well close to water. The entire tree is quite poisonous to humans with the exception of the flowers and the berries.

Folklore: Elder is the female fairy tree, hawthorn being its male counterpart. It is both a symbol of evil and of protection, it is said to be very unlucky and has the mischief of the *sídhe* within it, hence the triad 'Three signs of a cursed place — elder, nettle and corncrake'. It was considered ill fated to burn the wood. It was also advisable never to sleep under an Elder tree, to do so was to court evil or even death. Elder was said to make children ill and it was also believed that animals or children struck with an Elder rod would cease to grow. Despite its negative aspects Elder was also said to keep away witches and protect milk. Elder is associated with fairies, the land goddess and witches.

Practical use: The flowers have a pleasant smell and are used in making a cordial. The black berries are also safe and are used to make wine, note that all other parts of this tree are toxic and unsafe to use.

Therapeutic use: Elderberry wine is said to accelerate healing. The berries act as a laxative, they are also useful for treatment of coughs, bronchitis and dermatitis.

***Ailm* (Pine) A┼**

First vowel of the *Beith-Luis-Nin*
Second month of the Ogham Tree Calendar 29th Nov – 26th Dec
NOBLE OF THE WOOD (*Airig Fedo*)

Also known as *Ochtach* or *Giúis*, Pine is an evergreen conifer with an invigorating scent. It is a symbol of renewal, rebirth and eternal life.

Folklore: It was used in festivals associated with the sun – *Bealtaine* and the Summer Solstice. Bog pine logs or *Bloc Nollag* were commonly burnt on Christmas Eve in Ireland and Scotland. The bright flame of the burning pine was considered purification and protection against evil. It was known in Scotland as the harp of trees on account of the 'musical' sound of the wind blowing through the needles.

Practical use: Commonly used for resin, pitch and flaming torches and in recent centuries Pine is very popular for furniture. It has a lovely scent that is used domestically and in aromatherapy and disinfectants. Stockholm tar and turpentine are made from pine as too is oil of Terebinth.

Therapeutic use: It is used widely in aromatherapy and as a scent. It is used as an additive in herbal baths for exhaustion, nervousness and stress. A good treatment for insomnia and accelerates slows healing in skin conditions. Pine makes a good inhalant for catarrh and asthma. Supposedly, the ingestion of pine buds aids calcium absorption, which is relevant in maintenance of healthy bones. Used topically pine helps to improve blood flow to the skin and its mild analgesic action is used for treating muscular pain as well as rheumatism.

Onn (Ash) O ┼

Second vowel of the *Beith-Luis-Nin*
Eighth month of the Ogham Tree Calendar 16th May – 12th Jun
NOBLE OF THE WOOD (*Airig Fedo*)

Also known as *Fuinseóg* or *Uinnius,* Ash is a large tree with strong, flexible timber. Ash is associated with the mother/land goddess and also childbirth.

Folklore: It was said to be the first tree to be struck by lightning. In Norse mythology the first man was said to have sprung from an Ash. Ash is linked with kingship and sovereignty of the land, ashes also being commonly found by sacred wells. *An Crann Comhaita,* a mythical ash tree of power, was said to have miraculously borne apple blossoms (supposedly caused by St. Patrick). Three of the five great trees of Ireland were Ash: *Bile Uisnigh* (at Uisneach), *Bile Tortan* (at Ardbreccan) and *Craobh Daithi* (at Farbill). Of the five, *Bile Tortan* was the largest and also the most sacred. The Druid wand of ash was used in the healing of the sick, surviving into modern times: W. B. Yeats described a 'fairy doctor' who always carried an ash wand, keeping it on his knees whilst saying charms to heal patients.

Practical use: It has traditionally been used to make hurley sticks (for the Irish game of hurling) as well as spears. Ash is still used in modern Ireland for hurling but due to the shortage of Ash in

Ireland most of the wood is now imported. The bark of ash was used in tanning. St. Anthony's buttons, actually a fungus that grows on ash, were used as firelighters. Ash makes an excellent firewood and can be burned well 'green' unlike the wood of most trees which require drying over time.

Therapeutic use: Extract of the bark was used to reduce fevers and also on cuts. It acts as a laxative, purgative and diuretic. A decoction of the bark in boiling water (then cooled) is especially good for fevers. An external compress made from a decoction aids suppurating cuts and sores. The bark is best gathered in spring and stored in a dry place for later use. Ash buds were thought to aid energy flow in the liver. Ash can also be used to treat anxiety, gout and hypercholesterolemia.

Note: reassignment of tree from Furze to Ash

The word *Onn* was associated with furze or heather by medieval glossators however in Old Irish it means Ash, corresponding to the Old Welsh for Ash – *Onnen*. The name *Uinnius* replaced *Onn* in later times and the original word was forgotten. The glosses are not particularly clear although they fit Ash better than they do either Furze or Heather and besides Heather is not even a tree:

Congnaid congnamaid ech – wounder of horses
Fétham soíre – smoothest of craftmanship
Lúth fían – sustenance of warriors

Ash was used to make spears, hence the warrior or wounding connection, perhaps the second gloss is a reference to the art of hurley stick making, which is still done by hand and is a skill that has been passed down through countless generations. It is well known that the game was played in the Druidic era, Cú Chulainn as a boy (then called Setanta) played hurling with amazing prowess.

Úr (Elm) U ᚒ

Third vowel of the *Beith-Luis-Nin*
Associated with late spring (time of most growth)
COMMONER OF THE WOOD (*Aithig Fedo*)

Also known as *Leamhán* and *Ura,* it has rich foliage and sap associated with fertility. Elm does not rot in water and grows very well in bog land. *Úr* means 'moist'.

Folklore: Elm is said to give protection against evil and fairies. It is a nourishing and protecting tree that is associated with holy wells. In modern times, the Elm has become rare due to Dutch Elm disease.

Practical use: It was used in shipbuilding as it is so slow to rot. It was also used for furniture, coffins, longbows and divining rods.

Therapeutic use: Elm is a tonic, demulcent, astringent and diuretic. It was used in a decoction for the treatment of diseases on or in the skin such as ringworm. The water found in the 'bladders' of the leaves was believed to be very effective in cleansing the skin. Elm is also used as an essiac cancer treatment. Taken internally it is said to be good for digestive complaints and irritable bowel syndrome. It can also be used for colitis, colic, reflux and ulcers. Elm is also used to relieve chest and bronchial conditions, and urinary tract infections.

Note: reassignment of tree from Heather to Elm

The word *Úr* means not only moist but clay or earth. Although glossators refer to it as heather, I believe Elm is a better fit. Heather is not a tree, it was also associated with poor quality land and had relatively few medicinal uses unlike Elm which was a valuable tree with many uses and which grows well in a cold and damp climate. The glosses are fairly vague and do not seem to refer to qualities of either Elm or Heather, with the exception of one: *Úraibh adbaib — in cold dwellings,* which could fit reasonably well with Elm.

Eadha **(Apsen) E** ᚓ

Fourth vowel of the *Beith-Luis-Nin*
Associated with late autumn (the beginning if the time of death and hibernation)
LOWER DIVISION OF THE WOOD (*Fodla Fedo*)

Also known as *Crann Creathach, Fiodhadh* or *Edad,* it has flat leaves that rustle in the slightest breeze. It was considered to be an unlucky tree associated with death and misfortune.

Folklore: The sound of the leaves was considered to be reminiscent of the sound of the sea, it was thought to be a link to the otherworld/afterlife which was beyond the sea. The rustling of the leaves was meant to signify approaching death or the closeness of otherworldly forces. The wood was never used for fishing or farming implements because of its unlucky reputation and no one wished to even touch aspen wood unless it was one's role to use the *Fé* (funereal measuring stick). The Aspen is mentioned in Irish folklore in reference to illness or approaching death: Oscar of the Fianna is described as 'like an aspen tree that is falling' before his death. His father Oisín, returned from Tír na nOg and becoming horribly aged (after setting foot on Irish soil) describes himself as 'like an aspen, my leaves are gone from me' shortly before his death. Aspen is also referred to in the tale of Deidre and the sons of Uisneach.

Practical use: The *Fé* (aspen wand) was used to measure the dead and to measure out graves. In fact, the glossators refer to Aspen as 'the stick of woe' due to its connection with bad luck and death.

Therapeutic use: It was thought to cure fevers and had magical curative powers if used in the hours of darkness. However, due to its reputation and a general fear and abhorrence of this tree Aspen was rarely used therapeutically.

***Iodha* (Yew) I ᚔ**

Fifth vowel of the *Beith-Luis-Nin*
First month of the Ogham Tree Calendar 1st Nov - 28th Nov
NOBLE OF THE WOOD (*Airig Fedo*)

Also known as *Ibar* or *Iúr*, the yew is a highly poisonous evergreen tree that lives to exceptional age. All parts except the pink flesh of the berries are poisonous to humans and most animals, the seeds are especially poisonous with two seeds being sufficient to kill a child. Yew has a dark tough wood. It grows very slowly and can live for thousands of years.

Folklore: Yew is a symbol of death, eternity and the afterlife. These trees are commonly found in graveyards or by sacred wells, often of far greater age than the church or graves. Yew was associated with the *fidnemed* or 'sacred grove', is reported in several instances to be used by the ancient Druids in divination and has long since been connected with divining. Yew had many protective properties including protecting milk and protection from witches although it was also considered harmful. To rest or sleep under a yew could be fatal, perhaps due to its toxic nature. It was a symbol of great age — Fintan Mac Bóchna claimed that he had outlived a yew tree. The tale Mad Sweeney (Suibhne Geilt) features a yew, which he uses for shelter after running from the battlefield, driven mad by the horrors of war; perhaps his use of the tree is indicative of his madness given its poor reputation for such a task. The Spear of Assail, which belonged to Lugh (one of the four treasures of the Tuatha Dé Danann) was made from yew and if Lugh called its name 'Iúr' whilst throwing, it would be sure to hit its mark. Yew is linked to the goddess of the land and considered to have protective powers for both the living and the dead. Many tribe names are associated with yew. The yew is also strongly associated with war; the Druidess warrior Scathach trained Cú Chulainn in the art of war under a great yew tree along with her two sons Cuar and Cett. Various stories in Irish myth refer to the yew in relation to kingship or the protection of kings, the *Eo Rossa* (yew of Ross) stood close to the ancient seat of the kings of Leinster (in Co. Carlow).

Practical use: Yew was popular for weapons, particularly bows and spears. The oldest recorded wooden object in the world is a yew spear of approx 150,000 years of age, excavated in Clacton, England. Yew was also used in building although sparingly due to the long time for the trees to reach maturity.

Therapeutic use: Great care is required in the use of yew. It is used in minute quantities in homeopathic treatments for rheumatism and arthritis.

Supplementary Trees

Ébad, Eadha (Aspen) É or EA ⚹

LOWER DIVISION OF THE WOOD (*Fodla Fedo*)

This letter was originally É and was later changed to the diphthong EA. the glossators mention both honeysuckle and aspen in regard to *Ébad,* the glosses refer to water and fish, perhaps due to the fact that the pronunciation É sounds the same as the *gaeilge* for Salmon (*Éco*).

Ór, Feoras **(Spindle) Ó or OI** ᚖ

LOWER DIVISION OF THE WOOD (*Fodla Fedo*)

This letter was originally Ó again changing later on to a diphthong OI. The meaning here is clearly gold, a word that is still used in modern Irish. The glossators mention both ivy and the spindle tree. The spindle tree is a small tree (ivy is not a tree) which bears a bright orange fruit — close enough to golden. There is not much folklore relating to spindle however in one poem (from the *Dindshenchus*) the Druid of Caipre Lifechair, Bicne enticed the four birds of Aonghus Mac Og away from Cairpre, who were following him. Bicne tried singing a spell over every tree he could think of without success until he finally tried a spindle tree, which rose up attracting the birds away so that Caipre was able to elude them.

Practical use: It was used to make spindles, skewers and toothpicks. The wood is hard and spindle trees can be coppiced, providing multiple harvests for firewood or tools.

Therapeutic use: Used as a tonic, cholagogue, laxative and hepatic stimulant. In small doses spindle stimulates the appetite and the flow of gastric juices. In larger doses, it is a cathartic. It has slight diuretic and expectorant effects, but its major use is as a purgative in cases of constipation in which the liver is disordered, and for which it is considered particularly effective. It is especially valuable in liver disorders, which follow or accompany fever. It is mildly laxative and stimulates the liver without causing nausea. It also promotes bile production.

Uilen, Aiteal **(Juniper) UI** ᚗ

LOWER DIVISION OF THE WOOD (*Fodla Fedo*)

Juniper is a slow growing tree with highly aromatic leaves, wood and berries. *Uilen* means elbow or angle, giving its name to the Irish bagpipes. The glossators mention both honeysuckle and juniper however honeysuckle is not a tree and hence does not fit with the gloss *tuthmar fid* meaning 'most fragrant tree' despite its pleasant smelling flowers. Also known as *Crann Fir*, the word *fir* or *fiar*, meaning bent or twisted refers to the growth habit of juniper, which is often twisted.

Folklore: It was thought to have protective powers with regard to cattle and also the home. In Scotland it was often place over the door at *Bealtaine*. It was used to ward off witches and was burned to drive away evil and to purify.

Practical use: Juniper is still used for that purpose in modern aromatherapy and magic. It was often burned in hospitals or around sick people to aid their recovery. Juniper berries are used in the making of gin. The berries are also used to flavour pickling brine, sauerkraut and stuffing for game, ham and pork.

Therapeutic use: the berries can be used internally to treat cystitis, urethritis, kidney inflammations and water retention. It is also used for treatment of rheumatism, gout and arthritis. Juniper also aids poor digestion, excess gas, dyspepsia and colic. Used externally the berries are a treatment for rheumatic pain and neuralgia. As an essential oil, it is used for toning of congested skin and blocked pores, treatment of acne, eczema and psoriasis as well as skin inflammations. Juniper has anti-depressive, anti-spasmodic, astringent, carminative, depurative and insecticide properties.

Pín, Spinan **(Gooseberry) P or IO** ᚘ

BUSHES OF THE WOOD (*Losa Fedo*)

This letter was originally sounded P being changed later to the diphthong IO. The glossators refer to this tree as *spin* or *spinan*, which is the Irish name for gooseberry (meaning 'spiny one'). Gooseberry is native to Britain but not Ireland, however by the time these supplementary letters were added it most probably had become naturalised in Ireland. Although a bush, it can reach up to three metres in height and eleven metres in width if allowed to mature.

Folklore: There is no significant folklore in Ireland, what is known comes from Britain for example a chaperone was called as 'gooseberry' as it was a standard ploy to pretend to be picking fruit whilst keeping an eye on courting couples and gives rise the phrase 'to play gooseberry' meaning to be an unwanted presence. 'Old gooseberry' was a euphemism for the Devil. The saying 'born under a gooseberry' bush was a quaint explanation of how children arrived, which now implies foolishness or naivety.

Practical use: The only use I have found is the berries, used in pies and jams.

Therapeutic use: The juice was said to cure all inflammations. The light jelly made from the ripe berries was considered valuable for sedentary, plethoric or bilious patients.

Emancholl **(Hazel) CH or AE** ᚙ

NOBLE OF THE WOOD (*Airig Fedo*)

This letter means 'twin of hazel' or 'twin of C', which of course associates it with the hazel, which we have discussed already. CH, which effectively is a twinned or doubled C became the diphthong AE at a later date. It is interesting to note that in some later interpretations the Beech tree is given, along with the name *Phagos* from the Greek, however it is never mentioned in any of the early manuscripts, as it was not native to Ireland. It is generally accepted that Beech trees were introduced to Ireland around the year 1700 hence it truly has no place within the Ogham alphabet despite the fact that it is a fine tree with edible nuts and several practical and therapeutic used.

MacCoitir suggests a strong link between the senses and the supplementary letters and also the four cardinal directions and the centre, citing the story 'The Settling of the Manor of Tara' to substantiate his theory; although as a late addition to a well developed system I question the necessity or validity of these additional correspondences.

This completes my work here on Ogham as a system of knowledge. What I have provided here is a basic overview, there is a vast body of mythology, folk legend, practical and therapeutic knowledge related to these trees that goes far beyond the scope of this book. This subject merits further study for anyone who is seriously interested in fully understanding Ogham knowledge, see the bibliography for further reading.

Ogham as a Tree Calendar

The tree calendar has become an accepted part of modern Druidry and modern study of Ogham, however before Robert Graves 'invented' it for his epic *The White Goddess* this was not the case. Graves did correctly observe that the trees of the Ogham alphabet are connected with certain times or seasons of the year, however he failed to do his research properly using O'Flaherty's *Ogygia* as his only source for a thirteen consonant and five vowel alphabet. Having correctly noticed that there are thirteen lunar cycles or 'moons' to some years he decided to connect these thirteen trees to the thirteen moons and thus creating the tree calendar whilst at the same time rubbishing the Coligny Calendar as 'no longer regarded as Druidic'.

Unfortunately, this grave mistake (excuse the pun) was soon picked up by anyone with a reasonable knowledge of Ogham and who was aware that there are in fact fifteen consonants in the Ogham alphabet, thus immediately dismantling the cornerstone of Graves's theory.

Re-examination of the tree calendar in recent years by MacCoitir suggests that although greatly flawed as Graves' ideas were and incorrectly executed, he believes there is a case for creating a Tree Calendar, based on thirteen of the trees that exist within the twenty letter Ogham alphabet, even if one did not actually historically exist.

Graves' calendar began with birch at December 24th, MacCoitir suggests that it should start at the traditional Celtic year end/start i.e. *Samhain* – November 1st. MacCoitir also links his thirteen months with those of the Gaulish Coligny calendar as this is the only existing known Celtic calendar. However, MacCoitir gives a different list of Gaulish months from either of my (borrowed) suggestions in Chapter VI – Cosmology, which surely only further muddies an already confused and hotly disputed area. Therefore, I have decided to omit the Gaulish months, the jury being still out as regards a definitive answer to the question of their correct order.

MacCoitir gives actual fixed dates for his calendar, based on the festival of *Samhain,* which is today fixed at 31st October. I question this as, if there was in fact a lunar tree calendar, the dates would move each year depending upon the cycles of the moon, a fact that the Coligny Calendar itself accounts for. Furthermore, there is reason to believe that *Samhain* might well have been celebrated at the nearest new moon in ancient times, as it is by some modern Druid orders such as Ord na Drui, in Ireland. Nonetheless, I have decided to give MacCoitir's dates as a rough guide to placement. I leave it to the reader to decide whether to fix the calendar to lunar or Gregorian dates for *Samhain* or possibly astronomical dates such as the solstices or equinoxes. Either way I believe this model gives an approximately workable model based on what we known of the Celtic year.

MacCoitir's choice of tree is not based upon the (incorrect) consonant list but on the seasonal placing of the trees in Irish folklore. In some cases, such as *Luis* or *Huath* this is quite obvious, others require some justification which he makes pains to do. I am in agreement with his arguments and also with his belief that the Ogham Tree Calendar is of little practical value as a calendar, what it is useful for is as a seasonal reminder of our link to the land, symbolism and folklore of Celtic culture and of the need to reconnect with nature in our everyday lives.

1. *Iodha/Idad*	Yew	1 Nov - 28 Nov	I
2. *Ailm*	Pine	29 Nov - 26 Dec	A
3. *Beith*	Birch	27 Dec - 23 Jan	B
4. *Luis*	Rowan	24 Jan - 20 Feb	L
5. *Fearn/Fern*	Alder	21 Feb - 20 Mar	F
6. *Saille/Sail*	Willow	21 Mar - 17 Apr	S
7. *Huath*	Hawthorn	18 Apr - 15 May	H
8. *Onn*	Ash	16 May - 12 Jun	O
9. *Duir/Dair*	Oak	13 Jun - 10 Jul	D
10. *Tinne*	Holly	11 Jul - 7 Aug	T
11. *Coll*	Hazel	8 Aug - 4 Sep	C
12. *Quert/Cert*	Apple	5 Sep - 2 Oct	Q
13. *Ruis*	Elder	3 Oct - 31 Oct	R

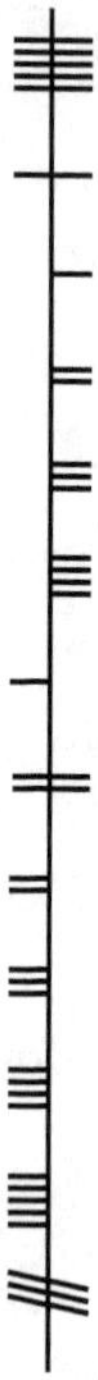

1. Yew – in berry at this time. Representative of the dark aspects of the land-goddess, protective of both the living and the dead. Associated with death and the otherworld hence the Samhain connection.

2. Another evergreen tree traditionally associated with Christmas and also the winter solstice. The Yule log was

usually of pine. Pine symbolised imminent rebirth and the promise of returning spring.

3. Birch is symbolic of new life emerging, the beginnings of a reawakening. Birch was associated with children and birth and also *Imbolc* which follows shortly.

4. The Rowan buds are beginning to swell by February. This tree, like Brighid, is associated with fire. The Quicken tree encourages new growth, this being the time when snowdrops appear and much growth occurs underground.

5. Alder is associated with war and blood. By now, leading up to the vernal equinox the sap that gives it its red colour is rising in the branches.

6. Around April the Willow is producing its catkins (flowers) that attract the bees. By now the milk is flowing well for the new lambs and calves. Willow is associated with protecting milk and butter.

7. Hawthorn is the Maybush, strongly associated with *Bealtaine,* which is also *Gaeilge* for the month of May.

8. Ash is in full leaf by June. Ash represents the land-goddess at the peak of her fertility. It represents the strength of the land that is continually renewed, being quick to regenerate if cut back.

9. The oak represents the rule of kings, its health tied to the justness and fitting behaviour of the ruler. The solstice fires, celebrating the triumph of the light were traditionally of oak.

10. Holly flowers around mid July, small as they are, from them the vibrant red berries will be generated. *Lughnasadh* falls in this month, a time of horseracing, games and sports; holly was traditionally used for chariots and spears – appropriate for this time.

11. Hazel produces nuts in August that are ripening. In Ireland, it is still traditional to celebrate the Pattern at this time, families gathering at shrines (grottos, holy wells) and graveyards. The hazel is most associated with holy wells and the mythical Well of Segais.

12. Apples are one of the most valuable and prized native fruits, ready at this time as the Equinox approaches and the grain harvest ends. This fruit helped sustain people through to the next harvest, as the otherworldly apple heals and renews those who taste it.

13. Elder the female fairy tree is associated with the *sidhé,* the otherworld and magic. It is also highly poisonous and can deal death as easily as it can sustenance as we approach the death of the year.

And so this concludes my investigation of Ogham, for a more complete understanding of this rich and complex area of Druidry, I refer the reader to the bibliography. I have merely skimmed the surface.

XIV

Medicine and Healing

This area of Druidry is one that requires particular care and discernment as it is an area that has been widely covered in modern esoteric literature and often wild and unfounded claims have been made about the practices of Druids and/or 'rediscovered' lost arts of Druid healing etc. There are both classical and Irish accounts of Druidic functions as regards medicine, however most of it is not very specific and certainly leaves a lot to be desired so far as building an accurate picture of their functions and practices in this respect. I shall attempt to present here an incomplete portrait of the Druid physician, using the sources that are contemporaneous with the Druids or retained in mythology, folklore and legend.

> Three things that constitute a physician: a complete cure, leaving no blemish behind, a painless examination.
> Irish Triad

Perhaps the best account of the Druids' powers of healing is gleaned from the story of *Cath Maige Tuired* (The 2nd battle of Moytira), which relates as a sub-story to the main plot how the full knowledge of herbs was lost. The Irish god of medicine, Dian Céacht, was filled with jealousy after his son Miach succeeded in completely recreating former king Nuada's hand when he himself was only able to make a silver replacement. His furious anger over his son's superior healing skills led him to strike his son down three times, from which Miach healed himself. The fourth and final blow proved fatal and from Miach's grave 365 herbs grew, that would heal every part of the body. These were gathered up by Miach's sister Airmeith (Airmid) and laid down upon her cloak so that she could classify them all according to their function. Unfortunately, her father (Dian Céacht) saw this and still being in a rage snatched up the cloak, scattering the herbs so that their function and properties would be unknown.

Dian Céacht, despite his murderous temper, used his skills to good effect by using his healing well *Tiora Sláine*, which contained all the healing herbs of Ireland, to revive dead and dying warriors of the Tuatha Dé Danann. The next day, they would emerge alive again and ready to resume battle, thereby managing to bolster the numbers of the Tuatha Dé Danann and save them from crushing defeat long enough for Lugh to kill his grandfather Balor and thereby win the battle.

There are numerous references to Druidic healing in Celtic literature that have survived into the modern age, but there are also several mentions of Druids' healing functions in classical sources. Pliny referred to the three classes of Druids as 'The Druids, and that race of prophets and doctors.' They certainly had some knowledge of herbs but this would appear to be combined with magical healing techniques, which might even have been considered as of equal or greater importance than the botanical cures, magical cures certainly endured into the late medieval period throughout Europe. Pliny gives some details of how the Gaulish Druids used herbs:

> Similar to savin is the plant Selago. It is gathered without using iron and by passing the right hand through the left sleeve of the tunic, as if in the act of committing a theft. The clothing must be white, the feet washed and bare, and an offering of wine and bread made before the gathering. The Druids of Gaul say that the plant should be carried as a charm against every kind of evil and that the smoke of it is good for diseases of the eyes. ...The Druids also use a certain marsh plant that they call Samolus, this must be gathered with the

> left hand, when fasting, and is a charm against the diseases of cattle. But the gatherer must not look behind him, nor lay the plant anywhere except in drinking troughs.
> Pliny (*Historia Naturalis*)

The above plants named by Pliny were native to western Europe and are called *Juniperus sabina* (Savin Juniper) and *Samolus valerandi* (Water Pimpernel) in their modern botanical (and common) names, although completely different plants have often been cited as those discussed by Pliny.

The Irish king Criomhthann Sciaithbheal employed the services of the Pictish Druid Trostan (of the *Cruithnigh*) to save his men from being poisoned by the weapons of British invaders:

> ...there was a skilful druid called Trostan among the Cruithnigh who could furnish himself and his people with an antidote against the poison with which the weapons of the Tuatha Fiodhgha were wont to be charged... "Get thrice fifty white hornless cows milked." said Trostan, "and let the milk got from them be placed in a hollow in the middle of the plain in which you are wont to meet them in battle, and offer battle on that same plain; and let each one of your followers who shall have been wounded by them go to the hollow and bathe, and he will be healed from the venom of the poison.

Criomhthannn did as instructed by Trostan at the battle of *Ard Leanhnachta* inflicting a terrible defeat upon the invaders. Although not explicitly stated, the milk was most likely magically enhanced by the Druid, milk alone generally not possessing curative power against poisons.

Another fine example of the use of herbs comes from the *Táin Bo Cuailgne* in the form of the tragic battle between childhood friends Cú Chulainn and Ferdia who trained in the arts of war together with Skatha (Scathach):

> At last the day came to its close. "Let us cease now". said Ferdia, Cú Chulainn agreed. Each then threw his arms to his charioteer, and the friends embraced and kissed each other three times, and went to their rest... the heroes sent each other food and drink and healing herbs for their wounds.

This act of sharing or 'equal division of healing' was called *comraind legis* in *Gaeilge*. In recognition of this communal spirit, the Irish Army Medical Corps use this phrase as their motto.

There are numerous other examples of animal and plant healing from Celtic myth such as restoration of the sick or wounded, healing 'fairy' herbs that restore feminine beauty and so on. In general, it would appear that a ritual method of collection was employed for plants that possessed special healing powers or were believed to be imbued with divine spirit. For example, vervain was gathered at sunrise after a sacrifice to the earth had been made to make amends for the taking of this sacred plant. It was thought that vervain rubbed upon the body would grant all wishes; it was also used to cure fever, calm the heart and as an antidote to snake bites. The dried form was burned as an incense at gatherings and banquets to facilitate a convivial mood. It was also considered a powerful protection against evil and was used also in divination, religious ceremony and ratification of treaties. Three herbs most sacred to the Druids were water-mint, meadowsweet and vervain.

It is clear that knowledge of healing was important Druidic knowledge and part of Celtic culture generally, hence its survival beyond the pagan era. The *lubgort* was the name given to herb gardens in ancient Irish and Scottish society generally belonging to nobility, prosperous farmers or monasteries. These were used for vegetables, some of which had medicinal properties, but also for growing specifically medicinal plants.

In Irish and Scottish tradition Chieftains were served by a physician (usually hereditary) who took care of the Clan's medical needs. This system survived, passing from the Druid to the physician, well into the Middle Ages with some manuscripts in Irish and Latin still in existence today for example the *Book of the O'Lees* from 1443 or the *Book of the O'Shiels* from 1652. Brehon Law in Ireland was applied to medicine, it being stated that a physician's bag should have many small compartments for the safe storage of herbs. It was also an offence to collect herbs from another's land, the fines for such offences as stealing wild garlic, apples or seaweed being the value of two and a half milk cows. Only in the case of a proven need for a seriously ill patient would there be an exception, this being the case, the physician could collect sufficient of the necessaries from wherever possible with impunity.

Another area of Celtic healing that has become resurgent in recent years is the Sweat Lodge or *Allus Bothan* in *Gaeilge*. Interest in this tradition has come primarily via modern Shamanism, inspired by the Native American sweat lodges that are used in Shamanic healing. As interest in Indo-European equivalents has increased it has led to the rediscovery of the Celtic tradition, most of what is known being gleaned from Ireland. There is, as far as I know, no documented evidence of use of the sweat lodge by the Druids but there was a strong folk tradition of the *Allus Bothan,* which was retained until the 19th century.

Unlike the portable American method it appears that only stone 'beehive' huts were used, however it is indeed possible that a temporary structure may have been used where sufficient stone or manpower was unavailable. The steam was generated from turf or wood fires and the hot steam inside the chamber infused with healing herbs. In recorded history the sweat lodge was used for physical healing, particularly relief of rheumatism and arthritis although much remains unknown about their use. This method of healing was not frequently undertaken as it would have been considerably expensive in terms of much prized fuel. It was probably necessary for this huge cost to be shared amongst the participants or the wider community as the majority of the common people in post-Norman Ireland lived in poverty. There are a few surviving examples of stone sweat lodges such as in Rathlin Island (between Ireland and Scotland) and also in counties Leitrim, Cavan and Kerry. Although slightly larger, these appear very similar in appearance to the monastic beehive huts, which had an entirely different purpose.

> Sweat houses were common in Ireland until 50 years ago. It was heated by fires of turf, when sufficiently hot the coals and ashes were removed, and some cool thing such as sods, rushes or stones put in for the person to stand upon. As many as six or eight men stripped off and went in, then all openings were closed except what afforded a little ventilation. When they could suffer the heat no longer they came out and plunged into a pool of water within a yard or two of the sweat house.
> Patrick Shields, 1890

It is quite possible that the sweat lodge had been used in a more spiritual sense in earlier times, as is the case with the modern Celtic and Native American methods. It has been suggested that herbs and fungi such as the magic mushroom or fly agaric were used in conjunction with the sweat lodge as part of a magical healing technique. Indeed the surviving secular Finnish tradition of the Sauna was earlier practised in a more spiritual form by the indigenous *Suomi* (Lapp) people, who themselves still have an unbroken Shamanic tradition. The absence of concrete information means that we can only guess as to the exact structure and purpose of ancient Celtic sweat lodges. After the famine, Gaelic practices in Ireland dramatically decreased, including the sweat lodge tradition and the knowledge of its use and purpose so that by the 20th century it was a distant memory with only occasional personal accounts received from previous generations and a few written references to throw light on the subject. However, the re-imagined Celtic or Native American sweat lodge seems to be growing in popularity and they have very much become a part of modern Druidic healing methods.

With the decline of the Gaelic order after the flight of the Earls, Celtic healing tradition began to die out in Ireland and a similar process took place in Scotland with the introduction of Anglo-Norman Lairds. Classical knowledge of medicine began to dominate, leading to a decline in indigenous healing among the higher echelons of the Celtic and ex-Celtic kingdoms. Despite this, some of the Druidic knowledge survived in folk knowledge, particularly among the *Bean na Luibheanna* or 'Herb Woman' to be found in Ireland or Scotland. Almost all modern Celtic/Druidic herbals are based on the work of Nicholas Culpepper or Margaret Grieve and not on Celtic folk medicine; however, we are fortunate that Michael Moloney collected much of what is still known in his 1919 work *Luibhsheanchus* or 'Irish Ethnobotany'.

There are other subsequent works that explore the genuine ancient medical traditions of the Celtic lands, but it must be admitted that much has been lost forever as the process of codification began far too late. To properly explore this subject requires a book in itself and I therefore refer the reader to modern sources such as D. Allen & G. Hatfield, Niall MacCoitir, J. Fleetwood and the Scottish School of Herbal Medicine.

Of course, much general information can be culled from the internet and general herbals for the large variety of plants that are known to belong to Celtic tradition, although in most cases it is impossible to know how they were used magically/medicinally by the Druids. In Ireland, seven herbs were considered immune to natural or supernatural influence if picked at noon on a sunny day, approaching or on a full moon: Vervain, St. John's Wort, Speedwell, Eyebright, Mallow, Selfheal and Yarrow. They could also be used for harm if collected at a particular time. Below is a list of plants that are known to belong within the

Celtic medicinal tradition, although it cannot be confirmed with many of them that they were used as far back as the times of the ancient Druids. For medicinal use of trees, see the previous chapter on Ogham.

English	Celtic (Irish/Scots)	Latin (Botanical)
Basil	*Lus mic rí*	*Calamintha* (genus)

Wild basil is common in Britain but relatively rare in Ireland. Herbally it was used for menstrual and sciatica pain, to prevent conception. Magically it provides protection in conflict and deters thieves. It can be used for purification and to dispel bad energy. Most of what is known comes from Culpeper and later sources.

Bilberry	*Fraochán*	*Vaccinium myrtillus*

A valued food in summer, it is associated with Lughnasadh and was a ritual gift to the *Ard Rí* at Tara. The berries were used as a diuretic for kidney problems, relief for jaundice, urinary infections, diarrhoea and as a general painkiller. Although rarely seen today billberries were a popular and vital fruit in Celtic countries up until the last century.

Blackberry	*Dris*	*Rubus fructicosus*

Another valuable fruit, it is also useful for dyes, kindling and wickerwork. It was considered bad to eat them after Samhain, and in England after September, most likely as they begin to turn at this time. Berry juice was used to cure dropsy, the leaves to aid swelling, cuts, sore feet, burns, boils and spots. Magically the plant was used to cure whooping cough, hernia and rickets, which was achieved by crawling under it. It was also used to protect milk, although it also had a malevolent side.

Bog-myrtle	*Raideog*	*Myrica gale*

It was considered a useful and blessed plant, used to flavour and strengthen beer throughout the British Isles and Gaul. It was also used to make dye and to deter insects, its dried flowers for fragrance and its fruit in soups and stews. Medicinally it was used for sore throats and kidney problems.

Bracken *Raithneath Mhór* *Pterdium aquilinum*
Viewed as a magical plant that appears to bear no flowers and fruit and has almost invisible seeds. Magically it is associated with invisibility, the otherworld and changelings. It was used in fires, as bedding, thatch and in brewing beer. Ash from bracken was used in soap, bleaching and also fertilizer. Medicinally it was used to treat parasitic worms although it is highly poisonous and hence generally little used.

Brookweed/Samolus *Falcaire uisce* *Samolus valerandi*
Described by Pliny as dug up by the left hand of a Druid who had fasted for days. It grows wild in the British Isles and France, it was used as a cure for a variety of illnesses in cattle and pigs. The leaves are extremely bitter but were eaten to prevent scurvy but it was rarely used internally by humans due to the horrible taste. A poultice from it was used in Wales for sore eyes.

Butterbur *Gallán Mór* *Petasites hybridus*
The large leaves were used to wrap up butter pats and also as protection from the sun. The root can be used to help break a fever as it induces heavy sweating. It was also used for the treatment of rheumatism.

Buttercup *Fearbán* *Ranunculus* (genus)
Associated with *Bealtaine* it was picked on May eve and also rubbed in cows' udders on May Day to protect them. Their fragrance was thought to induce madness yet if worn in a pouch around the neck they were thought to cure it. Medicinally their acrid juice is used to raise blisters and in rheumatism, relief of

headaches, curing warts, jaundice, heartburn and kidney problems.

Centaury *Drímire Mhuire* *Centaurium erythraea*
Valued for its purifying properties and believed to be particularly powerful if picked on May Day. It was considered an excellent protection against magic. It was used by the ancients in wound healing. It is regarded as a blood purifier and effective against liver, kidney, stomach and rheumatic complaints. It was also used in Britain and some parts of Ireland for indigestion relief.

Charlock *Praiseach Bhuí* *Sinapis arvensis*
Formerly a common food, especially in times of famine, it came to be regarded as a nuisance weed in more recent centuries. However, during the Irish famine it kept many people alive, as well as being boiled like cabbage, its seeds were used to make a rough bread. It was also used to cure jaundice. The juice was also taken as a spring tonic.

Crane's Bill *Crobh* *Geranium* (genus)
Reputedly named after St. Robert (Herb-Robert) who used it for healing, it was used to staunch bleeding, to cure kidney problems, treat coughs and sore throats and cure red-water fever in livestock.

Daisy *Nóinín Bellis* *perenis/ Leucanthemum vulgare*
Associated with the coming of spring and also childhood prophetic games. The larger ox-eye daisy is associated with the summer solstice and several medicinal uses such as treatment of abscesses and boils. Daisies can be used to treat fresh wounds, liver inflammation, burns, sore eyes, ringworm, chilblains and as sedative (Chamomile).

Dandelion *Caisearbhán* *Taraxacum officinale*

Associated with Imbolc and the goddess Brighid it was one of several plants used to protect milk from malign influence. It is famously diuretic but also was used in magical healing of warts and chickenpox. It was also used for coughs and colds, as a blood tonic, cure for jaundice, liver and stomach upsets, rheumatism and tuberculosis, cuts, swelling, styes, sore throats and parasitic worms. In ancient Ireland 'Diancecht's Porridge' containing Dandelion was used for fourteen types of stomach disorder.

Devil's Bit Scabious *Odhrach Bhallach* *Succusa pratensis*

Considered beneficial to cows' milk, and good to have on one's land, it appears in folklore often in association with the 'evil eye'. It was used in a magical potions to cure this and also as part of an incantation to summon the aid of fairies in the household. It was thought to have great healing powers, being used for plague, fevers, anti-poisoning, swellings, wounds, bites, bruised, blood clots, spots, coughs, inflammation, scurf, dandruff and sores.

Dock *Copóg* *Rumex* (genus)

Well known to ease nettle stings, it was also used to wrap up items such as butter and was even used as impromptu toilet paper. It was associated with good quality land despite being a troublesome weed. It was used to staunch bleeding and was a cure for bronchitis, colds and coughs, liver troubles including jaundice, to cure boils, rheumatism, diarrhoea and skin complaints.

Dog Rose *Feirdhris* *Rosa Canina*

An ancient symbol of love and beauty (especially in Ireland) it was also a valued foodstuff (rosehips) until modern times. Roses appear in some tales of the Fianna and also in the story of Tristan and Isolt. The gall was used to cure whooping cough and toothache and used magically to aid good sleep.

Figwort *Fothrom* *Scrophularia nodosa*

Said to have been used by Gaulish Druids in their midsummer fires, it was considered an important medicinal plant. In Ireland it was the 'queen of Irish herbs' and strongly linked with fairies, hence it was regarded with some trepidation and great respect. It was commonly found under Elder trees, from which it was thought to gain power and was collected with due ceremony and care. It was used for treating fits, sore throats, bronchitis, sprains, swellings, wounds, liver complaints, as a blood tonic and for piles.

Flag Iris *Feileastram* *Iris pseudacorus*

A symbol of beauty, purity and wisdom, it is associated with *Bealtaine,* being placed on windows or doorsteps and hung on the May bush. It is mentioned in Celtic myth and poetry in association with beauty. The leaves were used for bedding and thatch and a black dye was made from the root. Medicinally it was used to treat diarrhoea, toothache, colds, sore throats and jaundice. It was also used as a mild purgative.

Forget-Me-Not *Ceotharnach* *Myosotis* (genus)

A symbol of love and constancy throughout Europe, it however has few uses. A decoction of the juice was said to harden steel and a syrup from the flowers was used for pulmonary (lung) complaints. Related plants such as Speedwell were used to provide protection on journeys and against ill luck, it was also used to relieve breast feeding soreness, colds and jaundice.

Foxglove *Lus Mór* *Digitalis purpurea*

Believed to be a fairy plant, its affect on the heart could revive listless patients hence it was used on children under the 'fairy stroke', but equally it could kill if administered carelessly. It was collected around the summer solstice, the most auspicious time and believed to offer powerful magical protection from fairies (*sidhé*) and appears in otherworldly mythology. Medicinally is can calm the heart but also raises blood pressure hence is potentially dangerous. It was also used to cure colds, fevers, sore throats, skin problems, wounds, swellings and burns. It was also used as a diuretic.

Fungi *Fungais* *Fungi* (division)
Strongly associated with fairies, they often grow in gradually expanding rings, which it was believed the fairies used to dance in. Various folk beliefs of ill luck or harm are associated with fungi rings. The field mushroom was eaten and but many other types have hallucinogenic or poisonous properties. Puffball spores were used to staunch bleeding, mushrooms to treat jaundice and the fly agaric to kill flies.

Grass *Féara* *Gramineae* (family)
Grass seeds provide a huge variety of foods and the plants provide fodder. In folk custom hungry grass is associated with illness and fainting and in Ireland with famine victims. Grasses were used for ropes, thatch, mats, baskets and bedding as well as food. Medicinally it could be used to cure boils, urinary or genital infections, kidney problems and poisoning in dogs.

Great Mullein *Coinnle Muire* *Verbascum thapsus*
Believed to protect against magic and also against sickness at certain times of year. It was used by women to condition their hair, the stalks were used to make torches and the leaves as padding for shoes. Medicinally it was used to treat tuberculosis, cure toothache, colds, coughs, bronchitis, asthma and to treat bee stings.

Heather *Fraoch* *Calluna vulgaris/Erica* (genus)

Used for bedding, brooms, fuel, fodder and making beer, it was highly valued but conversely is associated with poor quality land. To this day, it is considered lucky to wear heather. Heather features in several legends including the failed attempt to learn the Viking method of making heather beer. Heather honey was especially prized and tea made from the tips was used to cure coughs and colds, weakness of the heart and asthma.

Hemlock *Moing Mhear* *Conium maculatum*

Part of the Umbellifers family, this famous poison was used to dispatch Socrates some two and a half thousand years ago. It often grows alongside brooklime and watercress and hence care was required not to pick it accidentally. However, despite its poison, it was used in poultices to cure swellings and sores and also used as a cure for rheumatism.

Henbane *Gafann* *Hyoscyamus niger*

Another highly poisonous herb, it is also highly hallucinogenic, hence its reputation as a magical plant. The Celts were fearful of its power, especially towards children, it was also used in charms such as to banish hares or ward off evil spirits. The Gaulish Druids used *belinimica* in their rites to medicinal god Rectenus, this being a species of Henbane according to Moloney's Irish Ethno-botany. It was used (in small doses) as a sedative, painkiller, toothache cure, for whooping cough, gout, arthritis and nervous disorders.

Hogweed *Feabhrán* *Heracleum sphondylium*

Used to feed pigs as the name suggests, its hollow stems were also used by children as peashooters. The seeds were burnt and breathed in to relieve lethargy and revive from coma. In Scotland, it was believed that it could break the power of fairies holding a child in their grasp or suffering from the 'fairy stroke'.

Honeysuckle *Féithleann* *Lonicera periclymenum*
A symbol of beauty and summer, its choking grip makes it a symbol of strength. It was believed to protect from malign influence and a decoction drunk was used to negate the effects of the 'evil eye'. It was used magically to heal tuberculosis and fevers and to protect livestock and milk. Medicinally a syrup from the flowers treated lung disorders and a decoction treated the liver and spleen. It was also used for inflammation, jaundice, whooping cough and fevers.

Houseleek *Lus an Tóiteáin* *Sempervivum Tectorum*
Believed to protect against lightning and fires, plants were attached to thatch roofs to protect the house, similar beliefs existed in Roman and Greek culture. It was used medicinally to cure ulcers, burns and inflammation, corns, warts and chilblains. It was also used to relieve sore eyes, cure headaches and also to induce premature birth (abortion).

Ivy *Eidhneán* *Hedera helix*
A symbol of enduring fertility, eternal life and loyalty, ivy was valued throughout the ancient world. It was used in love divination, especially at *Samhain,* it was used to protect against witchcraft and disease although it was considered unlucky in the house except at Christmas. It was believed that cups made of ivy would neutralise bad or poisoned wine. Medicinally it was used to treat corns, burns, inflammations, to staunch bleeding, cure colds, coughs and bronchitis, eczema, boils, abscesses and also as a painkiller.

Lady's Mantle *Dearna Mhuire* *Alchemilla* (genus)
It was believed that the dew that collected in the leaves had magical properties. It was used against the evil eye in Scotland

and Ireland. Alchemists also used the dew in their attempts to turn base metals to gold. It was also used for women's problems and particularly to encourage conception and also believed to cure sagging breasts and restore faded beauty! Medicinally the plant was used in treating wounds and staunching bleeding, to reduce inflammation, treat burns and kidney problems.

Lords and Ladies *Cluas Chaoin* *Arum Maculatum*
Regarded as an aphrodisiac due to the phallic shape of the spadix. The berries are in fact highly poisonous and it was believed that both snakes and bears ate the berries. A starch was obtained from the plant to keep collars and ruffs stiff. Medicinally it was used to cure tuberculosis, spots, blemishes and freckles. The root was used to cure worms in children.

Madder *Garbhlus na boirne* *Rubia tinctorum*
Common to Britain and Europe, it was used to make a dye for wool, giving various shades of red. The root was used to treat urinary tract infections, bleeding, inflammations, diarrhoea, fevers, liver conditions, jaundice, skin problems and to speed healing of bones.

Mallow *Hocas Fiáin* *Malva sylvestris*
In Irish tradition one of seven herbs that were immune to natural or supernatural influence. It was picked at midday on a sunny day, close to or on the full moon. Travellers struck by the mallow were said to be protected from illness or fairies. It was used as food but also medicinally by the Celts, Greeks and Romans. The root was made into a paste used in sweets, giving its name to marshmallows, although sugar and artificial flavours are now used. It relieves aches and pains, sore throats, coughs, sores, cuts, bruises, ulcers and inflammation. It was also used for sprains, urinary complaints and as a general tonic. It was used as a sedative; its calming effect also made it an anti-aphrodisiac.

Mandrake *Mandrác* *Mandragora* (genus)

Well known throughout the ancient world, it is native to southern Europe but not the British Isles. It was widely used in magic and was known to the Gaulish Druids if not those of further west. It can be used to induce a trance state. It was also considered an aphrodisiac and cure for impotency and sterility, protection against demons and repeller of disease. Medicinally it is a purgative and anaesthetic and strongly soporific. It was used for ulcers, pain and insomnia.

Marsh Marigold *Lus Buí Bealtaine* *Caltha palustris*

A symbol of May and linked to *Bealtaine* it protects against evil and particularly against the *sidhé*. Bouquets of Mayflower were hung in the house or left on windows and doorsteps on May Eve. Medicinally it was used to cure fitting, relieve heart ailments and reduce boils. Its uses were limited though as it is strongly irritant.

Meadowsweat *Airgead luachra* *Filipendula ulmaria*

A sweet smelling flower that was used to flavour beer and fragrance rooms, it was also considered dangerous as it was thought to send people into a deep and sometimes fatal sleep. It was used for cleaning milk vessels and to make a black dye. It was used magically to cure those believed to be wasting due to fairy magic. It was considered one of the three most sacred herbs to the Druids. Medicinally it was used to prevent diarrhoea and dysentery and to cure fevers, colds, sore throats, dropsy, kidney problems and as a nerve tonic.

Mint *Mismín* *Mentha* (genus)

Mint is common throughout Europe, water-mint was considered one of three most sacred herbs of the Druids; it was also well used by the Greeks and Romans. It was used in love charms, in protection from the evil eye and to dispel stomach diseases and infections. It was used to deter fleas, flies and moths and to keep away mice in corn. Water-mint was used for coughs, colds indigestion and stomach disorders. It was also used in Ireland to cure deafness, jaundice, measles and as an antidote to nettle stings.

Mistletoe *Drualus* *Viscum album*

Perhaps most famously associated with Druids thanks to Pliny, it's Irish name means Druid's herb although it is not native to Ireland. It was considered a symbol of fertility and regeneration, growing parasitically on trees (usually apple and hawthorn, rarely oak) although appearing to grow without any source of nutrients, with unusual growth habits and producing flowers and fruit at late winter and early winter respectively. Folk customs still survive today and it is strongly associated with Christmas. It has been found in Celtic graves in Britain and was also connected with the god Baldur in Norse myth. Medicinally it was considered a 'heal-all' despite the fact that it is poisonous if over-prescribed. It was used to cure nervous disorders such as St. Vitus's dance and epilepsy. It was used for heart palpitations, nervousness, hysteria, and also in salves and washes for cuts and wounds.

Mugwort *Mongach Meisce* *Artemisia vulgaris*

Valued throughout Europe for women's problems and nervous disorders, it was also believed, by the Celts, to offer protection against evil. It is associated with the summer solstice and St. John's Eve, often being hung on doors or windowsills or worn throughout the British Isles. It was also thought to magically protect against sunstroke, tiredness and wild animals. Medicinally it was used to restore menstruation, ease childbirth and cleanse the womb. It was also a popular divinatory plant due to its narcotic properties that can induce a trance state. It was used to treat epilepsy and other nervous disorders, to fumigate patients' rooms and the smoke from burning it was inhaled by the sick as a general remedy.

Nettle *Neantóg* *Urtica* (genus)
A potent symbol of desolation it does though have many uses as food, cloth and herbal medicine. In both Ireland, and South West England May Eve had a tradition of children stinging each other and passersby with nettles. The sting was considered effective against rheumatism, inflammation and also purified the blood. Nettle was used as a food – *Cúl Faiche* or 'field cabbage' and fertiliser was made from soaking them in water. Nettle juice was used to make a green dye. Medicinally it was used to treat skin problems, measles, poor circulation, bleeding, swollen limbs and the bite of a mad dog.

Orchid *Magairlín* *Orchis* (genus)
A symbol of fertility, its phallic shape led to its use as an aphrodisiac and as a love charm. Women would use the new tuber (root) to make a man fall in love with them; it was believed that to give the old (dying) tuber would send them mad. In Scotland, they were also used for love divination as well as for love charms. Much of their use relates to magic, including eating the root to strengthen the genitals, aid conception and to select the sex of the child. Medicinally they were used to treat tuberculosis and diarrhoea, in Scotland Salep (a drink made from the tubers) was used to sooth stomach and bowel problems.

Pignut *Cúlarán* *Conopodium majus*
Well liked by pigs, hence the name, it was also popular with children who roasted them, in recent centuries calling them 'fairy potatoes'. In Ireland, it was regarded as a fairy plant. Medicinally it was used as a blood cleanser.

Plantain *Slánus* *Plantago* (genus)
Believed to have great healing properties, in Ireland it was even thought to be able to revive the dead. It was considered dangerous to pick as a change in the wind could cause the collector to go mad. In Ireland and parts of Britain the flower heads were used to play 'fighting cocks' or 'soldiers' (similar to modern conkers), this game was still played when I was a child. Greater plantain is associated with St. Patrick, often used to heal wounds, although like many items attributed to this and other saints, it was probably used by Druids in the pre-Christian era. Plantain was especially valued for treatment of bleeding and wounds but also used for skin problems, corns, warts, headaches, coughs and jaundice.

Poppy *Poipín* *Papaver* (genus)/*Meconopsis cambria*
In Britain and Ireland it was believed that staring at them caused headaches or that children could lose their sight. In Ireland, young women had a fear of touching them, although it is not clear why. In Britain and parts of Europe it is linked with thunder and lightning. It was well known to the Egyptians, Greeks and Romans, linked with fertility of the land. The western poppy varieties are narcotic but not half so much as the opium poppy that grows in Asia. The European poppy was used as a painkiller, especially for ear or toothaches, it was also used for coughs, sore eyes and neuralgia.

Primrose *Sabhaircín* *Primula vulgaris*
In its wild form, it was considered a symbol of vitality of spring and of otherworldy beauty. It was also a powerful protection against malign influence. It is linked with *Imbolc*, Easter (vernal equinox) and *Bealtaine*, being widely used at these times for decoration or protection. They were often put around the outside of houses on May Eve in Ireland and the Isle of Man. Primrose appears in several myths in each case linked with fairies or other-

worldly events. Medicinally it was used to relieve nervous disorders, insomnia, induce relaxation, treat toothache, burns, jaundice, tuberculosis and coughs in horses.

Ragwort *Buachalán* *Senecio* (genus)
Although widely hated by farmers it had several uses. It was regarded as a vehicle for fairies, especially at *Samhain*, several stories relate to fairies riding them like horses and even abducting people whilst doing so. Ragwort is the national emblem of *Yn Ellan Shiant* – the 'Fairy Isle' or Isle of Man. It was stored with grains to deter mice and brooms and brushes were often made of Ragwort. Medicinally it was used to cure cuts, sores, burns, boils and ulcers. It was also used for jaundice, coughs, colds, sore joints and rheumatism.

Rushes *Luachra* *Juncus* (genus)
Used for thatching and floor coverings, they are also used for the Crois Bride or St. Brigid's Cross. They symbolise hospitality, protection and also the purity and cleanliness of water, they are strongly associated with *Imbolc* and Brighid/St. Brigid. They appear in folklore in relation to Brighid and also to holy wells, by which they could often be found growing. As well as thatch, they were used for candles, mats, toys and ropes. Medicinally their uses were few but they were used for jaundice, ringworm and shingles and magically to cure a crick in the neck.

Selago *Uilen* *Juniperus sabina*
Another herb referred to by Pliny. Often mistaken for *Lycopodium Selag*, which is not native to Western Europe, Selago is in fact a diminutive member of the juniper family. It was used to purify and drive away malign influence. Common juniper has many practical and medicinal uses (see page 239), savin juniper most probably shares many its attributes.

Scarlet Pimpernel *Falcaire Fiáin* *Abagallis arvensis*
Thought to be a source of magical power, it was said to give clairvoyance and clairaudience to a person holding it. It was also believed to give the ability to understand the 'speech' of animals and birds. It was also thought to enable the bearer to see through illusions, a property similar to the shamrock. Medicinally it was used as an antidote for snake and dog bites and was also used for depression, liver problems, eye diseases, jaundice, dropsy, kidney problems, rheumatism and toothache.

Searack *Feamainn* *Fusus* (genus)
Seaweed was a valuable fertilizer in Britain and Ireland, even well into the twentieth century. St. Brigid's Day/*Imbolc* was a traditional time for collecting it and also shellfish in Ireland. In the Scottish Highlands an annual sacrifice of ale was given at *Samhain* to the sea (Shony) to secure a good harvest of seaweed next year, this may well be Norse in origin in connection with Sjoni the god of the sea. Seaweed was eaten as food and used medicinally for rheumatism, bruising, pains and for coughs and colds: *Carrigeen* – a cure still in use today that I can personally testify is most unpleasant although effective.

Selfheal *Duán Ceannchosach* *Prunella vulgaris*
Gains its name from its reputation as a healer of wounds. It is suggested that the Druids gathered it at a dark moon at the rise of the Dog Star in a similar manner to vervain. It was used in magical healing, a particular example being 'fairy struck' children that were wasting away. Medicinally it was used for heart conditions, strokes, fever, worms and tuberculosis.

Shamrock/Clover *Seamair/Seamróg* *Trifolium* (genus)
Famously connected with Ireland it was valued throughout the Celtic world. It is commonly associated with St. Patrick but its value probably dates to long before his time. Usually three leafed,

the four leaf shamrock or *seamróg nagCeithre* was considered fortuitous in Ireland and Scotland and also a bestower of supernatural powers such as seeing through illusions/deceptions and being immune to witchcraft or fairy sight. Similar beliefs relating to clover persisted throughout the British Isles even in my childhood and my friends and I spent many hours searching for four or more leafed clovers. Shamrock or clover appears in Irish and Welsh myth in connection with fertility or the supernatural. Clover is valuable as fodder and enriches the soil hence it is valued by farmers. Medicinally it was used to cure coughs, liver complaints, to cure cancer and to relieve bee stings.

Spurge *Spuirse* *Euphorbia* (genus)
It was used magically in Ireland to rescue women from fairy abduction if collected at the appropriate phase of the moon during August. It was used as a quick method of catching fish in rivers and ponds as it poisons them. Medicinally it was used for warts and skin blemishes and as a general purgative, especially for diarrhoea.

St. John's Wort *Beathnua* *Hypericum perforatum*
Linked with the summer solstice and the Feast of St. John, this was an important magical and medicinal herb throughout the British Isles, still used today. Believed to provide great protection against evil, expel demons and bring abundance to the bearer. It was cast into midsummer fires and dried and smoked over them too. On St. John's Eve, children were given it to ward off sickness and it was also worn to protect against evil. It was also placed on windowsill and over doors of the home as protection from malign influences. In Scotland, it was said to be especially valued by St. Colmcille (Columba) and was valued as powerful protection from harm, placed under the armpit. At midsummer, it was used by girls in love divination and also in the making of love charms. In Wales, it was used to predict life expectancy.

Medicinally it was used for lung and bladder problems, dysentery, jaundice, diarrhoea, sore eyes, cuts and scratches. Its primary modern usage is as an antidepressant, although it has fulfilled this function in ancient times under the guise of hysteria, melancholia, cure for the evil eye, evil spirits and general 'insanity'.

Thistle *Feochadán* *Cirsium* (genus)
The Scottish national emblem, credited with saving Scotland from a Viking invasion although probably only known for this from the Middle Ages onwards. In Ireland, it was a symbol of good land despite being a troublesome weed. It appears in *Tain Bo Cuailgne* when Cailidín's children create an enchanted army from thistles and puffballs. It was used as fodder for livestock and poultry. The flowers of spear thistle were said to be able to curdle milk. Medicinally it was used for kidney infections, wounds and (in a tea) as a cure for depression.

Vervain *Beirbhéine* *Verbena officinalis*
Recorded as used by the Druids of Gaul, it was widely used throughout the ancient world. It had the reputation of being powerful protection against evil and enchantments and also being able to amplify beneficial influences. The Gauls picked it in July/August at the rising of the Dog Star (Sirius) after first making an offering of fruit and honey to the earth. It is native to Western Europe, except Ireland, becoming naturalised in Ireland at an unknown date hence it does not feature much in early Irish legend or folk cures. It is said the Druids used it in religious ceremonies, in ratifying vows and treaties and for divination. Vervain is one of three herbs held to be most sacred to the Druids. At *Bealtaine* it was used to protect farms from evil influence, and especially to protect cattle by tying it to the horns or tail. It was sown into babies' clothes to protect them from fairies and it was often carried by travellers and fishermen for luck and protection.

It was used magically to heal the 'evil eye', the 'fairy stroke', cure headaches and scrofula. It was thought to cure poisons, prevent disease, cure fevers and spread a convivial atmosphere where scattered or burned. Medicinally it was used for gout, swellings, sores, skin problems, jaundice, whooping cough, mastitis, oedema, lymphatic disorders, rheumatism and ear infections.

Vetch *Peasair* *Vicia* (genus)
Hated by farmers due to its tough roots, it can be eaten but has a bitter taste, although the young roots taste of liquorice. It was used as fodder for livestock and by the Scots to stave off thirst and hunger and also in advance of a drinking bout to reduce drunkenness. Medicinally it was used to heal wounds, for stomach ache, staunching blood loss and for back ache.

Violet *Sailchuach* *Viola* (genus)
In folk belief they are linked to sadness and death, it was considered bad luck, omen of sickness or an omen of death to see them flowering in autumn and it was bad luck to bring a single common dog violet into the home. Conversely, perhaps due to the sweet fragrance, they are associated with love and also are a symbol of modesty. In Irish myth it appears as a symbol of beauty and to the Gauls a symbol of virginity, meanwhile the Greeks linked the violet with Aphrodite. Violet was used in perfumes and ancient cosmetics. Medicinally the scent was used to revive someone who had fainted, for boils, headaches and also to cure cancerous tumours.

Watercress *Biolar* *Nasturtium officinale*
A valuable food that grows in abundance it also has medicinal benefits. In Scotland and Ireland it was believed it could be used magically to 'steal the goodness from milk' of other people's cows. In general though it was thought to be beneficial to health and mental well-being. Magically it was thought to protect

children from depression and improve intelligence if eaten. It was a valued food and a magical aid and is mentioned as such in Celtic myth. It was considered good for scurvy and as a blood purifier, being eaten raw, cooked or in soup for its health giving properties. Medicinally it was used for colds, coughs, rheumatism, women's problems, skin problems, swellings, heart disease and labour pains.

Water Lily *Bacán* *Nymphaeaceae* (family)
Considered somewhat dangerous, especially in Scotland, as it was thought it could cause children to become 'fairy struck' and also could nullify sexual desire in adults. It is linked with the Celtic water goddess Coventina of Britain, Iberia and Gaul who was depicted holding a water lily. In Scotland, the root was used to produce a black dye for wool and in England to deter cockroaches and crickets. Medicinally the root was used to calm sexual frustration or out of control libido, it was also used for reducing boils and to staunch wounds.

Water Pimpernel/Brooklime *Lochall* *Veronica beccabunga*
Sometimes confused with Brookweed (Pliny's Samolus) it is possible that this is the plant referred to but this cannot be verified. It is common in the British Isles and France. It can be used to prevent scurvy, as a poultice for itching, burns and wounds. The juice also acts as a blood tonic, diuretic and treatment for kidney stones. Magically it was used to increase psychic and visionary abilities.

Wild Carrot *Mealbhacán* *Daucus carota*
Associated with the autumnal equinox/Feast of St.Michael, in Scotland they were collected by women, it being thought they brought fertility. They were valued in Ireland and Scotland as they could be stored into winter. Medicinally it was used as a diuretic and in a poultice for treating sores and wounds.

Woad *Glaisín* *Isatis tinctoria*
An important plant to the British and Irish due to its blue dye, although it is now extinct in Ireland. It is referred to by both Pliny and Julius Caesar in reference to British people painting themselves with woad, especially warriors; it is likely that it was used for tattoos. It was probably used for the same purpose in Ireland as suggested by an 8th century poem referring to Amergin's blue tattoos. It appears that it was not used medicinally.

Wood Avens *Machall Coille* *Geum Urbanum*
Believed across Europe to protect against evil spirits, demons and wild animals, it was not widely used though in Ireland or Britain. It was used to flavour ales, as fly repellent and to protect clothes from moths. Medicinally it was used to prevent plague, for diarrhoea, stomach ache and sore throats.

Yarrow *Athair Thalún* *Achillea millefolium*
A popular plant for love divination in Scotland and Ireland by women, it was also used as protection from evil and diseases. In Scotland it was also thought it had the power to increase feminine beauty or make a man fall in love with the wearer. It was also believed to restore the goodness of milk that had been magically stolen. It is also one of the seven sacred herbs immune to natural/supernatural influence. Yarrow was called 'herb of seven cures 'because of its healing properties. Medicinally it was used to staunch wounds and cuts by the Celts, Greeks and the Romans. It was used to stop nosebleeds and also to cause them – as a means of relieving headaches. It was also used for toothache, coughs, colds, fevers, rheumatism and boils.

The above information on Celtic plants is just a short summary and merits much deeper investigation for those with an interest in Druid medicine or modern herbalism, some plant families are a vast area of study by themselves. In the case of fungi, this is a whole division of the plant kingdom and is the subject of many academic and nature books. It is widely believed that the Druids made use of *Muisiriún Mearbhaill* (Psilocybe semilanceata) the Magic Mushroom and *Agairg Cuileoige* (Amanita muscaria) the Fly Agaric. Certainly mushrooms and toadstools were (and often still are) associated with magic and fairies throughout the British Isles and there is an abundance of folklore relating to them.

In the case of grasses, an entire plant family, these were a great provider of food in the form of seeds and also food for livestock but they also had some medicinal uses. The water lily is another entire family of plants, the roots of which had several medicinal uses in Celtic culture.

Where I have used genus in brackets in the plant list it indicates that there are several species within this group (genus) that were used. In common usage one plant species can have multiple common names or conversely several different species of plant might have the same common name, which leads to great confusion. In modern botanical naming, developed by Carl Linneaus in 1735, every plant has a unique name in Latin, thereby avoiding any confusion. Almost all respectable modern books on plants and their usage avail of this system either exclusively or alongside the common names. This is obviously of great value, particularly in herbal medicine, imagine if one mixed up plant names and gave a patient the wrong herbs in the wrong dosage — this could potentially lead to complications or even death.

In modern Druid practice, there are various other healing methods such as Oracle cards (which I discussed earlier), Reiki, Acupuncture/Acupressure and so forth. These may well be worthwhile and complementary to the body of ancient Druidic lore; however, they are not strictly speaking Druidic as they have no basis in Celtic culture. Therefore, I have chosen not to include any of these additional methods in this book, and besides they are all very well documented elsewhere.

XV

Justice and Wisdom

It is well documented in both Classical and Celtic literature that the Druids performed an important function in terms of a judicial system and also in the dissemination of knowledge to royalty, nobility and also the people in general. Before going on to give specifics, I shall give a few examples from the literature:

> ...The Gauls, friends and foes alike, obey the rule of the priests and bards not only in time of peace but also during wars. It has often happened that just as two armies approached each other with swords drawn and spears ready, the Druids will step between the two sides and stop the fighting, as if they has cast a spell on wild beasts. Thus even among the wildest barbarians, anger yields to wisdom and the god of war respects the Muses.
> Diodorus

> ...The Druids also study the ways of nature, but apply themselves to laws of morality as well. The Gauls consider the Druids the most just of people and so are entrusted with judging both public and private disputes. ...Murder cases especially are handed over to the Druids for judgment.
> Strabo

> Indeed the Druids are judges on all controversies public and private. If any crime has been committed, if any murder done, if there are any questions concerning inheritance, or any controversy concerning boundaries, the Druids decide the case and determine punishments. If anyone ignores their

decision, that person is banned from all sacrifices — an extremely harsh punishment among the Gauls. Those who are so condemned are considered detestable criminals. Everyone shuns them and will not speak with them, fearing some harm from contact with them, and they receive no honour nor justice for any worthy deed.
Julius Caesar

...Druids make their pronouncements by means of riddles and dark sayings, teaching that the gods must be worshipped, and no evil done, and manly behaviour maintained.
Diogenes Laertius

They teach many things to the nobles of Gaul in a course of instruction lasting as long as twenty years, meeting in secret either in a cave or in secluded dales.
Pomponius Mela

Thus philosophy, a science of the highest utility, flourished in antiquity among the barbarians, shedding its light over nations. And afterwards it came to Greece. First in its ranks were the prophets of the Egyptians; and the Chaldeans among the Assyrians; and the Druids among the Gauls...
Clement of Alexandria

It was ordained in Cormac's time that every High King in Ireland should keep ten officers in constant attendance on him, who did not separate from him as a rule, namely a prince, a Brehon, a druid, a physician, a bard a seancha, a musician and three stewards... the Brehon to explain the customs and laws of the country... a druid to offer sacrifices and to forebode good or evil to the country...
from *The History of Ireland* by Geoffrey Keating

I see another band there. A sedate, grey-haired man in front thereof...

'Judicial and sage, by our conscience, is the despription,' said Medb.

'Sage and judicial the person whose description it is,' said Cu Roi.

'Who then is he?' asked Ailill.

'Not hard to tell. Sencha the Great... from Carn Mag of Ulster; the most eloquent man of the men of earth, and the peacemaker of the hosts of the Ulstermen...'

from The Intoxication of the Ulstermen

There are many more examples besides, although clearly some of the Druidic functions were distributed among several different classes of 'official' it would appear that some Druids performed several of these functions, perhaps some (such as a *Ollamh*) all of them. Despite regional differences, the basic structure of law, education, ritual, arbitration, advice, medicine and divination was performed in Gaul, Ireland and Britain by the Druidic classes. The classical accounts, spanning some five centuries, do not contradict what evidence and lore is to be found among the accounts produced later by the Celtic peoples themselves.

In Ireland, it was common that even the king would not speak without the consent of his Druid or without the Druid speaking first. Following the events related in the *Táin Bo Cuilgne*, Conor mac Nessa consulted his 'right illustrious' Druid Cathbhadh (Cathbad) in regard to his wish to avenge his humiliation at the hands of Queen Maebh of Munster, deferring to his judgment. Likewise, King Laegaire relied on the advice of his Druids, Lucetmail and Lochru in particular. In British mythology, Arthur king of the Britons relies on the advice of his Druid Myrddin (Merlin) who also advised the ill-fated Kings Vortigern and Uther (Arthur's father) before him.

Much of the Druidic wisdom is encoded in the form of poetry

or stories. This can be found intermingled amongst the convoluted fabric of the mythologies, collected histories or epic poems such as those found in the Metrical *Dindsenchas, The Book of Ballymote,* the *Ossianic* and *Ultonian* cycles, *The Book of Taliesin, The Red Book of Hergest, The Black Book of Caermarthen* or *The Book of Aneurin* and more. Unlike modern writing that often presents convenient 'sound bites' or 'bullet points' the corpus of Celtic literature usually requires the reading of entire myths or poems in order to extract the nuggets of wisdom contained therein. Only in the Welsh and Irish Triads will you find Druidic wisdom expressed in a succinct form and even these can be cryptic, often requiring some thought before they are fully understood.

Below you will find a few examples that I have selected, just to give a taste of what one might expect. However, I recommend serious study of the Celtic mythology, poems and triads in order to gain a thorough understanding of Druidic wisdom.

I am not headstrong and petulant.
I will not avenge myself on him who drives me.
I will not laugh in derision.
Under foot for a while,
My knee is stretched,
My hands are bound,
In the earthen house,
With an iron chain
Around my two knees.
Yet of the mead from the horn,
And of the men of Catreath,
I, Aneurin, will compose,
As Taliesin knows,
An elaborate song,
Or a strain to Gododin,
Before the dawn of the Brightest day.
From The Gododin in the Book of Aneurin

He who meddles with the mane of a wolf without a club in his hand, Must naturally have a brave disposition under his cloak.
From The Gododin in the Book of Aneurin

From First Battle of *Moy Tuireadh* in *'Lebor Gabála Érenn'*, the *Firbolg* Druid's dream foretells the coming wars, encapsulated in this verse (*roscanna*).

The Arrival of the Tuatha
A tale for you,
youths across ocean,
a thousand heroes will fill (web) the sea,
speckled (magic) ships will moor here,
all death declared.
A folk each of magic incantations,
a bad doom will strike false science,
good portents will ebb peaceful bindings,
contention will be routed.

Attributed to Lugh after the second battle of Moytirra (*Magh Tuireadh*):

It is established steadfast bright and accurate
(this) aftermath (of the battle).
O people of the world,
it has come that all has been made manifest
to our flowering ones.
Understanding of milkings will come.
Made great are those (who were) reduced
by my judgement/esteem
(by) my singing chants of oaks
to those of) youthful feats of riding
in quick (soon over) weeping.

Vanish sorrow!
Joy/welcome is bound on the men below me.
The sun gives home to (these) arrangements
to those cherished ones who are free.
Go forth O men to the banquet-halls.
I establish the frame-work of this home
(this) binding establishment
concerning (our) mutual angers in (the) heart.
The Fomors of the bright sea do vanish.
O turn great path/way!
Life to Ireland!
Destruction to foreign petitions/chants
and long-life to men,
bright games-playing be prosperous,
from today forever
be there peace between Fomor and Ireland!

The Druid Amergin recites on his arrival the following invocation to Ireland:

I request the land of Ireland
to come forth)
coursed is the wild sea
wild the crying mountains
crying the generous woods
generous in showers (rain/waterfalls)
showers lakes and vast pools
vast pools hosts of well-springs
well-springs of tribes in assembly
assembly of kings of Tara
Tara host of tribes
tribes of the sons of Mil
Mil of boats and ships
ships come to Ireland

Ireland high terribly blue
an incantation on the (same) wind
(which was the) wind empty of Bres
Bres of an empty cup
Ireland be mighty
Ermon at the beginning
Ir, Eber, requested
(now it is) I (who) request the land of Ireland!

Kenmare's Pacification Spell:

Melt away (expire, soften) fully, melt away completely.
I swear this myself to every prince.
Melt into sleep, melt in tranquillity.
Be borne a bright newness
to (the) head of the hosts of Fiacha of princes.
Melt clean(ly), melt (with) generosity
(all those) around an ignorant (unjust) king.
Melt away completely, melt away into sleep.
Be borne a fresh newness.
(But) of Mogh Corb
melt away his silver and gold and enamel (jewellery),
melt away fairy (allies of the king) and king and great ones,
empowered with you and from you to Mogh Ruith
and from (the) men of Corb
and to Buan
empowered himself
a sight (seen to be done) three times
with that a sight of wisdom
the (high) king made humble.
The draught will be drowned.
(Magical) energy will enliven,
each will be healed,
will transform into peace. Melt away.

From the The Testament of Morann (*Audacht Morainn*) translated by Fergus Kelly:

> *Darkness gives way to light. Grief gives way to happiness. An oaf gives way to a learned man. A fool gives way to a sage. The unfree give way to the free. The uncouth gives way to the illustrious. Stinginess gives way to generosity. Avarice gives way to openhandedness. Recklessness gives way to steadiness. Disquiet gives way to pacification. An un-sovereign gives way to a true sovereign. Conflict gives way to peace. Falsehood gives way to truth.*

From the Cauldron of Poesy, translated by Erynn Rowan Laurie:

My perfect cauldron of warming
has been taken by the Gods from the mysterious abyss of the elements;
a perfect truth that ennobles from the center of being,
that pours forth a terrifying stream of speech.

I am Amirgen White-knee,
with pale substance and grey hair,
accomplishing my poetic incubation in proper forms,
in diverse colors.

The Gods do not give the same wisdom to everyone,
tipped, inverted, right-side-up;
no knowledge, half-knowledge, full knowledge —
for Eber Donn, the making of fearful poetry,
of vast, mighty draughts death-spells, of great chanting;
in active voice, in passive silence, in the neutral balance between,
in rhythm and form and rhyme,
in this way is spoken the path and function of my cauldrons.

Where is the root of poetry in a person; in the body or in the soul? Some say it is in the soul, for the body does nothing without the soul. Some say it is in the body were the arts are learned, passed through the bodies of our ancestors. It is said that this is the truth remaining over the root of poetry, and the wisdom in every person's ancestry does not come from the northern sky into everyone, but into every other person.

From *Cú Chulainn and Senbaecc,* translated by John Carey, Ed. E. J. Gwynn:

> ...There are nine fair-bearing hazels from whose nuts he got imbas: it used to drop into the wells, so that the stream bears the imbas into the Boyne. Then Senbecc sang to him some of his lore, and a song:
>
> *I am not a lad, I am not a man,*
> *I am not a child in learning.*
> *The mysteries of God have made me gifted.*
> *I am Abcán, a sage of learning, a poet from Segais.*
> *Senbecc is my name, Ebrecc's grandson from the síde.*

(These are the names of the nine hazels: Sall, Fall, Fuball, Finnam, Fonnam, Fofuigell, Crú, Crínam, Cruanbla.)

There are hundreds of triads, or wisdom sayings, most referring to three items or qualities although a few exist in twos and fours. From the Triads:

> The three places of Ireland to alight at: Derry, Taghmon, Kilmainham.
> The three fairs of Ireland: the fair of Teltown, the fair of Croghan, the fair of Colman Elo.
> The three mountains of Ireland: Slieve Gua, Slieve Mis, Slieve Cualann.

The three lakes of Ireland: Lough Neagh, Lough Ree, Lough Erne.

The three rivers of Ireland: the Shannon, the Boyne, the Bann.
The three dark places of Ireland: the cave of Knowth, the cave of Slaney, the cave of Ferns
Three unfortunate things of husbandry: a dirty field, leavings of the hurdle, a house full of sparks.

Three unfortunate things for a man: a scant drink of water, thirst in an ale-house, a narrow seat upon a field.

Three rejoicings that are worse than sorrow: the joy of a man who has defrauded another, the joy of a man who has perjured himself, the joy of a man who has committed parricide.

Three slender things that best support the world: the slender stream of milk from the cow's dug into the pail, the slender blade of green corn upon the ground, the slender thread over the hand of a skilled woman.

Three hands that are best in the world: the hand of a good carpenter, the hand of a skilled woman, the hand of a good smith.

Three things which justice demands: judgment, measure, conscience.
Three things which judgment demands: wisdom, penetration, knowledge.
Three things for which an enemy is loved: wealth, beauty, worth.
Three nurses of theft: a wood, a cloak, night.
Three qualities that bespeak misfortune: weariness,

premature old age, reproachfulness.
Three laughing-stocks of the world: an angry man, a jealous man, a niggard.
Three ruins of a tribe: a lying chief, a false judge, a lustful priest.
Three maidens that bring hatred upon misfortune: talking, laziness, insincerity.
Three maidens that bring love to good fortune: silence, diligence, sincerity.
Three hateful things in speech: stiffness, obscurity, a bad delivery.
Three signs of wisdom: patience, closeness, the gift of prophecy.
Three things that make a wise man foolish: quarrelling, anger, drunkenness.
Three things that show every good man: a special gift, valour, piety.
Three things that show a bad man: bitterness, hatred, cowardice.

Four elements of wisdom: patience, docility, sobriety, well-spokenness; for every patient person is wise, and every docile person is a sage, every sober person is generous, every well-spoken person is tractable.

The three melodies of creation: the wind in the trees, the stream at snowmelt, the cry of a newborn babe.
Three sureties of happiness: good habits, amiability and forbearance.
Three followers of wisdom: imagination, purpose and endeavour.

Three things that resemble each other: a bright sword that rusts from long staying in the scabbard, bright water which

> sinks from long standing, and wisdom which is dead from long disuse.
> There are three foundations of wisdom: discretion in learning, memory in retaining and eloquence in telling.
> Three foundations of learning: seeing much, studying much and suffering much.

It is likely that in Ireland, where there was no prohibition against writing (unlike Gaul), that a great volume of literature once existed. It is stated that St. Patrick burned 180 Druidic books and encouraged royalty and nobility to do likewise, however it is also stated that the Brehon Law was written down at St. Patrick's instigation. A great many events and dealings are falsely attributed to St. Patrick so it is impossible to know if his involvement in recording the laws is correct or false, however the 'Annals of the Four Masters' states that he oversaw the process. Following the book burning there was still much that survived, but no doubt much has been lost through wars, colonisation and the passing of time. One aspect of Druidic knowledge that was retained more-or-less intact by the Gaelic order in Ireland long after the decline of the Druids is Brehon law. We are highly fortunate that the ancient laws of Ireland that have been in existence for thousands of years, have survived albeit in a diminished form.

In Gaul all traces of the Celtic law were obliterated by the Romans, the same becoming true of their language after four centuries of conquest. In Scotland and Wales, the situation was somewhat better. In Scotland the ancient laws survived until the decline of the Dalriadian dynasty (after MacBeth's death), after which a process of Anglicisation of the laws began. Medieval manuscripts do refer to the earlier laws — *Assisa terras* or the law of the land. Fragments of ancient law were recorded by James Balfour in his legal compilation *Practicks: or a system of the more ancient law of Scotland*, written in the late 1500s but published posthumously in 1754. Vestiges such as Tanistry, relating to inheritance are similar to the laws of ancient Ireland; however, what does remain is fragmented and corrupted to say the least. Despite largely adopting English practices, Scotland has retained its own legal system and unique laws to this day.

In Wales, a similar system to that in Ireland existed until the defeat of the Celtic order on the death of Llewelyn in 1282. Two years later Welsh law was abolished by the Statute of Rhuddlan and English law was introduced. The Celtic laws in Wales were called *Cyfraith Hywel* after Hywel Dda who is traditionally attributed with codifying the ancient laws between 942 and 950.

> Hywel the Good, son of Cadell, by the Grace of God, king of Wales... summoned to him from every commote of his kingdom six men who were practised in authority and jurisprudence... to the place called the White House on the Taf in Dyfed... And at the end of Lent the king selected from that assembly the twelve most skilled laymen of his men and the one most skilled scholar who was called Master Blegywrd, to form and interpret for him and for his kingdom, laws and usages...
> From the Book of Blegywryd

Like the Brehon laws, the Welsh law incorporated much earlier laws from the pre-Christian (and pre-Roman) era although it appears that they were updated and revised to a far larger extent. Unfortunately, the earliest surviving manuscripts date from the 13th century onwards, in Latin or a mixture of Latin and Welsh, many showing the influence of the church and Canon law. What we can be sure of is that society was divided into at least four classes/layers, land law, criminal law and the status of women originally bore far more resemblance to the Irish laws than they did to either the (Roman) church laws or those of the conquering Normans. So, it would appear that a similar system regarding government and law existed in all of the Celtic kingdoms, but only in Ireland (due to its remoteness and late colonisation) do we have anything extant that is not badly corrupted and forms the bones of a complete system.

This body of Irish law known as Brehon Law, or to call it by its correct name, *Feineachus*, is specific to Ireland, but it would appear that it is similar to the systems that existed in both Britain and Gaul, although this is difficult to prove definitively. In a wider context, the rule of law or *Recht* (in *Gaeilge*) was at least comparable to that of other great civilisations of the ancient world, by the time of Jesus of Nazareth much of the then known world had come under the yoke of Roman Law. However, as the Romans abandoned their territories leaving them to lawlessness, an unbroken rule of law continued in (most of) Ireland up until the Elizabethan era. Consider that the first codified English laws in the early 7th century, under Ethelbert of Kent amounted to a few scraps and even in the late 9th century under Alfred the extent and complexity of the laws was still meagre. The Welsh laws, codified in the late 10th century, were comprehensive but by this stage much influenced by church law and the later version that still existed are further diluted.

The body of Irish law was developed over an unknown period of time with references to events some four hundred years before the common era. It is clearly a system that originated in great antiquity but becoming fully formed around the mid 3rd century AD during the reign of King Cormac and it was written down in the early 5th century. Fortunately, the absence of the Romans during this period of development and codification meant that the Druidic system of law was not obliterated as it had been further east. It continued through the conversion to Christianity, the invasions of the Danes and the Normans. Only in what was known as 'The Pale' — roughly four counties of Leinster under English rule after the Norman invasion, was Brehon Law not observed and despite various attempts to impose English Law over the centuries, the Gaelic system continued until the flight of the Earls in 1607.

During this long period of time, the *Feineachus* was copied and elaborated upon. The original texts, in Old Irish, are lost to us but some portions of the original are retained in the books that transcribe, describe and discuss the original text. The process of transcription occurred many times so that those copies that survive are full of glosses, notes and elaborations in various old dialects and to a large degree Medieval Irish, to be found between lines, in margins or wherever they could be fitted in.

Unfortunately, due to the Elizabethan prohibition of the Gaelic language and books in *Gaeilge* it was necessary for those who wished to preserve their heritage to hide their manuscripts; the punishment for infringement being severe. Fear of reprisals led to the destruction of many Gaelic works and also to their loss through burial, concealment in walls, roofs and so forth. Only some two hundred years later was it again safe to speak *Gaeilge* or possess books in the language; however, by this time much of the vast body of literature, including some of the *Feineachus* was lost forever.

What has survived was translated into English by a Royal Commission (beginning in 1852) and published in five volumes entitled 'Ancient Laws and Institutes of Ireland'. Despite the loss of material from destruction, poor transcription and such things these five volumes still run 400 to 500 pages each, a considerable body of work even after truncation. The bulk of these volumes consist of the remains of the *Senchus Mór*. This in itself runs to almost three volumes of the work, however it is clear that portions of it are missing, reference being made in the four remaining copies to passages or sections that are no longer in existence. Of these four copies of the Senchus Mór only one is complete (in Trinity College, Dublin) the three others being fragments in Trinity College and the British Museum in London. The commencement of the original work is described below:

> The age of Christ 438. The tenth year of Laeghaire. The *Senchus Mór* and *Feineachus* of Ireland were purified and written... He requested the men of Erinn to come to one place to hold a conference with him. When they came to the conference the Gospel of Christ was preached to them all... And when they saw Laeghaire and his Druids overcome by the great science and miracles wrought in the presence of the men of Erinn, they bowed down in obedience to the will of God and Patrick, in the presence of every chief in Erinn. It was then that Dubhthach was ordered to exhibit the judgments and all the poetry (literature) of Erinn, and every law which prevailed amongst the men of Erinn, through the law of nature, and the law of seers, and in the judgments of the island of Erinn, and in the poets. Now the judgments of true nature which the Holy Spirit had spoken through the mouths of the Brehons and just poets of the men of Erinn from the first occupation of the island down to the reception of the faith were all exhibited by Dubhthach to Patrick. What did not clash with the Word of God in the written law and the New Testament, and with the conscience of believers, was confirmed in the laws of the Brehons by the ecclesiastics and the chief men of Erinn; for the law of nature was quite right, except the faith and its obligations, and the harmony of the Church and people. And this is the *Senchus Mór*.
> From the Annals of the Four Masters

So it is clear that the laws were written down and updated to suit Christian mores after the coming of Patrick. This account, written much later, probably by monks, is most likely not entirely correct, considering that Laeghaire himself died a pagan and the conversion of the country took some two hundred years to complete even though all ecclesiastical accounts describe a miraculous almost instant and non-violent conversion, here too there are likely to be some 'embellishments' of the facts.

Whatever the case may be, we have the bulk of the Celtic laws of the ancient Irish, with superficial alterations, sufficiently complete to be a working system, still with us today. This includes *Cáin* law, *Cáin* being a word synonymous with *Ollamh* (head Druid) and not referring to Cai, a supposed contemporary of Moses. This area of law was sanctioned by assemblies at which the *Ard Rí*, Druids and provincial kings would all be present and this law was universal over the entire populace and was administered by the Druidic class of judges (*Druí*). Also included was *Urradhus* law, which was related to local governance and could be adjusted by local assemblies and this was administered by the chiefs (*Flaith*).

National assemblies were convened at Tara (*Feis* of Tara) or other important sites (e.g. at Taillteann and Uisneach) and locally (called *Aenach*) in each of the four provinces. These *feis* were held for several purposes, not least of these being the administration of the law. This was taken extremely seriously, so much so that the penalty for disrupting such an assembly was death. These *Feis/Aenach* took place at the important seasonal/religious times of the year for example *Bealtaine* however it was also possible for them to convene in cases of urgency. In all these events, the *Senchus Mór* was used to uphold the rule of law on a national and local basis. One Gaelic account of the Laws gives the following:

1. The Law of fosterage
2. The law relating to free tenants and the law relating to base tenants
3. The law of social relationship
4. The binding of all by their verbal contracts; for the world would be in a state of confusion if verbal contracts were not binding.

The binding of all to their good and bad contracts prevents the lawlessness of the world. Except the five contracts which are dissolved by the *Feini*, even though they be perfected –

1. The contract of a labourer without his chief
2. The contract of a monk without his abbot
3. The contract of the son of a living father without the father
4. The contract of a fool or mad woman
5. The contract of a woman without her husband

From the above we can ascertain that the areas of life that are still of concern today were covered (although fosterage was formerly far more common). Contracts were expected to be honoured, although unlike today a verbal contract was valid, only with notable exceptions for the protection of those where circumstances dictated that it should be ended.

According to the *Senchus Mór* there were six general classes in society: various grades of kings, the professional classes, the *flaiths* (nobility), freemen with property, freemen without property and the non-free. The position of people within the clan and their rights to land and such depended upon where they fitted into this system; however, unlike the Hindu caste system of India, it was possible for people to rise or fall within the class structure.

The Clan was the basic structure of community in Celtic community, best preserved in western Scotland and Ireland – basically a tribal unit similar to an extended family. In Ireland known as the *Tuath, Cinel* or *Clann,* the clan was a complex organisation linked through ancestry consisting of septs and within these a number of *fines*. The *Flaith-fine* was head of the *fine* of up to sixteen men, with subsections of the fine, their responsibility and entitlement, depending on their relationship to the *Flaith-fine.*

Land was inherited amongst the clan and land (if it was saleable) was generally offered to those within the clan before offering it to others. Depending on status, clan members were entitled to a portion of land surrounding their home on which *ciss* or tribute was not payable — this comprised a distance (in all directions) that a spear like object could be thrown or multiples thereof, depending on status. Only the un-free were obliged to pay 'wearisome tribute', which corresponds closely to modern rent, but even those in slavery were able to pool their resources in order to buy land and eventually obtain a higher status. Hence, we can see that property was dealt with very differently from the Roman, Norman feudal or modern ways, enabling land to remain within the clan unless it was specifically intended to be otherwise.

Dealing with criminals was also very different from our modern methods. It was common for people to air their grievances against another by giving notice of a number of days and in the case of the defendant being a person of status for example *flaith*, *Brehon*, bard and so on, the plaintiff would also fast outside their house until their grievance was dealt with. In the case of debt, distraining, or payment by the seizing of land was a form of settlement, if a defendant refused to hear the grievance the compensation would be doubled. However, should the plaintiff (faster) refuse fair settlement they would lose all right to compensation, thus preventing abuse of this system. Such a practice is not unique to Ireland, it was practised in India and even in ancient Rome, a similar form of protest took place to shame the accused into facing their accuser.

In the case of crimes against an individual, the crime died with the criminal, but in the case of damage or loss of property the criminal's *sept* could still be held liable. It was common for crimes to be paid for rather than criminals be imprisoned, tortured, beaten or executed. Types and quantity of fines varied according to the crime — *eiric* (reparation usually for a death), *einachlan* (honour-price), *dire*, *coirpdire*, *smacht* and *airer*. If the criminal should abscond without paying their fines then their closest relatives became liable for these fines. For example a murderer might have to pay his own honour-price, an *eiric* of seven *cumhals*[24] for the killing and twice that again if malice was proven; if the murderer ran off his/her family would instead have to pay the family of the deceased.

There are hundreds more examples besides that illustrate a well conceived and community centred approach to justice, women's rights, marriage, inheritance and so forth, which can be found in the translations of the original works and various commentaries on them. To my mind, the Brehon Law demonstrates both fairness and wisdom and a thirst for justice to be observed — far removed from the mindless and illiterate savages that the Celts were sometimes portrayed as being. To labour the point further, it should be noted that the earliest Celtic writing dates from at least 600 BC: inscriptions of the Lepontii Celts of northern Italy were discovered on over one hundred stones in 1913, which were written in an early form of Gaulish using a script created by the Etruscans. Although the Celts practised some bizarre and gruesome habits, such as the preservation and collection of enemy heads, this was also common in Germanic, Norse and Sythian cultures. The Celts were fearsome and violent but they were clearly highly cultured, intelligent, artistic, philosophical and employing a complex social structure that belies any notions of savagery or unsophistication.

In a modern context, there are currently few/no recognised positions for Druids in respect to the moral, educational and guidance requirements of society. The role of lawyers, barristers and judges are professions for which one trains and practises, usually regardless of the personal flaws or merits of the individual. Likewise, the role of the Druid as possessor and transmitter of wisdom has become secularised - undertaken by a multitude of personnel such as teachers, historians, politicians, poets, doctors, scientists, philosophers etc usually in an impersonal context. It is likely that very few ancient Druids were truly exceptional in all the Druidic arts, it is clear that a level of specialisation occurred, however the Druidic approach to knowledge and wisdom appears to be far more holistic and integrated than the modern approach, that is centred on information more than it is on understanding or a broader context.

So where does that leave the modern druid if these functions are already fulfilled by secular practitioners/professionals? Despite the great difficulty, time and patience in acquiring a broad range of skills and knowledge, as was required of the ancient Druids, the benefits of such an undertaking are a more rounded and complete understanding of the human experience and the world around us. I believe that acquiring knowledge in the Druidic way brings wisdom in itself because it requires a way of thinking that is non-linear.

It is popular to link failures of modern society to over-rationalisation, a high degree specialisation and division of knowledge, not just amongst the 'alternative' fringe but also amongst some respected economists and academics. A way of thinking and a world-view that is compartmentalised and that is short-term or ignores the broader consequences of actions is guaranteed to create problems for humanity and the world at large. Perhaps the problems of unbalanced economic systems, corrupt government, inequality, and lack of freedom and justice has led to a resurgence in interest in alternative (often earlier) models for living.

In the past decade I have witnessed the increasing acceptance of Druidic and Shamanic practitioners in healthcare, the official acceptance of Druids in religious functions and legal matters (e.g. marriage), the provision for Druidic burials and Druids as a voice for environmental and social concerns. There is still a long way to go before Druids are respected members of mainstream society but I believe this is fully possible, especially given the increasing failure of many of our professions to practise within the bounds of accepted morality and public expectations.

Much of the problems of modern humanity arise from totally

linear and insular perspectives – a fact that is only now coming to be fully understood. This problem is exacerbated by the frequent absence of a moral or spiritual framework to underpin important functions within much of western society. Most professions have a code of ethics that should be adhered to, but the reality today is that corruption, incompetence, lack of responsibility and lack of accountability is far too common. Solutions to our problems as a species require a change of attitude and thinking, especially amongst those in positions of power and influence. Perhaps this need will provide an opportunity for Druids and others on similar spiritual/wisdom paths to have a greater and hopefully insightful input into the future of human society.

After all, if having collected a body of knowledge and wisdom, what use is it if this is never put to good use? This is where the concept of service is of great relevance in modern Druidry. Having studied, worked hard to gain an understanding of oneself and the world in which we live, it becomes the responsibility of the Druid to be of service to others. The process of self-transformation is key to the Druid's path and requires a long period of looking inward, but ultimately the journey should not end at self-fulfilment and self-improvement. All of this introspection and work on the self is wasted if the Druid fails to manifest the fruits of their inner journey in the world beyond themselves. In fact, one could justifiably say that anyone who does not live their truth and practically demonstrate their path by the way that they live life is not actually living the path of a Druid.

Afterword

All that is written here in this book is just words. Words are easy; words alone are worth little or nothing. When words inspire new ideas and new actions then they have meaning and value. If these words here mean anything to you then let them take root inside you and bear fruit in your thoughts and actions – change happens from the inside before it manifests on the outside.

The path through the forest of life is full of wonder and beauty but also distractions, sorrows and danger. Without a light to see by it is hard to find one's way through the dark times in this forest, but there are many routes to the inner light inside us that guides us and illuminates the way.

Perhaps THIS route is one that you might follow towards that inner light. In finding that inner light it will shine clearly upon the way forward and all you need do is continue to follow it. Where there is light, there is hope, and where others see a beacon of light in you they might also be filled with hope to find their own inner light and right path through life.

Whichever spiritual path you choose, know that this light is within all living things and connects us to the divine in all that exists. Find and keep this light burning brightly, bring it out into the world and there will be no greater service you can perform to the gods, to creation or to your own true self.

Some contact information for a selection of Druidic Orders (correct 2011).
See www.druidnetwork.org for a more comprehensive listing:

France: Assemblée Druidique du Chêne et du Sanglier. Website : http://www.druides.org
International: Ancient Order of Druids in America. Website: www.aoda.org

International: Order of Bards, Ovates and Druids. Website: www.druidry.org
Ireland: Ord na Druí. Website: www.druidschool.com
Scotland: Order of the White Oak (Ord na Darach Gile). Website: www.whiteoakdruids.org
Scotland: The Gaelic Druid Order. Website: www.gaelic-druidorder.org
UK: British Druid Order. Website: www.druidry.co.uk
USA: Ár nDraíocht Féin. Website: www.adf.org

Notes

1. The Welsh king Aedd Mawr is cited in the Welsh Triads as one of the founders of Britain, thought to have lived around 1300 BC. He may well be linked with Addedomarus, ruler of the Trinovantes in southeast Britain around 35-5BC. Britain supposedly takes its name from the warrior Brydain, who is said to have settled the British Isles.
2. Julius Caesar was Proconsul of Rome and conducted a conquest of Gaul from 58-51BC. His book *Gallic War* or *Commentarii de Bello Gallico*, describes his long campaign and also gives some details of the Celts themselves. This was written with political purpose to further his own career in Rome and hence must be read with considerable discernment. Two years after his conquest of Gaul, Caesar instigated a civil war in Rome and after his victory was proclaimed Dictator of Rome for the remainder of his life. He brought to an end the Roman republic and for this he was murdered in the Roman Senate in 44 BC.
3. Patrick (Pádraig) was Welsh, he first arrived in Ireland as a slave but eventually managed to escape back to Britain, where he became a priest. He left two Latin letters which are now available in English, the most important – *Confessio* gives no indication of a violent conversion (see *St, Patrick the man and his works*) . The 7th century *Annals of Ulster* describe Patrick - drawing an account from the *Book of Ultan* which now lost, again non-violent conversion is indicated. A modern version of his life story can be found at www.saint-patrick.com.
4. See *The Anglo-Saxon Chronicles* for a map of the ancient British kingdoms.
5. According to an oral account I received from an Elder of the Irish Esoteric community there were 'Druidic Triads',

remnants of the pagan oral tradition in Ireland as late as the mid 1990s. The person in question related to me how he was called to meet a very old man on his deathbed who claimed to be *an Druí* (the Druid) and who explained that he was the last of his triad, himself being the gardener & herbalist. The Brehon and the Poet/Historian who comprised the rest of his triad had already died so he explained. He also stated there were a few other remaining triads he knew of, however he did not know if any of the people who comprised them were still alive.

I am also aware that there was one young Scots Gaelic (*Gáidhlig*) speaking Bard who was residing in the Scottish islands in the 1980s, he was a teenager at the time and newly trained. He would now be the last known person to be trained in the oral tradition of poetry in his native tongue and should be around his mid to late forties as of now (2011) but I am not aware of where he lives or if he still practices his art.

6. See *Religion of the Ancient Celts* by J. A. MacCulloch.
7. See *The Book of Druidry* by Ross Nichols.
8. See *The Philosopher and the Druids* by Philip Freeman.
9. The Welsh Bard/Druid Taliesin underwent several animal transformations subsequent to his accidental tasting of the three drops of *Awen* from Cerridwen's cauldron. He was reborn of Cerridwen after she ate him (in seed form) and was set adrift inside a crane skin bag/coracle, finally landing on a salmon weir and emerging still a child but a fully formed Bardic poet and powerful seer.
10. For instance The Bardic/Celtic Seer/Druid Source Books by John Matthews.
11. See *The Philosopher and the Druids* by Philip Freeman and *The Celtic Heroic Age* edited by John T. Koch and John Carey. Both books provide a wealth of Celtic and Classical source material.

12. See *The Book of Druidry* by Ross Nichols.
13. Theory formulated by author Garret S. Olmsted. He based his ideas on Pliny's remark that the Gauls began their month on the sixth day of the moon, and not the first. He estimates the calendar system was 1000 years old by the time the Coligny calendar was made, although this is disputed by academics. His theory implies that the system predates Celtic invasion of Gaul and was a survival from an earlier culture.
14. See *Religion of the Ancient Celts* by J. A. MacCulloch. Also see Michael Scott's *Irish Folk and Fairy Tale Omnibus* for several examples of werewolf stories.
15. See *Archaeology Ireland,* Vol 25, No1 for further detail on the Irish Crane.
16. Alexander Carmichae'ls *Carmina Gadelica* or *Ortha nan Gaidheal* is a collection of hymns, prayers, songs and incantations of the Gaelic speaking people of the north and western islands of Scotland. Carmichael, a Gaelic speaker himself, spent approximately forty years in collecting this unique cultural heritage from the elderly islanders — the last generation to live in this way. It was published in the late 1800s and records practices that would be completely lost otherwise.
17. See www.megalithicireland.com for full details on Newgrange and other ancient Irish sites.
18. See *Lugh, Lughnasa and Celtic Sun Magic* by Con Connor at www.druidschool.com
19. 20. See *Where Three Streams Meet* by Seán Ó Duinn.
21. See *Carmina Gadelica* by Alexander Carmichael.
22. This is according to Duchas, The Heritage Service (in Ireland).
23. From the medieval text *Auracept na n-Éces* (The Scholar's Primer).
24. *Cumhal/Cumal,* in English means a slave woman or the equivalent value thereof.

Bibliography

I used the following books and articles as source material (listed in alphabetical order), together with the oral knowledge and wisdom I have received through my teachers and colleagues in Druidry and other esoteric disciplines. Most of these books are easily purchased (often as facsimiles of the original publications) and are reasonably cheap, although many of the Revival texts and Celtic texts translated into English are long out of print and hence are extremely expensive. Fortunately there are a number of internet resource sites that offer these non-copyright translations (and often the original text too) free of charge as HTML pages or PDF files. Also a number of these books, in their original imprint, can be viewed at national libraries such as The British Library, The National Library of Ireland and other places.

Allen, David E. & Hatfield, Gabrielle. *Medicinal plants in folk tradition: An Ethnobotany of Britain & Ireland* (Timber Press)

Bain, George. *Celtic Art, The Methods of Construction* (Constable)

Bardic Grade Course, (2nd Edition, OBOD)

Benigni, H., Carter, B. and Ua Cuinn, É. *The Myth of the Year* (UPA)

Boutet, Michel-Gérald. *Druidical Astrology primer* (CURA article)

Berresford Ellis, Peter. *The Fabrication of Celtic Astrology* (The Astrological Journal article)

Brennan, J. H. *Astral Doorways* (Thoth)

Caesar, Julius. *Gallic War* (James Brodie Ltd)

Calder, G. *Auraicept na n-Éces — The Scholars' Primer* (Edinburgh)

Carmichael, Alexander. (Tr.) *Carmina Gadelica/Ortha nan Gaidheal* (extracts: Floris Books/Liguori/Triumph)

Carr-Gomm, Philip & Nichols, Ross. *In The Grove of The Druids* (Watkins)

Carson, Ciaran. (Tr.) *The Táin* (Penguin Classics)

Connor, Con. *Lugh, Lughnasa and Celtic Sun Magic* (druidschool.com article)
Connor, Con. *The White Mare of Tara* (Indymedia article)
Conway, D. J. *By Oak, Ash and Thorn* (Llewellyn Publications)
Cotterell, Arthur and Storm, Rachel. *The Encyclopedia of World Mythology* (Lorenz Books)
Cruise O'Brien, Máire & Connor. *Ireland, A Concise History* (Thames & Hudson)
Culpeper, Nicholas. *Complete Herbal* (Foulsham)
Dictionary of The Celts (Geddes & Grosset)
Druid Grade Course (First Edition, OBOD)
Duchas, The Heritage Service – *Ogham* (poster & booklet, Duchas)
Eastwood, Luke. *Crainn na hÉireann* (OBOD project, unpublished)
Eastwood, Luke. *Magic, The Inconvenient Truth* (unpublished article)
Ferguson, Sir Samuel. (Tr.) *Lays of the Western Gael* (Bell & Daldy)
Fortune, Dion. *Psychic Self Defence* (Weiser)
Freeman, Philip. *The Philosopher and the Druids* (Souvenir Press)
Frazer, Sir James. *The Golden Bough* (Wordsworth)
Gilroy, John. *Tlachtga: Celtic Fire Festival* (Pikefield Publications)
Ginnell, Laurence. *The Brehon Laws: A Legal Handbook* (Biobliolife)
Goodenough, Simon. *Celtic Mythology* (Tiger)
Graves, Robert. *The White Goddess* (Faber and Faber)
Greer, John, Michael. *The Druidry Handbook* (Weiser)
Gregory, Augusta. (Tr.) *Gods and Fighting Men* (John Murray)
Gregory, Augusta. (Tr.) *Chuchulain of Muirthemne* (John Murray)
Greywolf. *A Little History of Druidry* (BDO article)
Guest, Charlotte, E. (Tr.) *The Mabinogion* (Drover Publications)
Hopman, Ellen Evert. *A Druid's Herbal* (Destiny Books)
Howe, Stephen. *Ireland and Empire* (Oxford University Press)
James, David and Davis, Courtney. *The Celtic Image* (Cassell & Co.)
Joyce. P. W. (Tr.) *Ancient Celtic Romances* (Parkgate Books)

King, John. *Kingdoms of The Celts* (Cassell & Co)

Kinghan, Wil. *The Hallows and the Quest* (*Immrama* article Vol.5 No.5)

Kirkey, Jason. *Druidism and the Way of the Dán* (OBOD article)

Kondratiev, Alexei. *Celtic Rituals* (The Collins Press)

Koch, John T. & Carey, John. *The Celtic Heroic Age* (4th Edition, Celtic Studies Publications)

Kruta, Venceslas. *Celts, History and Civilization* (Hachette)

Laurie, E. R. (Tr.) *The Cauldron of Poesy* (?)

MacAlister R. A. S. (Tr.) *Lebor Gabála Érenn* (Irish Text Society)

MacAlister R. A. S. *Newgrange, Co. Meath* (Dublin Stationery Office)

MacAnnaidh, Séamus. *Irish History* (Starfire)

MacCoitir, Niall. *Irish Wild Plants: Myths, Legends and Folklore* (The Collins Press)

MacCoitir, Niall. *Irish Trees: Myths, Legends and Folklore* (The Collins Press)

MacCulloch, J. A. *The Religion of the Ancient Celts* (Constable)

MacEowen, Frank. *The Spiral of Memory and Belonging* (New World Library)

Maclean, Magnus. *The Literature of the Celts* (Senate)

MacUistin, Liam. (Tr.) *Celtic Magic Tales* (The O'Brien Press)

McGowan, Joe. *Echoes of a Savage Land* (Mercier)

McGrath, Liam. *How to Use the Ogham Trees* (Private pressing)

McManus, Damian. *A Guide to Ogam* (Maynooth Monographs)

Magnusson, Magnus. *Scotland, The Story of a Nation* (Harper Collins)

Matthews, Caitlin. *Celtic Wisdom Sticks: An Ogham Oracle* (Connections Book Publishing)

Matthews, John. *The Bardic Source Book* (Blanford)

Matthews, John. *The Druid Source Book* (Blanford)

Memory Paterson, Jacqueline. *Tree Wisdom* (Thorsons)

Meyer, Kuno. (Ed., Tr.) *The Triads of Ireland* (Todd)

Meyer, Kuno. (Tr.) *Selections from Ancients Irish Poetry* (Constable)

Murphy, D. (Tr.) *The Annals of Clonmacnoise* (Llanerch)
New Everyman Illustrated Encyclopedia (Octopus)
Nichols, Ross. *The Book of Druidry* (Thorsons)
Nicholson, Francine. *Fictions, Facts and Mysteries: Druids* (web article)
Noodén, Lars. *Animal Symbolism in Celtic Mythology* (University of Michigan)
Ó Catháin, Séamas. *Irish Life and Lore* (Mercier)
O'Connor, Ulick. (Tr.) *Irish Tales and Sagas* (Town House)
O'Curry, Eugene. *Manners and Customs of the Ancient Irish* (Williams & Norgate)
O'Donovan, John. (Ed.) *The Annals of the Kingdom of Ireland by the Four Masters* (CELT)
O'Dubhain, Searles. *Ogham Divination* (Summerlands Press)
Ó Duinn, Seán. *Where Three Streams Meet, Celtic Spirituality* (The Columba Press)
O'Hogain, Dr. Daithi. *Myth, Legend & Romance* (BCA)
O'Loughlin, Thomas. *Saint Patrick The Man and His Works* (Triangle)
Ovate Grade Course, (1st & 2nd Editions OBOD)
Piggot, Stuart. *The Druids* (Thames & Hudson)
Preston, Richard. *The Wild Trees* (Penguin)
Robertson, Colin. *The Druidic Order of the Pendragon* (Thoth)
Rolleston T. W. *Celtic Myths and Legends* (Senate)
Royal Horticultural Society. *Encyclopedia of Gardening* (Dorling Kindersley)
Savage, Anne. (Tr.). *The Anglo Saxon Chronicles* (Coombe)
Scott, Michael. *Irish Folk and Fairy Tales Omnibus* (Warner Books)
Skene, W. F. (Tr.) *The Four Ancient Books of Wales* (Kessinger)
Smyth, Daragh. (Tr.) *Cú Chulainn, An Iron Age Hero* (Irish Academic Press)
Tír na nÓg website. *Druids: Their Functions and Powers* (web article)
Treharne R. F. *The Glastonbury Legends* (Abacus)

Williams Ab Ithel, J. (Tr.) *Barddas* (Welsh MS Society)

www.wikipedia.org. Various entries on Celts and Druidry (web articles)

Winwood Reade, W. *The Veil of Isis or Mysteries of The Druids* (Newcastle Publishing Co.)

MOON
BOOKS

PAGANISM & SHAMANISM

What is Paganism? A religion, a spirituality, an alternative belief system, nature worship? You can find support for all these definitions (and many more) in dictionaries, encyclopaedias, and text books of religion, but subscribe to any one and the truth will evade you. Above all Paganism is a creative pursuit, an encounter with reality, an exploration of meaning and an expression of the soul. Druids, Heathens, Wiccans and others, all contribute their insights and literary riches to the Pagan tradition. Moon Books invites you to begin or to deepen your own encounter, right here, right now.

If you have enjoyed this book, why not tell other readers by posting a review on your preferred book site.

Recent bestsellers from Moon Books are:

Journey to the Dark Goddess

How to Return to Your Soul

Jane Meredith

Discover the powerful secrets of the Dark Goddess and transform your depression, grief and pain into healing and integration.

Paperback: 978-1-84694-677-6 ebook: 978-1-78099-223-5

Shamanic Reiki

Expanded Ways of Working with Universal Life Force Energy

Llyn Roberts, Robert Levy

Shamanism and Reiki are each powerful ways of healing; together, their power multiplies. *Shamanic Reiki* introduces techniques to help healers and Reiki practitioners tap ancient healing wisdom.

Paperback: 978-1-84694-037-8 ebook: 978-1-84694-650-9

Pagan Portals – The Awen Alone
Walking the Path of the Solitary Druid
Joanna van der Hoeven
An introductory guide for the solitary Druid, The Awen Alone will accompany you as you explore, and seek out your own place within the natural world.
Paperback: 978-1-78279-547-6 ebook: 978-1-78279-546-9

A Kitchen Witch's World of Magical Herbs & Plants
Rachel Patterson
A journey into the magical world of herbs and plants, filled with magical uses, folklore, history and practical magic. By popular writer, blogger and kitchen witch, Tansy Firedragon.
Paperback: 978-1-78279-621-3 ebook: 978-1-78279-620-6

Medicine for the Soul
The Complete Book of Shamanic Healing
Ross Heaven
All you will ever need to know about shamanic healing and how to become your own shaman...
Paperback: 978-1-78099-419-2 ebook: 978-1-78099-420-8

Shaman Pathways – The Druid Shaman
Exploring the Celtic Otherworld
Danu Forest
A practical guide to Celtic shamanism with exercises and techniques as well as traditional lore for exploring the Celtic Otherworld.
Paperback: 978-1-78099-615-8 ebook: 978-1-78099-616-5

Traditional Witchcraft for the Woods and Forests
A Witch's Guide to the Woodland with Guided Meditations and Pathworking
Mélusine Draco

A Witch's guide to walking alone in the woods, with guided meditations and pathworking.
Paperback: 978-1-84694-803-9 ebook: 978-1-84694-804-6

Wild Earth, Wild Soul
A Manual for an Ecstatic Culture
Bill Pfeiffer
Imagine a nature-based culture so alive and so connected, spreading like wildfire. This book is the first flame...
Paperback: 978-1-78099-187-0 ebook: 978-1-78099-188-7

Naming the Goddess
Trevor Greenfield
Naming the Goddess is written by over eighty adherents and scholars of Goddess and Goddess Spirituality.
Paperback: 978-1-78279-476-9 ebook: 978-1-78279-475-2

Shapeshifting into Higher Consciousness
Heal and Transform Yourself and Our World with Ancient Shamanic and Modern Methods
Llyn Roberts
Ancient and modern methods that you can use every day to transform yourself and make a positive difference in the world.
Paperback: 978-1-84694-843-5 ebook: 978-1-84694-844-2